Divine Consciousness

The Secret Story of James the Brother of Jesus, St. Paul and the Early Christian Church

Divine Consciousness

The Secret Story of James the Brother of Jesus, St. Paul and the Early Christian Church

Reena Kumarasingham

BOOKS

Winchester, UK
Washington, USA

JOHN HUNT PUBLISHING

First published by O-Books, 2020
O-Books is an imprint of John Hunt Publishing Ltd., 3 East St., Alresford,
Hampshire SO24 9EE, UK
office@jhpbooks.com
www.johnhuntpublishing.com
www.o-books.com

For distributor details and how to order please visit the 'Ordering' section on our website.

ISBN: 978 1 78904 436 2
978 1 78904 437 9 (ebook)
Library of Congress Control Number: 2019943739

A CIP catalogue record for this book is available from the British Library.

Design: Stuart Davies

UK: Printed and bound by CPI Group (UK) Ltd, Croydon, CR0 4YY
US: Printed and bound by Thomson-Shore, 7300 West Joy Road, Dexter, MI 48130

Contents

I found the Divine within my heart. – Rumi

For all the souls standing strong in You
Keep shining your radiant light.

Acknowledgements

I would like to thank and acknowledge these amazing people, without whom this book would not have been possible:

To the regressees who participated in this book – for your volunteered time, commitment and permission to using your sessions for the creation of this book. This was a real team effort and this book could not have been produced without you.

Andy Tomlinson, for your loving and unwavering belief and support that have sustained me.

Michael Mann, whose vision and loving mentorship inspired this book.

Sanja Jovic of www.sanjajovicart.com, the talented Artist of Light who painted the image for the cover.

The team at O-Books – for your time, care and love.

Last but certainly not least, my amazing friends – my soul family – for supporting and holding me through this journey.

I am so deeply grateful.

Introduction

Christianity two thousand years ago was very different to the Christianity that we are familiar with today. It was a time of big changes and upheaval politically and socioeconomically in Jerusalem and in Rome. It was a time where cultural conditioning, authority and belief systems were challenged. Those who wanted change and challenged status quo were subject to persecution and punishment. It was at this time that new teachings which promoted a different way of being were introduced by Jesus and his followers. At the beginning, there were multiple, diverse forms of Christian teachings, spread by multiple teachers. However, two dominant types of churches rose to prominence at that time. Two structured, organized, churches, each with respective uniformed set rituals, ceremonies, teachings, established leadership, meetings and events:

a. Pauline / Gentile Christian Church
b. Judeo / Jewish Christian Church

Bart Ehrman, theological scholar and currently the James A. Gray Distinguished Professor of Religious Studies at the University of North Carolina, in his book *Lost Christianities*, claims that in the second century, Christians were reading far more sacred literature than we would think. They were not only reading books that made it into the New Testament. They were reading other texts as well.[1] Unfortunately, most of these ancient forms of Christianity are unknown in the world today, as they were eventually reformed or stamped out.[2]

All forms of modern Christianity that we are familiar with today go back to one form of Christianity that emerged victorious from the conflicts of the second and third centuries. According to Ehrman, this form of Christianity decided what the "correct"

Christian perspective is, who exercised authority over Christian belief and practice, and what forms of Christianity would be set aside or marginalized.[3]

In my opinion, it is very sad that the world has lost the rich tapestry and diversity of teachings, world-views and intellectual thinking of the early centuries of Christianity.

Five years ago, I embarked on a journey that was filled with synchronous meetings and events that led to the birth of *Shrouded Truth*. It recounts the events before, during and after the crucifixion of Jesus through the eyes of eight different souls, via their past-life memories. These regression sessions were not planned, and the people who participated in this book were from different countries, and had very little, if any, connection to one another. These memories popped up spontaneously, at different points in time over a period of four years, in different parts of the world, by ordinary people who were experiencing sessions for different intents and purposes. They had varying prior knowledge of the biblical stories – some none at all, and some rather in depth. Through serendipitous and synchronous events, all their sessions were recorded, and by their good grace and permission, *Shrouded Truth* was produced.

While writing *Shrouded Truth*, there was a glimmer of diverse teachings, belief systems and established churches that occasionally peeked out from the dramatic life stories of these participants. Though faint, it was clear in *Shrouded Truth* that many of the people who lived during the biblical period had rather different interpretations of the teachings and discourses of Jesus. In addition, as I was doing some research, I realized that not only the life stories were different from what is commonly known nowadays, but the teachings and belief systems were as well. They were so diverse and different, and many of which seemed to have disappeared. They appeared to be a lot more complex than modern-day teachings that revolve around the New Testament.

I am therefore grateful that synchronicity and serendipity chose to step in again. In *Shrouded Truth* we met Mia and Greg (not their real names) – who respectively regressed to the lives of James (the brother of Jesus), and Paul (the Evangelist).

I first met Mia as a client, nearly five years ago, for a between-lives spiritual regression session. This is a process propagated by Dr. Michael Newton, where clients in deep trance are facilitated to go to a space in-between lives, to discover plans and purpose for this, their current life. (See Appendix for more information.)

Mia is a mother, wife and businesswoman living in the south of Britain, so it was by virtue of close proximity that she opted to come to me as a client. During the between-lives session, we spontaneously discovered that Mia had experienced a past life during biblical times.

She went back to a life as a man in his late twenties with bandages around his feet, wearing a smock that fell just below his knees. It was dark and he was in a cave with friends. She became visibly distressed – pale and tearful, and was feeling scared. "We have to get Jesus away… It feels like it has all gone wrong," she declared.

At that point, I, having grown up as a Hindu, had very little knowledge of the New Testament. So while the information was fascinating to me, the session was facilitated to maximize the between-lives experience for Mia.

Two years later, after I'd had a few different clients who spontaneously regressed back to biblical times, Mia agreed to participate in the conception of this book with her past-life recollection of a man who turned out to be James, the brother of Jesus. Through his regressions, compelling information of the Judeo-Christian Church emerged, as well as some of their teachings, which is different from what we are familiar with today. Another surprising piece of information that emerged is that James was also asked by Jesus to lead this church after his death.

There exists quite a number of non-canonical writings from the earliest days of the Church that provide reliable evidence that it was Jesus' blood brother James who was considered by many of the early Christians to be the first "bishop" of the Church, the successor to Jesus.[4] James is cited several times in the book of Acts, where he plays a huge role in the leadership of the disciples in the time following Jesus' death.[5] Bishop Clement of Alexandria had written that Jesus' brother James, as the appointed Nazarene Bishop of Jerusalem, was the "Lord of the Holy Church and the bishop of bishops," thereby setting this Jewish-Christian movement far higher than the Roman offshoot, Gentile Christianity.[6]

How could such an illustrious person have disappeared into oblivion in written biblical history or, at best, be seen as a minor figure who played a minuscule role during those times?

Through James' life story, Mia's regression gives us a unique insight into the teachings of Jewish Christianity, the similarities and differences with Gentile Christianity, as well as some practices according to the old religion.

Greg was one of my long-time clients, and we'd explored many of his past and current life memories. Greg wanted a session to work on a personal current life issue. To the surprise of both of us, he regressed back to the biblical character – Paul the Evangelist – as the source of his current life challenge.

After a year, Greg agreed to be regressed to Paul's life, to focus on his story for *Shrouded Truth*. At this time, I started to see a glimmer of how his teachings came about – his intent, his motivations and his methods. When I asked Greg if he would participate in the research for *Divine Consciousness*, he was happy to oblige, as he too was keen to know more. He is not a churchgoer, nor has he had too much exposure to Christianity. This meant he was the ideal candidate, as he did not have many preconceived ideas or prior knowledge.

Through a mixture of life events and his teachings, this

regression gives us a glimpse into Paul's life as a fledgling teacher, a leader of the Pauline Church, an evangelist and an author.

It is unanimously agreed amongst biblical scholars that Paul, to spread the teachings of Jesus to non-Jews, conceived the Pauline Church. Also known as Gentile Christianity, the premise of Pauline Christianity is that through the belief of and faith in Jesus' death and resurrection, the salvation of the Divine Christ applies to all people, Jews and Gentiles alike.[7]

Paul is both the most well-known and also the most mysterious biblical figure. Not only was Paul one of the most ardent evangelizers, where he travelled far and wide preaching his message, he was also a prolific author, writing the most number of letters in the New Testament. His teachings are the foundation of one of the biggest religious movements of our modern day. He is both adored by believers and practitioners of the faith, and at the same time reviled by those who are convinced that he had twisted and manipulated the pure teachings of Jesus.

How could both these souls have developed such contrary reputations for themselves? What happened in their lives, in their teachings, and in their churches, to have caused this?

When it comes to the life story and teachings of Jesus, all we have are memories. According to Ehrman, there were no stenographic notes recorded on the spot and no account of Jesus' activities were written at the time. Ehrman, and scholars like him, agree that the Gospels, which are popularly known to be a surviving record of Jesus, are not memories recorded by eyewitnesses. They are memories of later authors who had heard about Jesus from others, who found out from others, who in turn found out from others.[8]

Through oral traditions, stories were passed down that shaped and carved the perceptions of his person, his life, his teachings and those closest to him.

Past-life regression is another way to explore the perceptions and memories related to Jesus, his teachings and the biblical times. I am grateful to Mia and Greg that they agreed to be regressed back to their respective biblical lives, to gain more information about their teachings. I was curious to see if their teachings were in fact as diverse as they appeared to be in *Shrouded Truth*. I was also curious to investigate how their teachings were developed, what drove them, and how their individually antithetic reputations came to be. Mia, Greg and Maya, again, generously and graciously, agreed to participate in yet another journey. Their fascinating accounts, and my corresponding research, produced this book.

Before we delve into the story, it is prudent to first address the big question: Reincarnation, past lives and regression – are they real?

The immortal soul is such an important part of all religions. The Egyptians had such elaborate beliefs about death and the afterlife that they built complex rituals around preserving the "ka" and "ba" (soul) of the person after death. Many modern-day Christians and Muslims believe in heaven and hell, that souls will be judged accordingly based on their deeds on Earth and that they will spend all of eternity in one or another as a result. Nearly 350 million Buddhists and 800 million Hindus believe that the immortal soul incarnates over and over again until it reaches the state of Nirvana. The Quran and the Zohar, the mystical texts of Judaism, both mention reincarnation:

> And you were dead, and He brought you back to life. And He shall cause you to die, and shall bring you back to life, and in the end shall gather you unto Himself.
> – Quran 2:28

> All souls are subject to reincarnation; and people do not know the ways of the Holy One, blessed be He! They do not know that they are brought before the tribunal both before they

> enter into this world and after they leave it; they are ignorant of the many reincarnations and secret works which they have to undergo, and of the number of naked souls, and how many naked spirits roam about in the other world without being able to enter within the veil of the King's Palace. Men do not know how the souls revolve like a stone that is thrown from a sling. But the time is at hand when these mysteries will be disclosed.
> – Zohar II 99b

The early Christians, including some of the first popes of the Church, believed in reincarnation, however, the original references to reincarnation were removed from the Bible. St. Gregory of Nyssa believed that "it is absolutely necessary that the soul be healed and purified; and if that did not occur during life on Earth, it should be done in future lives."[9]

St. Clement of Alexandria also supported this belief; but perhaps the person most associated with the principle of reincarnation was his pupil, Origen, who included the reincarnation doctrine in his book *On First Principles*: "Each soul comes into this world strengthened by the victories or weakened by the defeats of its previous life... Your actions in that world determine your place in this world (on Earth) which must determine the next one..."[10]

The Fifth Ecumenical Council of Constantinople in 553CE, three centuries after his death, reportedly decided against Origen and declared the doctrine heretical. Some believe that the Emperor Constantine removed all these references from the Bible at the Council of Nicaea in 325CE, and that the only evidence is under the ashes of the Alexandrian library, which was destroyed.[11]

Saying that, there are surreptitious references to reincarnation in the Bible, including John 9:1-2 which states: "As Jesus was walking along, he saw a man who had been blind from birth.

'Rabbi,' his disciples asked him, 'why was this man born blind? Was it because of his own sins or his parents' sins?'" The only way that this man's sins could have caused him to be born blind is for him to have sinned before he was born in his current body.

Before we get into interpretive discussions around these religious texts, in a survey conducted by the Global Research Society and the Institute for Social Research (Ipsos), who surveyed more than 18,000 people in 23 countries, seven percent of people believe in reincarnation, while 23 percent believe that we only will "cease to exist." A 2009 survey by the Pew Forum on Religion and Public Life found that 24 percent of American Christians believe in reincarnation.[12]

Let's not forget too that respected academicians in the twentieth century believed in reincarnation. Carl Jung, in a lecture that he presented in 1939, said, "This concept of rebirth necessarily implies the continuity of personality. Here the human personality is regarded as continuous and accessible to memory, so that, when one is incarnated or born, one is able, at least potentially, to remember that one has lived through previous existences. As a rule, reincarnation means rebirth in a human body."[13]

Dr. Ian Stevenson, a Canadian psychiatrist who worked for the University of Virginia School of Medicine for fifty years, as chair of the Department of Psychiatry from 1957 to 1967, Carlson Professor of Psychiatry from 1967 to 2001, and Research Professor of Psychiatry from 2002 until his death in 2007, spent forty years of his life researching 3,000 children from Africa to Alaska, who claimed to remember past lives spontaneously. Some of the anecdotes came from children who lived in rural areas, who had no access to mass media and are so detailed and personal that the account could not have been imagined but only recalled. His work was collated and written up in around 300 papers and 14 books on reincarnation, including *Twenty Cases Suggestive of Reincarnation* published in 1966. His work, plus Jim

Tucker's (his successor) and that of many others since who have documented past lives of children, is a strong indication of the existence and authenticity of reincarnation and past lives.

The first known writings that mention past-life regression – to access memories in past lives – is in the ancient Indian literature the Upanishads, but the Yoga Sutras of Patañjali (written in the second century BCE) consider the concept in greater detail. The Hindu scholar Patañjali discussed the idea of the soul becoming burdened with an accumulation of impressions as part of the karma from previous lives. Patañjali called the process of discovering these impressions past-life regression, or prati-prasav (literally "reverse birthing"), and saw it as a means of addressing current problems through memories of past lives.

Past-life regression rose to prominence in the West in the early twentieth century through the works of mediums and spiritual practitioners. However, around the middle of the century, psychologists, psychotherapists and academics started to conduct research into past lives and past-life regression, and use it in a therapeutic setting, and they developed a more standardized framework that most practitioners work with now. Noted experts in this field include Dr. Brian Weiss (psychiatrist), Andy Tomlinson (psychotherapist) and Dr. Roger Woolger (Jungian therapist).

Coming back to *Divine Consciousness*, Mia and Greg participated in multiple regression sessions to their respective biblical lives. What emerged from this set of regressions are two very distinct and diverse sets of teachings and belief systems that both these individuals either led or evangelized that formed the basis of two distinct Christian Churches two thousand years ago. What was even more compelling, is that when I set out to research Christianity in antiquity, there was much research that scholars had published which correlated with the claims made in these regressions.

Pauline or Gentile Christian Church

A Gentile is simply anyone who is not a descendant of Abraham, Isaac and Jacob. Gentile refers to non-Israelites, and collectively designates the peoples and nations as distinct from the Israelite people. Also known as Pauline Christianity, Gentile Christianity was evangelized by the Apostle Paul, who opened Jesus' teachings to non-Jews.

Mainstream Christianity relies on Paul's writings as integral to the biblical theology of the New Testament and regards them as amplifications and explanations consistent with the teachings of Jesus and other New Testament writings. Christian scholars generally use Pauline Christianity to express the Christian origins and the contribution made by Paul to Christian doctrine.[14]

Jewish Christian or Judeo-Christian Church

Jewish Christians were the original members of the Jewish movement who accepted Jesus as the Messiah (Christ). This movement was influenced by the Dead Sea Scrolls, which are widely believed to have been authored by the Essenes. The members of the Essenes who first adopted Jesus' teachings were considered the first Jewish Christians. Jewish Christians are seen to be the original Christians. As Christianity grew and developed, Jewish Christians became only one strand of the early Christian community, characterized by combining the philosophy of Jesus as Christ with continued adherence to Jewish traditions and the observance of Jewish laws and customs.[15] They rejected the teachings of the Apostle Paul, especially as they did not adhere to the Jewish laws.

While the regressees did not use these terms in the sessions, for ease and clarity of reading, based on the correlation of the regressed accounts to the research, I have attributed the same categories to the teachings by the regressees:

a. Paul was the founder of the Pauline or Gentile Church, the precursor to proto-orthodoxy, which evolved to modern-day Christianity. Both "Pauline Christianity" and "Gentile Christianity" are used interchangeably throughout this book.
b. James, the Brother of Jesus, was the leader of the Jewish Christian Church. The term "Jewish Christianity" is used interchangeably with Judeo-Christianity and "Ebionite/ Nazarene" in this book.

Divine Consciousness is divided into two parts, each of which is comprised of the respective definition, regression and research into that particular belief or interpretation of Christian Churches:

a. Part One – Gentile Church
b. Part Two – Jewish Christian Church

Divine Consciousness offers a fascinating insight into how the diverse interpretations of Christianity emerged after the disappearance of Jesus from the public eye in the first century. It also offers a unique perspective into how these beliefs came about and what drove these different individuals in their respective interpretations of Jesus' teachings, and the development of their Churches.

Divine Consciousness also highlights pertinent parables, stories and practices that these different individuals taught. There are very practical and helpful suggestions and techniques that emerged from both regressions for us to employ in our daily lives moving forward. These segments are interwoven throughout this entire book.

A difficulty with the subjects in trance is that they sometimes repeat themselves, and their grammar can be poor, particularly for those who did not have English as their first language. So some minor adjustments have been made to improve the readability. For clarification I have occasionally added some of my own comments in square brackets. The overriding intent has been to present transcripts that are readable yet as accurate as possible to the original content.

Divine Consciousness is not produced to be contentious or offensive. It merely expands modern-day perspective by giving insight into the rich tapestry of diverse beliefs within Christianity in the ancient world. For those of you who have picked up *Divine Consciousness,* I ask that you have an open heart and mind as you read through – to put preconceived notions on the back burner.

Part One

Gentile Church

When you are a flame in darkness, it does not matter how big you are, you light the whole room.

Paul

Chapter 1

The Meeting

In his first session, Greg dropped into the life of a bearded man, wearing a dirty cloth draped around his shoulders, with a rope tied around his waist, and bare feet. He is looking at a man with white cloth draped over his arms and body, who was standing with his arms out, like a cross-type position. It was getting towards the end of the day and they were outdoors, amongst a group of twenty or thirty people, watching and listening.

Reena: And tell me more about this man with his arms out.
Greg: Seems to have this big glow around his head.
Reena: What color is the glow?
Greg: It can't be said that it has a color. I just get the feeling there's an energy or just a presence around him. There's almost like a saint-like quality that he has.
Reena: Who is this man?
Greg: Jesus.
Reena: Who is he in relation to you?
Greg: I don't know, but the thought that came into my head was "brother." He doesn't seem like a brother, he seems different.

Within the context of Jesus being part of the Essene community, this term would not seem so controversial. Within this community, a male member addresses another male member as "Brother," thereby denoting equality, filiality and mutual respect for one another.

It is also interesting to note that, while the other people who were regressed perceived Jesus as a man with special qualities,

Paul's first perception of Jesus was that he was almost like a saint – which is in line with his portrayal of Jesus as the Son of God.

The regression continues.

Greg: I'm just listening to him talking, we all are.

Reena: And how do you feel listening to him talking?

Greg: Really inspired. Almost like a feeling of reverence, it's like not being able to say anything in case it breaks the special magic of the moment of what he's saying – of the moment of where we are... He's just talking about love. And needing to spread the message of love.

Reena: And how does this make you feel?

Greg: Quite inspired.

Wanting to know a little more about his younger years, to ascertain more details about his identity, he was taken back to his first significant memory in that life. He went back to the time when he was five or six, being in a small room running and playing with other children around. He felt happy and contented being in that "lovely wonderful place." He identified having three other brothers, a mother and a father, and this is where he names himself as Paul.

The next significant event saw Paul at fourteen, participating in a Jewish ceremony.

Greg: There's someone in front of me, a priest of some sort, holding like a kind of cup, no, more like a bowl, a goldish/light-colored bowl. He is draped with different-colored clothes and a scarf-type thing, a religious type of scarf. They are singing a song that I am having to join in with. I think this is a ceremony of my coming of age.

Reena: How does the song make you feel?

Greg: There's something about it that feels false. It's like I am going through this ceremony to keep everybody happy but it's not something I particularly enjoy... It's about me embracing the Jewish religion and it doesn't quite work for me...

Finally, it's over and I can come back again. My brothers are looking at me a bit distant now like I am not a child to play around with. They are treating me like an adult and I don't really like it. I don't feel any different to how I was before... makes me feel a bit sad.

Reena: What's the age difference between you and your younger brothers?

Greg: I get the feeling that one of them is about eight and the other is about twelve.

This recollection is interesting because it clearly shows that though Paul was participating in a Jewish ceremony or ritual, he clearly did not feel comfortable with it. This goes against the tradition and common perception that Paul was in fact a Pharisee, who adhered strictly to Jewish rituals and traditions and persecuted the early Christians who went against the Jewish teachings.

Reena: What happens next?

Greg: I have to wear different clothes now... like a loin cloth with a belt. But it's clean material so I have to be careful not to dirty it. I can see this bright light. It's like I am part of a bright light... It's outside, I am by myself.

Reena: Is this after the ceremony?

Greg: It's a few days afterwards. I have been walking out in the desert. I think you'd call it a desert. It's quite barren in the area there. I have sat down and am reflecting on everything that happened in the ceremony and the changes at home. I have this feeling of a bright light all the way around me. It's like a very religious type of spiritual experience.

I just feel very serene. Almost like nothing else really matters... I am just getting the feeling that there is something special that I have to do and this is what this experience is about... I think it's some sort of teaching that I have to do. Not a lot of detail, just the experience of realizing the contrast between [this and] the ceremony that I went through. That meant nothing inside, despite all the people and the fancy clothes they were wearing and the gold cup. All that they had and here I was in the middle of this desert area by the small tree and this amazing experience came through. Almost teaching me what's real and what isn't real.

Reena: Where in the body are you feeling this feeling?

Greg: It's an experience that I am feeling in my head... it's almost like I have transcended out of the human body and I'm just having a spiritual experience of connecting with other spiritual bodies. It's like an experience of floating, almost like telepathic communication... It's to remind me who I really am.

Reena: And can you share who you really are?

Greg: It's to remind me that there is a spiritual part, that the world is magnificent, and it's also to remind me that there is a world of ceremonies and physical things and that they have to coexist. Both ways are trying to represent spirituality but one is just experiencing and being whilst the other is doing things with traditions and process.

The common story about Paul is that he, or Saul as he is referenced in the Bible, discovered spirituality from Jesus, after the crucifixion, while he was on the road to Damascus. Interestingly, this recollection brings to light that Paul had his own spiritual awakening and experience at the age of fourteen, before meeting Jesus.

In the next significant event, Paul is 23 or 24, sporting a black beard and wearing a whitish cloth over him. It's quite loose, to let the air circulate. He finds himself on a donkey with his legs tucked into stirrups, not free to move. He has got a leather bag with writings in it and taxes that he is collecting. Bags hang off the side of the donkey too. He is feeling fearful as he is carrying quite a bit of money and there is no one to protect him. Although he is confident that, as the local people know that he is doing the work for the Romans, they are all terrified.

Reena: How do you address the local people?

Greg: Hmm, well a lot of them are Jews, but I just address them by their individual names. I have a list before I come to each town of who the prominent people are and then I have to work out how much tax they need to pay. By the time I've finished in that town, or part of the town, I go back with the money and go back [to the town] again. It's like I am doing this all the time. I'm a bit young to do this sort of work, but I am good at doing it so that they've given me a free hand.

Reena: And what happens next as you are riding on this donkey?

Greg: Well, I'm coming to a commotion because there is a big group of people and I'm a bit concerned because I've got some of the money I've been collecting, not a lot but… I'm a bit concerned that this is some sort of trap. Some of the people who do my sort of work have been robbed before and been left to bleed…

Reena: And this big group of people – are they men and women?

Greg: Yes, but they don't seem threatening at all, they seem to be quite elated, they seem to be almost jostling to get into the center of a crowd. It's almost like they are ignoring me so I feel really interested in what could be happening.

Reena: OK, so what could you tell me about the scene around

you in terms of the weather and the ground?

Greg: On the ground, it's rocky, not much grass at all, just a few strands here and there, almost look like weeds rather than grass. There's dust and it's hot. The crowds, they are dressed in various clothes, most of them are in lightish colors, some have got little bits of color like it's been dyed. So they've got a little bit like tea cloths that we have these days, you know this sort of marking on it, it's not a very thin cotton, it's a more coarse-type cotton, it's a real... I think it's more of it keeps them warm at nighttime as well but keeps the sun off the body during the day... I really feel the excitement in the air.

Reena: So what happens next?

Greg: Well, before I am able to decide what to do, the group seems to be parting and there's this man coming towards me. He invites me to get down, to leave the donkey, the money and all of that behind and just embrace him.

Reena: Tell me more about this man?

Greg: He's dressed similar to the others but he's got very clear, piercing, loving eyes and he's got a black beard. Nothing's on his head, it's like the clothes are around the top half of the body and then draped down, he's got bare feet. He has the sort of clothes of someone who isn't very wealthy, [something] the poorer people, would wear. He's stood firm and bold. He's got a smile and it's almost inviting me to go up and let him put his arms around and hug me, and so I do that. And I just feel all this amazing energy flowing through my whole body.

Reena: Where is this energy coming from?

Greg: It must be coming from him. So I just, well, I just go with it, I mean it's so totally unexpected.

Reena: What does this energy do to your body?

Greg: It's almost like it's washing away things, it's like a lot of the worries and concerns and getting the job done and getting the taxes… I just don't care about that anymore. I'm quite elated.

Reena: What happens next?

Greg: He finishes the embrace and he says, "Come and join me." And a few other people are saying, "No, why do you say that, he's a tax collector?" And he's saying in the sea we're all… all the fish are the same, some are larger and some are smaller but they are all fish. And it's the same with people, all people are the same, they may just have different jobs and roles.

So I just walk off and leave all the things behind and it's as if, almost like, I just become one of the others. It's almost like the identity I had of collecting taxes was only when I had the donkey and the bags and all my written records of who I collected taxes from, and that was my role and I left that behind.

It's like I could become somebody new and they've all just accepted it now, and other things are coming up and we're starting to walk along and the crowd are following. It's almost like they're all wondering where they're going or what's going to happen and no one's really bothered, it's almost just like going for a fun walk except you don't know where you're going to.

Again, Greg's account of Paul meeting Jesus for the first time digresses wildly from the Bible and many other sources on the subject. The New Testament in Acts 9 (Acts 9:4-6) states that Paul did not travel with Jesus, but met him on the road to Damascus, after Jesus' resurrection. While Acts was written anonymously, early Christian tradition suggests that the same author who wrote the Gospel of Luke also wrote Acts. New Testament scholars have debated the accuracy of the portrayal of Paul in the book of Acts. There is no certainty that Acts presents an accurate account of Paul's mission and message. Some scholars claim that Luke created a more subdued Paul to mediate conflicts between early Christian communities. So this suggests that Acts was composed in the second century, hence the author knew almost nothing about Paul and used his letters as a source for the Acts narrative.[1]

There is also little mention of Paul's earlier life in the New Testament. Common knowledge holds that the tax collector that Jesus recruited into his team was Matthew, who was a disciple. However, neither the Gospels nor early sources name the tax collector as "Matthew." In fact, the only person that the Bible identifies as a tax collector that Jesus sympathizes with is Zacchaeus. The Gospel of Luke claims that this causes outrage from the crowds that Jesus would rather be the guest of a sinner than of a more respectable or "righteous" person.

In fact, there is not much in any source that provides accounts of Zacchaeus' later life, and what is available is contradictory. According to Clement of Alexandria, in his book *Stromata*, Zacchaeus was named Matthias by the Apostles, and took the place of Judas Iscariot after Jesus' ascension. On the other hand, Luke told us that Matthias was with Jesus since the baptism of John.[2] "Matthias" is the Hellenistic version of the name "Matthew." Could Zacchaeus therefore be the "Matthew" that Jesus recruited to be an apostle?

The later Apostolic Constitutions identify "Zacchaeus the Publican" as the first Bishop of Caesarea (7.46).[3] It is interesting to note that Caesarea was an important center for Paul as well, who used it as a hub for his missionary journeys, and he was allegedly imprisoned here before being taken to Rome.[4]

Could Zacchaeus and Matthew in fact be the same person – as per Greg's account of Paul? The regression continues.

Reena: And what happens next after your walking? [Very long pause.] Do you only walk with this man?

Greg: Well, I'm just part of the crowd now, no different from the others, and that feels really good.

Reena: How many in the crowd do you think?

Greg: It was really solitary before but this just feels totally different. Hmm, about twelve, fifteen? It's hard to count the number. It's like there's enough people to be interesting but not too big to be overwhelming.

Reena: Who are the people of this crowd?

Greg: I dunno! But they all seem excited and chattering... There's two women and the rest are men. Similar sort of age, similar to me, young twenties. It almost feels like there's going to be something achieved. I don't quite know what it is and we've been given the choice of whether we become part of something, we just don't know anything at all, but it just seems exciting to be part of it. It's not like me at all to go off and leave all the taxes and the donkey behind, it's almost like I don't care anymore now.

Reena: And what happens next?

Greg: We need some food, so we're stopping in a small house. I say house, it's a very cheaply-built thing, like white smooth walls that have been made with some sort of clay or something. It's just a doorway, I don't even think there's a window – it's very small. We're sat outside and the person inside has brought out a bit of food and is sharing it, so we all have a little bit of bread.

Reena: What else do you eat? Only bread?

Greg: No, there's some water and there's a bit of fruit, like dates. There's also something on the plate, I'm not quite sure what it is but it's like a dried fruit, some sort of plant or something. Something which he's perhaps collected wild. The bread's very lumpy and has grains in it. But it just seems so perfect.

The next scene saw Paul on the move with the same group of people, having left the house. The crowd is bigger now, people seemingly coming from different directions. They are following the person who hugged him.

Reena: How do you address this person who hugged you?

Greg: Well, I'm not sure, they kind of have slightly different names for him and he responds to all of the names, so it's a bit confusing. Some of them call him something with a "Yeyal" … not too sure what that is. It sounds strange but I just call him The One. It's almost like he feels [like] the special One. Yeah, I think we all have different names for him because it's almost like, I kind of feel like each of them have a different type of relationship with him and they kind of like to have a name that fits him. He responds to all of them, he… But for me I call him The One. I like that.

Interesting how Greg refers to Jesus as "The One" here, and "Jesus" earlier. Normally, when people experience multiple regression sessions to the one life, they become more comfortable and sink into the memories more. As Greg became more comfortable and embraced the memory more deeply, he shifted from referring to Jesus as "Jesus" to "The One." Also, "The One" sounds like a very personal term that he used to address Jesus, so the more associated with the memory he became, the easier he was able to access his personal term for Jesus.

Reena: Hmm… and they are all coming to see The One? These people?

Greg: Yeah.

Reena: And what's drawing all these people to The One?

Greg: Well, some people are talking about… perhaps he's going to be making some sort of plan, some of them are talking about him being the person to get rid of the Romans. Some of them say this word "Messiah," but I don't think they… words like that… it feels like… not sure. They don't like anything that's overthrowing the

Romans because they… I've seen what they've done with people before and they are all very frightened of them. It's almost like it doesn't matter when you're with The One. It feels almost like nothing can be defeated – you don't need swords or arms – just the group of us are able to almost do anything. It's almost like the Romans would wilt if we walked towards them, so I just go along with it and see what happens.

Reena: Are you a Roman or are you something else?

Greg: Well, I'm not a Jew, they call me a Gentile. I'm not really religious. I grew up in a village where there were Jews, it's just that we didn't do any of the things they do, so therefore they shunned us and that's why I was quite happy to do the job of collecting taxes from them, teach them a lesson.

This account once again contradicts the common knowledge that Paul was a Pharisee who held strongly to the Jewish traditions and rituals. It is the first time that Paul referred to himself as a Gentile. While I did not ask, this could imply that Greg's Paul held Roman citizenship due to his position as a Gentile, and his work as a tax collector, which is consistent with the accounts in the Book of Acts.[5]

The regression continues.

Reena: Tell me more about the crowds that came to see The One.

Greg: The crowd? Hmm, well there's young and old, there's some women carrying babies, some children, not many, the children are with the parents and holding their hands, there's some older people having difficulty walking. There's some of them that have got wounds, there's one person who's like lost an arm, but they're all coming along.

Reena: What's drawing them to The One?

Greg: Well, there's going to be some kind of talk maybe, some of them are saying, plans to get rid of the Romans, but I don't think that is the case. But we'll just have to see what he's going to talk about.

Reena: And so just tell me what happens next.

Greg: The One is standing on a raised bit of land. I say land, it's all rocks but it just means his feet are at the same height as the nearest ones' heads but the hill is further down so people aren't all at the same height. And he's gesturing for everyone to sit. So we all sit and he's starting to talk.

He's just talking about how things can be done differently, how powerful love is. I don't quite understand what he means by that, but it's what he did to me and that's pretty powerful. He's telling some stories.

He's telling the story of someone who had three sons, and the youngest son leaves home because he's not happy with how things are and feels that he's not getting a fair share. And how, when he comes back a little later, his father just gives him food and clothing. His other sons said, "We stayed with you and we all did the things you asked for, yet you give all these presents to him and he did nothing, it's not fair." And we all think to ourselves (well, *I* do), "That's not fair, is it?" And he's explaining that with love you can forgive people and you can give them things that they need, it's not about giving everybody the same thing, you just give people what they need, when they need it; that's what love is.

So this is quite a different way of thinking about things. It's certainly got me thinking. A few people are chatting to each other about it, almost like it's an idea that no one's ever thought of before. It's almost like, "Wow, yeah, we could do [that]." It certainly got me thinking.

Reena: And what happens next?

Greg: Well, there's a woman with The One and she comes

close to him and I guess I'm feeling a bit uncomfortable about why he's drawing women quite close to him, when this is men's work talking about these sort of things. It's not the sort of thing women do and yet he's drawing her up and he's saying how women are just as important as men. Well, this is a different idea altogether, women the same as men? They're supposed to stay at home and look after the babies and do the cooking.

Paul's way of thinking really is in line with both the Jewish and Romans' strong patriarchal cultures and systems at that time.

Reena: How does that make you feel?

Greg: Ah, a bit strange really. And he's talking about how it's not what job you do or who you are that's important, it's about how everybody can come through to the Kingdom of Heaven. It doesn't matter if they are young, old, male or female, they are all the same. And if all of them can come through to the Kingdom of Heaven, why are they treated differently when they are not in the process of going through to the Kingdom of Heaven? Hmm, that's got us all thinking about that one.

And then he says, what about someone who has a lot of money, can they take that through to the Kingdom of Heaven? They are saying, "Well, no." So then he says, well, if you can't take that with you, why do you need to collect it and hold it when you can help others? Oh my goodness… this is a bit of a new idea.

And he's walking forward and there's someone who's got some kind of disease, I don't know what it is. They're not well, they're like on a stretcher, I've never seen them before because of the crowd but they are always there. And he's moving his way forward and he's putting his hands on them and he's talking about bringing the Kingdom of Heaven down to them so that even the poor and the dying can feel it too. And he's saying how they can just go through to the Kingdom of Heaven in the same way as everybody else.

Well. He [the person with the disease] is certainly opening up his eyes and he's lifting his head up, others are helping to prop him up so he is partially sat, he's got such a smile on his face, it's almost like he's being touched, and there's a part of him that's about to change. I don't know, certainly quite an amazing effect he's having on everybody, including me... some sort of buzz.

It's almost like... thoughts of new ways of doing things, new ideas and more... no one ever talks about ideas – well, come on, let's have more of them! Nobody ever talks about these sort of things. Everybody is always on about how to survive and keep out of the way of the Romans. We all have our little jobs to do and when we feel emotionally unhappy, we take it out on whoever's around and this is what everybody does... and [this is] someone doing something completely different.

Reena: Tell me what more you are aware of.

Greg: Things are coming to an end now, walking away and the crowd dispersing. He's just called a few of us over.

Reena: Is that woman included as well?

Greg: Yeah. I think he's got a special relationship with her, I'm not sure. He seems to put his arm around her which... it's not like a permanent thing, it's like when you meet someone you hug them, it's like that. It's brief and then it's finished, but he does it like it's a sign of affection. Everything's new so I just need to find... he seems to be pulling a small group of us to one side, it was some of the ones who were together before the others joined us. He's calling us off and wants to talk to us as a group.

Reena: And roughly how many are in this group? [Long pause.]

Greg: About eight I think.

Reena: And what does he say to you?

Greg: He's saying something about we need to be fishermen for men or something. Do what he's doing, and, oh my goodness, how can we suddenly go through and do what he's doing? This is something entirely new.

We follow him and we find another house and get another bit of food given to us. One or two of them have brought some food with them and we're sharing it. It's not a lot, but it always seems to be just enough for what we need.

Reena: And what happens next?

Greg: Everyone's going to have to rest but we're all chattering and talking, the group are all quite excited. This is the first night, the first day, oh my goodness, if every day is like this… this is going to be exciting stuff.

It gets even more fascinating as the following accounts takes us back to Paul, listening to Jesus talk with a group of twenty to thirty people, and that their relationship seems to be a close one. This again contradicts the common story that he met Jesus after the crucifixion.

Greg: The things he says make so much sense. It kind of just feels right… The talk's finished now so I go up to him and put my arm round him and we walk off together. There are lots of people wanting to talk to him and spend time with him. But it's almost like a family reunion with him… He's full of excitement about all the places he's been to and the things he's learned. I just stay quiet and just listen… a bit in awe.

Reena: What happens next?

Greg: We're discussing plans. He's telling me that he has to leave and go to another part of the country. I ask him if I can come and listen. He says of course. So I have to go back and tell everyone at home that I'm going to go.

Reena: And what was the response?

Greg: A lot of sadness. My other brothers want to come too but they are too young. I pack my things, not that I have many, and I go out and join him and we go off together. There's a group of about twelve or fourteen people walking with him. I've got something on my feet now, they are sandals.

Reena: These people following him…?

Greg: They are just following him, listening to him. Doing things like sort out food and clothing and finding places to stay at night when they go to villages. Helping out.

Reena: Are there any women or only the male gender?

Greg: No, there're women, two or three women. But there's no one in relationships. They are just all independent people.

Reena: OK, just tell us what happens next.

Greg: We are just going from place to place. Starting to know a lot of the things he's talking about. It's like I've heard it a few times and it makes sense… and it's like, "Oh, that's a different way in which he's telling that now," and, "Oh, that's interesting." And I'm just doing a little bit of talking to others myself. I've got the general idea of how he does it so I am speaking to a few others. And if they don't understand what he just said I am going over the story again, until they get it. A lot of it is stories.

Reena: Does everyone do that in the group that is walking with him or just you?

Greg: Some do, some are just pleased to be there, some just like to be in the energy, some are doing practical things. It's almost like there aren't any rules about what they do or don't do.

Reena: It's whatever they want to do. Can you tell us what happens next?

Greg: It's an evening and a number of us are settling around a table… I was going to say eight or nine but I think there're a few people who aren't quite at the table who are within earshot. But there're eight or nine people around the table that are actually eating.

He [Jesus] is talking about how things are going to get difficult in the future... He's saying that there are a lot of people that don't like what he's saying, that he's too much of a threat. At the moment we've been more in the outskirts of things, [so] it's been less of a problem. But as you start to go into some of the cities, and some of the towns, there's going to be more resistance. There's going to be more people who try to stop it from happening. He's just talking about what to do.

Reena: Whereabouts are you now? Which part of the world?

Greg: This is in Judea.

Reena: And so are you going to go into Judea, into the proper center?

Greg: That's part of the discussion, who is going to go with him and who is going to leave... I say I want to stay. A few of the others are going to stay in some of the places where we've been and reinforce some of the things that we have talked about. So the group is going to get quite small.

Reena: Do some of them leave?

Greg: Well, they're not planning to, when we leave in the morning, they're not planning to come. Not right away but they may come a little later. It's like we're all part of the same thing but we're doing it in different ways. Just, it's not like leaving in terms of going away forever, it's almost just like a parting.

Reena: Do you know who the other people that are gathered around this table are?

Greg: Hmm... There's James.

Reena: Who is James?

Greg: I don't know; he's just called James.

Reena: Are there any women present?

Greg: Yeah.

Reena: Do you know who they are?

Greg: I'm not too sure of what their names are... Sarah... and... I'm not getting any more.

Reena: Is there a meal involved here?

Greg: There is. Every evening we get together. It's part of the ritual. It's almost like during the day we're all working, giving information and help and teachings to others and in the evenings it's kind of like, not a pep talk but it's kind of like any concerns anyone has, they can raise them.

It's almost like getting a deeper motivation. Or just talking through potential problems of where we're going. It's just keeping everyone together as a group. So the evenings are very similar. There's not one evening that is greatly different than the other.

Reena: Is there anything else of significance this night?

Greg: I kind of get the feeling that things won't be quite the same afterwards and I think the others feel that too. There's not a sadness, more of an acceptance.

The next event sees Paul and the rest of the followers in a larger place with lots of buildings.

Greg: We're walking there and there's lots of people looking at us. It's almost like they're not sure who we are, or what we do. But there is a curiosity overall all the same. We're just passing messages on to come along to a talk.

So there's like a hill, a small way outside. I am quite amazed at how many people are coming. I've not seen as many people as this. It's quite surprised all of us 'cos there appeared to be a bit of, not quite hostility, but there was certainly no warm welcome. So it's quite surprising how many people are coming. We're all a bit surprised by this.

So I'm taking my place, near the front, just so I can

keep an eye on things. I just don't really know what to do with so many people. When it's been smaller groups I've taken one or two people to one side and talked to them and helped explain it but it's such a big group, almost a hundred people, I don't really know what to do. I can't count them there are just so many faces... And there's like a quietness. You can hear that some of the people are moving about, settling down, sitting down. It's like there's no banter or arguing or anything of that nature; it's almost like they know what they are going to get almost before they come. Very unusual. So I sit at the front, just float about and see what happens.

Reena: And what happens next?

Greg: Well, Jesus starts doing one of his talks, really excelling this time. He's got lots [of ways] of telling his stories, which I always found interesting to listen to anyway... When he's finished talking they [the crowd] all want to touch him or speak to him but I've got to try and keep them away just to kind of give him a bit of space. It's a bit dusty and we're all still over-thirsty because we haven't eaten or had much chance to drink. This has all caught us by surprise so we all try to break free from the crowd so we can have our evening meal and talk.

Jesus just wants to keep talking and talking to them all. Eventually they break free and we usher them away and get into the house where we're staying and close the doors. We wash our feet and hands and drink and there's a meal ready for us.

Reena: Who does this house belong to?

Greg: It's one of the people in the town that's allowed us to stay. Some of the others are staying in other houses and some of them are sleeping outside... people just sleep wherever they can.

We are just discussing the bigger crowds, and how to

handle it. I make the suggestion that we encourage people at the next talk to bring food and water with them. So if they can go on for longer, they can even eat there rather than having to rush to come back.

Evening's the main meal of the day. You don't have much chance for the rest of the day so if you don't have a main meal you can get hungry.

Reena: Can you remember any of the stories that Jesus told during this?

Greg: He talked about the Pharisees I think. He thought of them as friends. He treated them differently, though they shun him. And that surprised a lot of people because they don't like the Pharisees…

He explains how certain traditions get in the way of these acts of kindness and how it's important to understand that the traditions are just simply that, they are a guidance, but it's important that these acts of guidance should be done as people need them. And that surprised a lot of people too.

He talked about women too. He talked about a woman who cared for a man who had leprosy and instead of shunning him, she just cared and gave him water and food and eventually the leper went off. He went off with a smile on his face.

He's just explaining about these acts of kindness and they were forgotten and how anybody can do it, wherever they are. The leper went off to the leper colony but at least for that day he had a wonderful memory to take with him. So these are the sorts of stories that he tells.

Here, it is interesting to note how much attention Paul paid to how and what Jesus was teaching. It was the most prevalent in his memories. This is in line with his passion for evangelizing and teaching Jesus' message.

Paul

Chapter 2

The Parting

The next event saw us moving forward four years – seeing Paul in a group, at a table, eating with The One.

Greg: There's a group of us, the ones who are closest to him. I'm in this house with a big table and we're sat around eating our evening meal and he's saying this is going to be the last time we're all together and that he's going to die but it's for a reason. We're all a bit quiet about that. A few of them said no, we can't have that.

But we just learned to accept whatever happens, happens, however unusual, because that is part of the journey that we seem to be on at the moment. Anyway, that's what I think, that's my view. The others may have different views. I don't talk much to the others about it. I'm more "think about it."

Reena: And it was a meal... what sort of meal were you having?

Greg: We had some water. There's some fish – it's like a dried fish that's cooked somehow. There's some bread – there's bread with everything – and there's some other things in with the fish and there's some vegetables of some sort, it's a bit like stew. Slapped onto a plate, it's very simple food but feels very filling.

Both fish and goat were predominant foods that were eaten during those times. Fish was caught from the Sea of Galilee, and transported around the country. As with goat, fish was also served to honored guests by rich patrons who could afford the delicacy.[1]

Reena: Are there men and women here at this meal?

Greg: Yes, there's Mary, who's sat next to Jesus – well, some people call him that... I call him The One. And then there's the other group of followers sat around him.

Reena: You are friendly with one another? What is your relationship like with the other followers... Mary and the others?

Greg: We all accept each other. It's almost like we treat each other how we've been taught to treat others. This seemed at first strange, treating people who were Jews or non-Jews, or women or men, all the same. But it's quite nice. I like it.

The next event sees Paul witnessing Jesus dragging a cross.

Greg: And we are just at the point where Jesus is carrying the cross. I can't help being a bit frightened by it all even though I knew what was going to happen so I just kept quiet in the background... So it's all like a bit of [a] state of shock nevertheless.

It's still not easy to see it happening and what is hard is that all the people who are shouting and jeering at him, they are the very people who were listening to his stories and it's almost like they didn't get it. I wonder if they get this though, that despite all the things that have been done to him he's still showing kindness.

The One is dragging a cross... he's got two hands to one of the pieces of wood and he's like pulling it behind him. And there are two or three Romans around him. One of them hits him occasionally. There's blood all over him, it's hard to recognize him like this. He's covered in blood, he's been beaten and whipped and his face has blood running all the way down it. There's blood coming from his head and shoulders. It's just that I know this is something the

Romans have done to him. And I'm just kind of stood there. I just don't know what to do. It was so obvious just following before but now something's happening to him. It's almost like I don't know what to do and the rest of the crowd are like that. And we're just kind of stood, almost like shocked, like paralyzed with the fear and the shock. How could this happen? So I keep a bit of a distance away.

Reena: So just tell me a bit about the wooden cross.

Greg: It's not very big, it's like the wood is like circular, not very thick, maybe three inches thick and probably about the length of a person and a bit more. There's another piece that's been tied to it and there's like rope around the two pieces of wood in the center. But as it's been dragged one of the pieces has been twisted so that it's not quite in line with the other piece but at a slight angle. The One is holding one of the pieces and dragging it behind.

Reena: Is it a dark wood or a light wood?

Greg: No, it's a light wood. It looks like some of the bark has been taken off it. I've got a feeling this has been used before for crucifixions.

Reena: Are both pieces of wood the same size or are they different?

Greg: Well one of them is slightly bigger than the other one and they are slightly, not entirely straight, a slight kink in them. But we all know what it's going to be used for.

Reena: And you're so confused, you don't know what to do…

Greg: Just shock and horror. Just devastated how such an amazing person can end up like this.

Reena: What's your understanding of how The One ended up like this?

Greg: That he was tried and found guilty. Of course it was all stage-managed by the Pharisees and the Jews. Some of the Jews who don't like him want to get rid of him. I wasn't involved in that, but I am just following the procession.

There's a few people on the side who've come to see this (all of them look equally shocked and devastated, frightened) and they are getting to a small clearing.

Reena: And what happens next?

Greg: Well, this clearing has got a small wall, very rough and ready, and the wood is on the floor and The One is being held. He's on top of the wood and they're taking nails and hitting the nail through each of his... his wrists? Somewhere between the wrist and his palm, I think they're being careful not to cut open a vessel. They've been told to be careful where to put them, they do it to his other hand and feet. Almost like it's a cross but it's like an X instead of a cross. Then they pull this up to the wall and the cross is like leaned against the wall and he's just got his head drooped down.

Reena: In between the cross?

Greg: Yeah, his arms are in the air, his head's in the air and his feet aren't quite touching the ground because there's some wood slightly longer than his feet so his whole body is dragged on the wood. And there's blood coming out of where the nails have gone in.

Reena: What is his behavior like? I mean, is he aware of the pain? Is he shouting?

Greg: No, he's not saying anything, he's just... it's like all the energy has gone out of him and the Romans stand around there. There're two others that have been treated in the same way so there's these three Xs where the three people are. All of them are hanging there. All of them have been nailed to the wood.

Sometimes I've seen these crucifixions where they've done them against the walls of Jerusalem and they're actually put on the big walls of Jerusalem, but for some reason they wanted to take him out of Jerusalem away from people so they found this little rocky outpost to do it. The Romans are just stood around, just keeping people at a distance.

In the interest of full disclosure, Greg, during the debrief, admitted to watching a documentary on television about ancient Roman crucifixion methods, and thought that this description of the position of the body may be more from conscious mind recollection of the documentary, rather than his own memory. However, according to Laurence Gardner, in the Dead Sea Scrolls the original holy sign of the cross was an X mark, which is now known as the St. Andrew's cross. By way of later Roman influence the new cross sign was devised.[2] Maybe Greg's account was not far from the truth after all.

Reena: What else are the Romans doing apart from standing around and looking at the people?

Greg: Well, they're just Romans. They don't care about the people who've been crucified. They've been told what to do is to keep people away, so that's what they're doing. A few of them are taunting The One and taunting some of the others too.

Reena: How do they taunt The One?

Greg: They're saying that if you're special why can't you come off the cross and walk away? One of them is prodding with a spear.

Reena: Whereabouts?

Greg: In the body, but it's not like it's going in deep, it's just going in a little bit. It's almost like having fun, this is their way of having a bit of amusement. There's not many people around, I'm one of the few people there.

Reena: Who else do you recognize from the group who are there?

Greg: Well, there's Mary, that woman who is special to him, who he told me he was married to. There's a couple of the others who've been with him… men. I'm in the crowd so I just leave too… [feeling] very sad. And we troop away. I know he can't do anything; he'll have to die. So I suppose that's what I can do perhaps. That's the biggest way of thanking The One for everything I've gained and learned, is to go and do the same to others. Although my mind's not really on that at the moment.

Reena: When he was put on the cross, where were you situated?

Greg: I was just in the crowd.

Reena: Was there anyone near him?

Greg: I couldn't see an awful lot. There were some soldiers there. I'm just so sad and overwhelmed by it all.

The next event sees Paul being ushered into a small room the day after the crucifixion, where there are four or five people.

Reena: Who is ushering you?

Greg: James, I think. And there is Jesus, he's quite badly hurt so that he's resting. It's definitely him and he's alive.

Reena: Who is there?

Greg: There's Mary. That's his wife… There's James who has brought me in. I think there's Peter and Judas there. Judas is the one who… Well, he's saying he betrayed [him] but Jesus is saying that you did what I asked you to do. I asked you to do those things, someone had to do them and it was a really difficult job. But he's full of grief. He's full of grief because even though he did it, he thought there'd be a different outcome.

Judas is leaving, Jesus is explaining that Judas is going to kill himself and we're saying but why, you're alive, he's seen you're alive… I just can't understand it. Jesus is explaining that even though Judas was asked to do it and what the reason was, he feels guilty for all of the hurt and pain that Jesus has been through.

Jesus can't be around to teach, we all know that, 'cos if anyone sees him, then there won't be a chance to rescue him a second time.

It feels almost like Judas has betrayed the whole cause of trying to get this message out. Even though it's been explained to him that it's just going to happen in a different way, he just doesn't seem to understand it and Jesus is saying that things are just going to have to unfold as they unfold and don't try to force anything.

I am just confused by the whole thing, it's just too much. First of all, seeing him being killed and I didn't know that he was going to be taken down and I'm just asking him how it was done and he explains that another body was put in there. Someone had died and soldiers were bribed, and they were quite happy for that as long as there was a body there for people to look at. They looked very similar.

Reena: Who bribed the soldiers and masterminded the rescue?

Greg: The whole plan was Jesus', of course. He asked different people to do different tasks. It's almost like this was all known, like it was all pre-planned, completely, it was almost like everybody knew the part they had to play.

What emerged in *Shrouded Truth* was that Jesus survived the crucifixion, and that James had masterminded the plan to save Jesus, unbeknown to Jesus. There were three levels of information that were shared about the "Resurrection of Jesus." The first level of what really happened was known only to a close-knit circle comprised of James, Mary Magdalene and Mother Mary. The second level was disclosed to the Apostles and disciples, where they found out that Jesus was indeed crucified but nursed back to health. In *Shrouded Truth*, Jesus emerged, hurt, to inform some of his disciples who were still around that he was not dead. For the safety of Jesus, they were instructed to inform everyone else, the third tier, that Jesus had died on the cross, so as to not attract attention from the Romans and the Pharisees.

It was clear from these regressions that Paul was privy only to the second level of information. So, it is interesting to note that Paul reflected the perception of knowledge received by the second tier – the disciples – which is why he thought it was Jesus who was carrying the cross and was crucified. This is important as this knowledge precipitated the teachings that he eventually would evangelize.

It also makes sense that Jesus was to shoulder the responsibility as the main decision-maker, as opposed to James, who still had a reputation to protect, as we will see from his accounts.

Reena: Can you describe Jesus' appearance [at] this time... is he badly wounded...?

Greg: Well, they did put nails in his hands, he has the wounds from that. He has the wounds around his head and where he was whipped. I think [he's] in quite a bad state, he's going to need a lot of nursing. I think the plan is to take him to a place... it's like a plank with wheels, a trolley, that can take him to a safe place and he'll just be nursed and looked after.

I think Mary Magdalene is going to be the one to look after him. They are going to keep it quite small to start with. The plan is we all go our different ways and then come back in a few months' time. I don't think there's any need, we've all made a note of where we're going. I've got a cousin I can stay with so I'm going there. They know where I am going.

Reena: Is this cousin in Judea?

Greg: [nods] ... And then we regroup in two or three months' time and that is how we'll find out from Jesus what he wants to do next.

The next event finds Paul at a meeting of eight people over a meal in the evening. He sees Jesus standing there, with a smile on his face, like old times, with many of his wounds around his face healed.

> Greg: Jesus is asking each of us what we'd like to do. I am saying that I'd like to go to the island of Cyprus. I've heard about this island and I'd like to take some of his teachings there. The others are talking about the other places that they'd like to go to... Someone wants to go to Turkey, someone wants to go to North Africa and someone wants to stay in the area and continue the teachings. It's almost like they don't know exactly where they want to go, it's like approximate directions, and then they'll just flow with things. Jesus and Mary kind of go off together... I think I get the feeling that he [Jesus] is going to just go off. He's got his own plan of where he's going to go off to, but he's going to have to stay in hiding certainly from the Romans.

So Paul parts from Jesus. As we proceed, it is fascinating to observe how he constructed and evolved his teachings based on how he clearly loved and idolized Jesus, and what his perceptions of the events around the crucifixion were.

Paul

Chapter 3

The Start

In the next significant event, Paul is wearing brown sandals and a rough, dirty, white cotton robe. He is in a village north of Galilee. He took three days to get to the village he is in now, travelling predominantly in the early morning and late afternoon as it is too hot to do so in the middle of the day. He explains that he relies on the kindness of people for accommodation, or sleeps in the open, in the cold.

The village he is at now is a new village that none of the Apostles had been to. Paul just went into the village and asked for the Elder, introduced himself, and explained what he was doing. The Elder's interests were piqued when Paul spoke about Jesus, and how he had worked closely with Jesus, travelling with him.

Intrigued, the Elder invites Paul to stay with him and asks everyone to put his or her tools down to listen to what Paul has to say. There are several groups of people, who are nervously half-talking and half-waiting for something to happen. They are open-minded, and have come to learn and listen to what Paul has to say. They want to see if there is anything Paul can say that will change their lives or help them in some way.

Greg: I am feeling a bit nervous. Before, I have said only a few things to complement other talks. This is the first time I have done an entire talk by myself.

After the people had gathered in groups, Paul finds a little rock to stand on and get everyone's attention. They stop talking and look up expectantly at him.

Greg: I start by saying who I am and what I have done with Jesus. It goes deathly quiet when I mention his name. Then I just start. I explain that I am a follower of Jesus and listened to all his teachings. I am going to share some of them along with some of my own observations. I told everybody to listen very carefully and that they could go through and share with other people.

I start off by just asking them, "Are you happy with your life? Do you have joy? Do you have people who bring love into your life? Or is life a long hard struggle with no light at the end?" It is not a large group, so I can talk like this. There are about twenty people here. They are still listening, so I ask them to put their hands up if they have joy in their life. No hands go up. So then I tell them a story... I start off with one of the stories I learned from Jesus.

Paul's Parable 1: Treat Others as You Would Like to be Treated

This is a story of two men who are friends, neighbors. One day one of the neighbors noticed that some of the sheep he was looking after had disappeared. He went looking to see where they had gone to – and found them amongst other sheep in his neighbor's field.

If you were that man who had lost his sheep – what would you say and what would you do?

Would you get angry, demand them back?

Would you just pick them up and take them and ignore your neighbor?

Would you suggest that as the sheep have found the way there, that's where they need to be and you can keep them?

Would you suggest that perhaps the two of you take one

of the sheep that has wandered over, cook it and have food and invite the families around to share it?

As they were yours, you have every right to go and demand them back. Would you take them or ask your neighbor if he knew why they were there?

Maybe your neighbor did not know why they got there.

If you took them and the neighbor thought they were actually his sheep – how would he feel and act? Do you think you would have a friendly neighbor or would you have someone who assumed you were taking his sheep and then he, in return, would retaliate?

Would you think that the sheep have found their way to you so perhaps that's where they need to be, and you would just claim them? What would your neighbor say if you did that?

What do you think your neighbor would say if you said there seem to be extra sheep, and you did not know if they were yours or his? What would happen if you offered to divide them between you and the neighbor, have a meal and enjoy being neighbors? How would you like to be treated if you were the neighbor?

This is the message that Jesus had – Treat other people the way that you would like to be treated. If you like to be treated by having kind things done for you… or sometimes be offered things to you beyond what you expected – then that is what you must do to others.

If you look after your sheep and give them the food and water they need, why would they want to go off in the first place?

If you treat the sheep the same way you treat your neighbors, you bring joy into your life. Even though work may be long and hard, you have happy sheep, you have happy neighbors. There will always be enough sheep for everybody.

Reena: How do they respond to that story?

Greg: A little bit with shock and horror, because their natural reaction is to go and demand their sheep back. It is the natural way. To say that there are alternatives is a surprise. To think that sheep can be treated in the same way as we treat humans gave some of them a shock. And of course that's what it was meant to do. We have exhausted that story. So then I go on to another story. It's a variation of a story that Jesus told and I quite like it, but I have altered it slightly.

Paul's Parable 2: Love Through Letting Go

This is a story about a man who had three sons. All three sons worked really hard and helped their father. The father taught them all the skills that he had. They made and sold furniture, and it took great skill to make furniture from wood. That takes many years to master… picking the right wood, using the different tools, making some of the tools. All three sons were learning the trade. The man's heart was full of joy at the thought that he'd been able to pass on all of his skills to his sons and give them something that they really wanted to do, and to have a place in the village and in the community. They were well respected, as very few people had those skills in those communities. Often people had to go further afield to get the furniture that was needed.

One of the sons had heard of faraway places from one of the travelers who had passed through. As he had never seen anyone like them, he wanted to travel. He asked for his father's blessing. His father really did not want him to go, claiming it was dangerous out there, with waterless deserts, where people were killed. At home, he had all the food and water he needed, as well as a highly skilled job. Why would he want to leave?

His son thought about this and said, "I have a yearning to go, to discover and to see. Even with all these frightening things you talk about, I still want to go. Can I have your blessing?"

The father started to get quite angry at this point. He had put all this work and effort into teaching his son how to do this job… and here he was asking for permission to leave? He could be killed. His other brothers wouldn't be able to enjoy his company. How could he treat his family like this?

If you were that man and that was your son… what would you say? Would you give him your blessing or would you demand he stays?

The father still forbade him to go, and even got a Pharisee to tell him that it was the duty of the son to stay with his father – but the son still went.

He was not seen for three or maybe four years. During that time one of the other sons died. Another damaged his hand and could not do the carpentry. The father was too old to continue.

The family was in real poor times, having to rely on the generosity of the other villagers for food.

Meanwhile the young son that had left had ended up in a new place and found that there was great demand for his skills, as no one else could make furniture like he could. He was able to sell far more than he had done before and he had accumulated quite a bit of money. After four years, he decided he would go back to his family to see them. He came back, pockets bulging with money, and found his father too old to work, his brother with one deformed hand, unable to work, and the other son deceased.

This son was someone who was threatened with disownment if he left, but left anyway.

If you were that young man who came back rich, and saw your family in trouble, but they told you were no longer part of the family… what would you do?

One option is that he could give them a few coins and go back to that place where he earned all his money and enjoy his new lifestyle.

But in this story, he takes all the money that he has, gives it to his father and says, "I have not been around for the last four years to help or be with you, but I just want you to know that for the remaining years of your life, you'll have all the money you need to look after your family, all the food that's needed. All those years you looked after me and gave me all the things I needed, now this is my turn to give you all the things you need."

If you were that old man, what would you think of a son who did that?

If you put out love in the world you get love coming back. You can't control love any more than you can control that young son's journey. You can give them your blessings. Let them go on with their life. If people help each other when they have something they can give, they give, and when they need, they can openly receive it from others. There are times when we all have things to give and there are times when we need to receive. Just flow with that and allow people the freedom to form their own lives.

Greg: That was not quite one of Jesus' stories, but it was an adaptation of one. I told several other stories like that. It was all about love. Love was all that Jesus used to talk about, because that was all that there is. Sometimes we just surround it or obscure it. The job of the teacher is to just take away those aspects of life that stop it from coming through and shining. Stories are the hallmark of Jesus. This is what he taught us. We have our own stories and this is how it should be too. I talked for about two hours, until it started to get dark. We finished for the day.

Reena: What makes you use stories as a way of teaching?

Greg: Because stories are being taught all through life. When we are children we are taught stories about how to live amongst others, stories about how our ancestors survive difficult situations. Stories are part of the culture. Simple people can understand them far more than theories and concepts. It is just that we have to tell a lot of stories when the change is great.

Reena: Tell me more about the change.

Greg: All the people that I go to live in fear. There is the fear of breaking the laws of the Romans, when we are in lands that the Romans control. There is fear of breaking the laws of the ruler who ruled at that time. There is the fear of breaking the ways of the community or the village that you are in and risking the other villagers' condemnation. There is the fear of survival when just finding food each day is not easy. Of course, there is the fear of the Pharisees and breaking the rules of the religion. So fear ripples through everybody's lives, and people living simple lives have to weave this thread through all of these fears. When they were outside all these fears, they had no guidance on what to do in what little space they had. If they happened to be in a community or a family where love prevails, then they would learn about love that way. If they were in a family where their father beat their children, then that is what they did. There was no ability to learn about spiritual things. Current religions have fixed laws about what to do and what not to do, giving a level of organization in family life. However, people just simply followed the laws to the letter without understanding the deeper meaning of it. This is the difference between the teachings of the religion and the teachings of Jesus. He taught people to think about what it really means to love and how to do it.

Reena: How did people respond to stories of love?

Greg: With all of them there was a certain amount of shock and horror initially. By using the stories and asking them questions, it got them thinking about the points that were being made. There was a yearning to learn more. This is different to when people are in the synagogues or whatever place of worship that they are in. They were being told what the rules were, of what they had to do and what not to do. It's almost like the projection of fear… except for being in a very caring family, there was no one who could teach about love. This is why it was almost like their hearts were crying out to hear it. Of course, not everybody would implement it. Not everybody came. The village I was at, only about half the men came to the first talk. No women. But it's a start. The Elder went through and invited the men. It was his decision to do that. I think at the next one I will ask the Elder to extend it to women as well. As this was the first talk, I needed his help.

Reena: What motivated him to only invite men?

Greg: Men were the leaders of the family. If you had people there who were not the leader of the family, it's almost a sign of disrespect. If the leader of the family, the father, the man, invited his wife and others along, or was encouraged to do that, then it is different. Whether that is the same in the other villages, I do not know. But this is how it was in

> this first village I spoke at. When Jesus did his talks he got both men and women – sometimes more women. I think that people heard about him and they just came and did not always tell others that they were going.

After the two-hour talk, the group wanted to gather round, talk and ask Paul questions about Jesus and about the stories that he talked about. Paul explained that the message which he had given them is the one that Jesus gave. However, the stories were adapted. Paul then offered to spend the next time telling them Jesus' stories, if a larger group of people would make it. He encouraged the participants to invite whomever they wanted.

He then went back for a meal, hosted by the Elder and his family. The family asked Paul questions about Jesus' teachings, to most of which Paul suggested they attend the talk the day after, as he was too tired to repeat it all for them. They then asked questions about Jesus himself.

> Greg: They asked whether he rose from the dead. In which case I said yes and I saw him after he had been crucified. That he was the Son of God and how I was carrying his messages.

This is the first time that Paul broaches the subject of Jesus assuming a divine-like status, where he confirmed that Jesus arose from the dead. Compared to the other main teaching branches of Christianity that we are going to look at, Gentile Christianity is the only branch that focuses on Jesus himself being God, or the Son of God. The debate of Jesus' divine status raged for many centuries through the echelons of the establishment within the proto-orthodox church, and it seems that it started here, with Paul. We cannot be sure if Paul introduced this by himself here, at his first solo talk, or whether he picked it up from another source. However, what is clear is that this is how he saw Jesus.

Reena: Did you see him being raised from the dead and know that he is the Son of God or did you just mention it as part of the story?

Greg: I just talked to the Elder and his family. I simply said that I'd seen him after he'd been crucified. I could see the wounds and hear him talking before he disappeared again. And that only the Son of God could do that.

Reena: What was their response?

Greg: This is something that they had all heard and is one of the reasons that attracted a lot of people to the message of Jesus. I was just the messenger of it. I was simply using my stories to convey his message but it is just as easy to use his stories too. Then the meal was finished and that was the end of the day.

Within modern-day Christianity, while thirteen letters were attributed to Paul, only seven have been authenticated by scholars to be written by him, known as the undisputed letters. In them, Paul constantly refers to the resurrection of Christ. His intent was not to prove that Jesus was physically raised from the dead. Instead he just assumed that his readers knew that Jesus had been resurrected, and had appeared to some of the Apostles, including himself.[1] When Paul speaks of Jesus' spiritual body, he is emphatic in 1 Corinthians that the body was transformed into an immortal being, and he concurs with the earliest followers that Jesus had come back to life in a body, and that this was a body that could be seen and heard.[2] This is in line with Greg's account of Paul's version of Jesus' resurrection at the very humble start of his ministry.

The regression continues on to the next day. People are assembling a couple of hours before the sun went down, just as it started to cool down a little bit, at the same place as before. Paul was delighted that this time there was a larger group of people, comprising the same group of men as the day before, with some family members, sons and women – wives and daughters. There were about forty or fifty people. So he decided to make this event a little different and tell them stories from and about Jesus.

Paul's Parable 3: Joy of Giving

The first story is about the son who left his father and came back. His father had a feast of fattened calf to celebrate his return. His other sons asked why their father had a feast for the son who went away, when they had been with him all this time and yet he never had a feast for them.

If you were the father, what would your answer be?

The message was that when there is a joy in your life, you can celebrate it. When there is someone who has returned you thought was dead, then celebrate it. This is not about trying to share things equally amongst people. This is about the joy of giving, and how when everybody can join in that joy of giving without comparing themselves with the other person, then it can bring joy into everybody's lives. But if people hold on to the resentment, it's not going change people's joy. It just means they are unable to fully participate in that joy.

As it was a bigger group, Paul did not ask too many questions but gave a small interpretation, just enough to make people think about it. Then, he went on to the next story, which is one of Jesus'.

Paul's Parable 4: Flow with Change

This story is about a man who was fishing and just could not find any fish at all. Jesus walked up to him and told him that he was not fishing in the right spot. He advised the man to throw his nets on the other side and he'd get all the fish he wanted. The man did that, and his nets were full and bulging with fish.

Jesus was able to help people gather all the things they needed in life in abundance, but they had to be prepared to change the way they were doing things. If they kept throwing their nets on the same side that has been well fished, they would not get any fish. Only when they were prepared to do something new and different would they suddenly discover new delights, new joys.

Then he went on to the last story for the night.

Paul's Parable 5: Forgiveness

This is about a man who was sick. His sickness grew worse, and he did not know what he was going to do. He had no family, no friends. He could not even work because of his sickness. He would just lie there with a begging bowl. People would walk past and ignore him. Occasionally some people might give him the smallest coin denomination they had with an "It was the most you deserved" expression. One day, a man stopped and looked at him and said, "What is it that you need?" He said, "I am thirsty; I need water." So this man took out his water bottle and poured some water into his mouth.

Then he said, "What is it that you need?" He said, "I need food." So the man opened up his own food container and gave him food, his meal for that evening.

When the man who was sick had eaten, the other man asked, "What is it you need?" He said, "I need to be kept warm, I am not well." So the man took out his own blanket that kept him warm at night and put it over the sick man.

Then he asked, "What is it that you need?" The sick man said, "I need forgiveness because I was not able to look after my family when I was younger and I had to leave them." The kind man said, "I cannot give you forgiveness... you can only get that from the people involved. If you say you want forgiveness, then God will hear [for] them. You've got food, you are warm, you've had something to drink, and God will hear your forgiveness – what else do you need?"

The sick man said, "Nothing, but I just want to say one thing to you." The man said, "What's that?" The sick man said, "You did not recognize me, but I am the father you used to have. I left home when you were quite young and I recognized you and I am so proud that someone that is coming to this life can treat people the same way you treated me." With that, the sick man died peacefully with love in his heart.

To give so much and yet to discover that in giving you can make such a difference in someone else's life. It's about love... it's about giving and receiving equally. It's about breaking the cultural conditioning of looking at the same things.

Reena: How did the group respond to that story?

Greg: The group was mesmerized. A little bit of shock and horror at times, but realizing just how powerful it is to do things for other people.

Reena: Did the Pharisees not teach them this before? Doing

things for other people?

Greg: Not in the same way. When people went to the synagogue they had to donate money, which was taken by the church to be used by the church. The church would look after some poor people but most of it was for the church to look after the church and the Pharisees. People were told that by giving that money, their souls would be saved.

Reena: They were told this by the Pharisees?

Greg: Yes. Not all Pharisees are the same. Some of them genuinely cared for the people. If they did that, it was because that is something they wanted to do over and above what was needed of them. A lot of the time Pharisees would settle disputes. People would go and ask for advice. A small fee would have to be paid for the Pharisees to make the decision. Not so much about land or cattle – but more about interpretation of the scriptures that were used and taught to the children.

Reena: How do you recollect your stories?

Greg: Well, Jesus' stories are easy, because I can simply say that these are the stories that Jesus told, and help people interpret them. With my own stories, it's using stories that people can relate to. Maybe situations that people typically have in their lives. Where I am at the moment is a community with sheep and desert. So the stories I tell include sheep and desert, so people can understand them all. To tell a story about things they don't know about means that the story is not so easy to understand.

And so it is that the most prolific evangelizer of Jesus' teachings started in a humble village, three days' walk north of Galilee. During this time, Paul travelled from village to village, focusing on spreading this message through telling stories – both his own and Jesus'. While he only alluded to Jesus' divinity once during his early days, he focused most of his time on spreading spiritual messages. Clearly a gifted storyteller, it was his favorite format of teaching people who lived simply in the country. This is so that they were able to relate to, focus on, digest and absorb the underlying spiritual message.

Chapter 4

Rome

The next significant event sees Paul in Cyprus. It is as though Paul gained his experience and confidence teaching in North Galilee, and moved further afield to continue evangelizing.

Greg: I'm in Cyprus and I'm going from village to village trying to do the same as what Jesus was telling. I'm finding that some villages accept me and some villages don't, but that's exactly the same as what happened to Jesus. I think it's quite hard doing that. It seemed so easy following Jesus.

It's quite hard because it's almost like you have to be aware of everybody and everything and when you're saying things you are saying it to everybody. But I persevere. I've been there for a few years and I've got a small community going in one or two places to pass on the stories that they've been told.

I'm feeling a bit restless that there's no big towns in Cyprus. It's all like tiny villages and people are like... it's a bit like when we first started out with Jesus. It's almost like this is to just teach a little bit about "how to teach things and do things."

A lot of the times I am talking about what Jesus said and what he did. It's a lot easier to refer to him than say it's coming from me. It has much more of an effect; it's almost like he creates an eternal ring. A bit like a god, they're so used to having things that are really spiritually important that they can't see but they get told about. In those times I could say it would be my truths that I pass on as Jesus' truths, and that works really well and it honors him for the work that he did.

But I am getting a little restless because things aren't really flowing in the way that I thought they might do.

Reena: So what happens next?

Greg: I am catching a boat and I am going to a bigger place and I am going to the mainland. I'm going to Italy. I'm going to do things a little differently in Italy. In Cyprus everything was done quite casually, in other words. Everybody listens to the words but it's up to them how they interpret them or how they do things.

It was almost like they needed to have some sort of structure in place for the message to be retained. It's almost like it was too pure for them to understand and relate to. It's like they have to keep being reminded of it on a regular basis. So in Italy I'm going to take it a little bit differently to make it a bit more formal – going to get some of what he said written down. Try to create places where people can come to once a week, a little bit like how the Jewish religion works.

Reena: How did going to Italy affect you in terms of the fact that there were some Romans who had issues with Jesus?

Greg: I can turn up. They think Jesus is dead.

Reena: How about your teaching?

Greg: Well, I have to be careful of that, but people are receptive to it out in the countryside. It's almost like out in Rome, there's lots of difference in Rome itself… but when you get out in the countryside, it's almost like it's a different country. So you can be in Italy and it's a lot like being in a bigger version of Cyprus. But the Italians seem to be much more receptive to doing things in a structured way, whereas in Cyprus they were a slightly simpler people, simple fishermen or herders looking after goats. They were kind enough to listen to the words and I'm sure it helped them a little bit, but it didn't really make much impact at all.

So in Italy they seem to have more trade, more specialists in different areas, so that their ability to think and be able to relate to what they've been told... it's not quite as simple as people in Cyprus. So that I'm spending time giving that message, the bit that really worked well, was to talk about Jesus and about Jesus' messages. So that's how I'm going to do it.

It works out quite well and the people come every week, so that you can reinforce the messages. That part works really well with that bit of structure in place... Makes it seem so much more impressive and particularly telling the story of Jesus dying. We can't tell them what really happened, but that seems to work out really well.

It's a little bit of a mistruth but, I mean, we're trying to get the message out there about his kindness. We try to be as honest as with all those stories and the other things, it's just we have to be careful about the death part because if we said what [did] happen, that he didn't die, then obviously it's going to create problems with Jesus wherever he is because they're looking for him.

Reena: Do you know where he is?

Greg: No. So I just keep going from place to place in Italy and get quite a following... It's going really well. People are helping and working with me. The crowd is getting quite a few Romans. That's interesting getting the Romans in there.

The very first one that came was a soldier, a centurion, he came in camouflage so we couldn't see his soldier's clothes but we knew what he was. He just sat and listened and understood. It's nice to know that the message gets there, even to a soldier. He explained how he has to do as he's told, being a soldier. But... the thoughts he has, they can't control. They might be able to control his actions, and what he does, but they can't control the thoughts of what's inside him.

So he passed a message to a few others and there're a few other soldiers that come. It seems to spread like wildfire, more and more people are spreading the message. Yes, it seems to be quite a momentum going now.

One of the fascinating things about this account is that we get an insight into how Paul started to teach outside Galilee. Again, his behavior is consistent with the enthusiasm that all he wanted to do was to spread the teachings of Jesus – and his way of effectively reaching people was to write down the teachings and also establish a formal way to meet to spread the teachings.

The next significant event, Paul is surrounded by big buildings, on smelly, filthy streets, with lots of people. People were walking up and down, with animals and carts, as were soldiers. It is noisy. Paul is in Rome, the "center of the known world," as he refers to it.

Paul is walking along with two other men. They wear sandals and whitish, cotton garments draped over their shoulders. Some of the material was draped over an arm to hold it up, so it would not get dragged on the filth on the floor. A piece of brown leather runs down the shoulder, to a belt wrapped around the waist, that would have held a sword, but is empty at this point.

Greg: I am walking behind them and the two of them are taking me to a place to have a meeting. We go inside and there is a group of four or five other people. They stand up when we come in, shaking our hands and clasping and hugging – general pleasure of seeing us. They are all men and some of them have some colored robes – but mainly whitish color. One man has a walking stick. We sit down and they ask [for] the stories about Jesus.

Reena: Who are these men to you?

Greg: One of them, the man with the leather, has got something to do with the army, but not in the army. Some of the others are merchants. They have all travelled and they have heard stories about Jesus. They want to know more about it. They know that I talk about the teachings of Jesus and that I was with him. So they quiz me to find out as much as they can.

Reena: How did they hear about Jesus in the first place?

Greg: One of them came to one of my talks in North Galilee and was a traveler. He invited me. He said that there will be some people who'll be interested in what I have to say, and gathered this small group of people. I did not go immediately. He came back later and I had finished talking to all the people in the different villages. He arranged the boat trip. He was some sort of merchant and had boats. So I was taken to Rome, which is where I am now.

It is interesting to observe how Paul started his ministry in Rome. This is the start of Paul's development of Gentile Christianity, of making Jesus' teachings universal and accessible to people who did not adopt the Jewish faith.

While Paul is generally credited to have started and strengthened the Christian Church in Rome, in his letter to the Romans, Paul indicates that not only was he not the founder of this Christian community, but that he had never visited Rome. According to Bart Ehrman, Paul wrote the letter to the Romans in order to drum up support for his mission, and to clear up any misunderstanding among Christians of his view, that he was preaching an anti-Jewish Gospel, and that Gentiles could make right with God without being a Jew.[1]

However, this is in conflict with our regression where Paul was invited to come to Rome to teach his version of the teachings. There might have been a small, disparate community in Rome, but it was Paul who started the ministry in earnest in Rome, and thus became the leader of Gentile Christianity that we are familiar with today.

Going back to the regression, once in Rome, Paul realized that everything had to be done in secrecy because the Romans were suppressing the teachings of Jesus.

Greg: I have to be very careful because all these people are known to the traveler who invited me. I go through and explain a little about what I've been doing and what happened to Jesus, and went through some of his talks.

Reena: What do you say happened to Jesus?

Greg: I say he was crucified and he was brought back to life by God before he ascended to join with God. I said I'd seen it with my own eyes so I know it to be true. Seems to be important to a lot of people to know this. Because he has done godlike things, his teachings must be from God as opposed to just a normal human being doing them. Because of his godlike nature, it is easy for people to be open to listen to different ways, and different ways of acting. So I tell them all about my time with Jesus and the history of it.

Reena: How do they respond to your talk of Jesus?

Greg: They seem to be more concerned about whether he was really the Son of God or not. Me – I am much more interested in what the actual teaching is. That is the thing that is important. All the religions have got all the different gods, what they say ought to be done or not. To play one god against the other is not productive. But to introduce completely different ways of how you can respond to people in difficult situations, that is worth talking about. This is what I prefer to spend my time doing.

Here, we see Paul continuing to bend the truth to make his teachings that much more compelling, retainable and relevant to his followers. He introduces Jesus and elevates his divine status as the Son of God – which is the version of Jesus that we are most familiar with in current times.

This is consistent with Laurence Gardner's account in *The Grail Enigma*: "In his unbridled enthusiasm, (Paul) invented an inexplicable myth and uttered a string of self-styled prophecies that were never fulfilled… all social values professed and urged by Jesus were cast aside in the attempt to compete with a variety of pagan beliefs."[2]

In *The Magdalene Legacy*, Gardner does stress that Paul had a tough job to do. His allotted task was to progress the Christian message in the Greek-speaking countries and the heartland of Rome. So, he had to compete with a variety of pagan beliefs in gods that were all of supernatural origin and had astounding powers over ordinary mortals. Paul encountered problems that the others never faced in their native environment. His route to success against such odds was to present Jesus in a way that would transcend these paranormal idols – which led to the Divine Jesus of orthodox Christianity.[3]

According to the regression, these indeed were the conditions when Paul started his mission in earnest, during his time in Rome.

After this first event in Rome, the group organized a talk for Paul the following day. The organization had to be done carefully so as to not raise any awareness of what was going on. They held the talk in a larger room of a private home, which looked like a cellar. There were twenty people in the room, tightly squeezed up. The people were very careful in arriving, so as to not draw attention to the meeting. It was too dangerous otherwise. Paul talked to them about Jesus – who he was, what he did and about his teachings.

Greg: There is a longing for something different. They have all had a lifetime of everything being about fear of gods that wreak vengeance. This is completely new and they just want to get more. After two hours, I answer some questions but they seem to want more and more, so we have agreed to have another meeting in a few days. It's too risky to have it every day. They have been asked to go off and think about the talk. If they have got any questions, they are encouraged to come back to the next meeting to talk about it. There is care not to disclose where the meeting will be taking place too early, just in case it gets the attention of the authorities. So they will be told whereabouts the meeting will take place just before.

Bart Ehrman mentions that for more than two hundred years, churches in Rome met in private homes, not specially designated buildings, so the groups had to be small – no more than two or three dozen people per meeting.[4] Churches were principally established in Gentile territories where the vast majority of converts were former pagans who had worshipped the many gods of Rome, and the gods of their own localities.[5] This explains their fear of the vengeful God, and great interest in the divine standing of Jesus, as the Man God.

Reena: What sort of demographics are the people who come to meetings?

Greg: There seems to be a mixture… there is the wife of one of the people there. The other is a man, there are two looking like they are about 21 – so they may be sons – elder sons. The rest are a mixture of people. Most of them are not rich people. More like the merchants or working class. A few people may be servants. They've been invited too. I don't know a lot about all of them. Just a little bit based on observation of their clothing and the questions that they ask. Some have education and some have not.

Besides talking about Jesus at these meetings, the people talk about the Romans, their experiences with them, and what needs to be done about them. Paul tells them a story to help give them perspective.

Paul's Parable 6: Standing in Truth

A servant was accused of stealing some food and was taken away to be beaten by a Roman. What he stole was of so little value that his master could have easily paid for it. His master went to the Roman to plead with them on his servant's behalf.

The Roman said to him, "You have a choice – you can either have him back and we will beat you. Or you can stand and watch your servant being beaten for the crime he has done."

The master said, "Well then, beat me. But if you beat me then be aware that all of my colleagues will know what's happened to me. I am a man of standing in the community. If there are any consequences then you need to be responsible for it."

The Roman did not like this at all. So he said, "Hmmm… OK… in that case we won't touch you, we will not beat your slave. We will take your son and beat him."

The son was brought forward and bent down, held down. One of the soldiers there had this whip with a lot of tongues on one end, used for ripping skin off the body. The other end of it was a stick that they used for breaking bones. The Roman said, "What do you say now about your son being beaten?"

The man said, "Well… if you beat him, this is your choice. All I did was to come in and ask you to find forgiveness for the slave whom you were about to beat.

When you said you were going to beat me, I made you aware of the consequences of what you did. Now you take my son and you are going to beat him. Again, these are your consequences. It is your choice to do that, not mine. You must do whatever you think fit. Although my son will feel the hurt and the pain, in a few months he will get over that and will be fine. But you will carry the hurt and pain that you have done for the rest of your life. I forgive you for doing that."

The Roman did not want to lose face. So he said, "If this ever happens again, all three of you will be beaten. Now go." And they left.

Questions to think about:

Was the man right to defend his slave?
Was he right to take the beating himself?
Was he right to be prepared to have his son take the beating?
When you offer no violence but make the consequences quite clear to the person who has all the power, it touches them deep in their hearts. Standing for your truth and having the power of forgiveness can transcend even the most difficult of circumstances.

Reena: How did people react to the story?

Greg: They want to talk about it or debate it. These stories are intended not to have an answer in themselves but to make people think. Through the power of the stories, they are able to work through their natural responses and hear other people's opinions, as well as to discover for themselves how to respond to these difficult situations. If you tell people what they have to do, it gets lost at the first sign of trouble. If you just tell them a story, it inspires them. If you tell them a story and allow them to debate it, it goes deeper inside them. This is what I do, what I am good at.

There are a lot of people who want to come, so I have to start arranging these talks very carefully. Even though the stories are very similar, they are different people. Sometimes I just change the story a little bit here or there. But all of them are about things that could happen to people. Through using stories rather than named individuals, it is a lot easier for people to accept it and the message gets out.

Reena: How long do your meetings last for in general?

Greg: All the meetings I have had in the outdoors normally finish when the sun goes down. I normally start them about two hours beforehand. Can't do it any earlier because people have their work to do. They sometimes bring food with them, as it would normally be their mealtime, and they eat whilst the talk takes place. In Rome the meetings can go on for far longer, as we have candles to light the rooms. We have to be careful though when groups of people are going out on the streets late, when most people are asleep. It arouses suspicion. So they don't normally last more than three hours. Of that, an hour is the talk and the rest of the time are questions and people debating and asking more questions. But I try not to give them answers. I try to let them find the answers themselves. It is much more rewarding and effective to do that.

Christians have been subjected to local persecution since the inception of the religion. This started with the punishment and crucifixion of Zealots in Judea, who were fighting for independence for their kingdom on behalf of their rightful Messiah. It was politically motivated. Jesus himself was sentenced to death for treason for his claim to being the Messiah or King of Jews, and anyone claiming to carry his word was also punished for political insurrection, predominantly in Judea.

In Rome, there were sporadic periods of persecution that were inconsistently enforced. Many Romans, who were pagans at that time, took their religion seriously and it was widely believed that the gracious and kind gods would anger if they were offended. Nothing offended them more than not being worshipped. Christians and Christian converts who did not worship the pagan gods were blamed for famine, war, drought and disease, natural disasters, political setbacks and economic difficulties.[6]

In the beginning of the fourth century, 303CE, two pagan emperors, Diocletian and Maximian, ordered the empire-wide persecution of Christians and the elimination of the religion. They called for the burning of Christian books, demolition of Christian churches and imprisonment of high-ranking Christian clergy. Christians were also forced to worship Roman gods, on punishment of death or forced labor. This "Great Persecution" went on for a decade, until the official tolerance for Christians was pronounced in 313CE.[7] The time of Paul, and nearly three hundred years after, was clearly a dangerous time for Christians.

Paul

Chapter 5

Son of God

Next, Paul finds himself, in his early to mid-thirties, in Rome. He is with a group of people, who are trying to get the teachings of Jesus established. However, it is proving to be a bit difficult. If they get caught by the Romans, they get thrown into the arena or beaten. So they have to be careful where they meet.

Reena: How long has it been that you have been doing your talks?

Greg: I started the talks immediately after Jesus was crucified. There was about a period of three months when I was devastated and just wanted to be by myself. I spent time in the area north of Galilee and I had a boat trip to a large island [Cyprus] and went along there for a period of time. Then I went from there through to Rome. So three or four years.

Reena: Where do you meet?

Greg: We meet in the cellars, or we meet in… once we met up in a barn on the outskirts of Rome, but then that's harder to get to. The cellars are easier because we can meet in smaller groups and it's harder for people to stumble in on us because we're out of sight. There're not many houses with these cellars but we have a few that open theirs. But the difficulty is that – and I tried to get some of these teachings established before on some of the islands – people started to go through and interpret them in lots of different ways and they started to lose their true meaning. At least now we're in a place where it's hard to keep this alive because of the Romans but trying to teach it in a way that is much stricter. It's more trying to keep what we've been taught but in a consistent way, because we can't meet in a more flowy way of the islands where it was up to us and people could come or not come. It was quite easy doing it there, but in Rome we have to be much more careful, so we have to teach it in a way, even if people are in small groups or they are going to a different small group, they'll get taught the same, otherwise they'll just get confused and we'll lose the message.

Reena: Do you just talk predominantly, or do you record your talks in different ways?

Greg: No – nothing is recorded. It is too dangerous. Everything has to be remembered. Once everybody leaves, there has to be no sign that the meeting has taken place.

Reena: What is the penalty if someone finds out?

Greg: Well... one or two people that have been our brethren have been put into the arena and sorrowfully treated. So we have to be really careful. But the numbers are growing and other people are starting to do the talks other than myself. They won't be able to stop it.

Rome was a warrior state at that time. Gladiatorial shows and public executions via games in the arena were held for popular entertainment. The games also reaffirmed the moral order, by the sacrifice of human victims – slaves, gladiators, condemned criminals or impious Christians. Public executions helped inculcate valor and fear in the men, women and children left at home. Public killings of men and animals were a Roman rite, with overtones of religious sacrifice. The religious component in gladiatorial ceremonies continued to be important, where attendants in the arena were dressed up as gods. During the persecutions of Christians, the victims were sometimes led around the arena in a procession dressed up as priests and priestesses of pagan cults, before being stripped naked and thrown to the wild beasts, especially if they went against the religious order of Rome.[1]

There are records that Ignatius, the Bishop of Antioch in the second century, had been arrested for Christian activities and sent to Rome for execution in the arena, where he was thrown to the wild beasts.[2] This is in line with these accounts that Paul was giving – albeit nearly a century afterwards. Convicted criminals were made to fight fierce and exotic animals as part of entertaining a crowd of delighted onlookers.[3] But it also played another sinister role in publicly showing what happens to Christian insurrectionists in the Roman world.

The regression continues.

Reena: These other people who are doing the talks – do you know them?

Greg: Of course. I know all of them. They have been ones who have been coming and listening to my talks and now they want to spread the word.

Reena: Do they spread it from memory?

Greg: Oh yes… nothing gets written down.

Reena: The people who spread the message, what sort of demographics do they come from?

Greg: They are all men – quite well-educated men. It seems that they are heard far more, and they have more resources available to them, so it is easier to reach all the social levels in Rome. If a slave or servant was passing a message to his masters, it just would not be accepted. With the other way, it is much easier to accept. So I deliberately encourage having a higher class, if you can call them that, the educated, with their own homes and servants. There is one who was originally a gladiator who was given his freedom. He takes the message through to some of the other people in that part of the (gladiator) world. It is easier for him to get access to that world and to talk to people, and because he has the freedom now, he can move in and out of that world. He is of both worlds. Again, he has to be very careful, but he still gets it there and people still listen.

Reena: Do they also have meetings that go on for about three hours?

Greg: No, their meetings are a lot shorter. The gladiator only has meetings that last ten minutes or a quarter of an hour. It's just too dangerous to have anything longer than that. Just whispering a few things. Whispering a story. Whispering some inspiration. It's almost a little bit like a hierarchy. They start off drawing people in. Once they have got more knowledge, they come to me and I deepen their level of knowledge. It works quite well. Then when they go out, they talk to other people – not quite as teachers, but they inspire people. They put a comment here, or a comment there. They look for potential people that could be drawn in. They act as filters.

Reena: How would people know that you and your group of fellow men talk about these things? How can they identify you if it is all done in secret?

Greg: First of all, we know each other. If a person comes to me and says, "I've been studying with 'John' and he suggested to come through to see you," then we take him. There are some people who have been going in there to root out the "Christians," as we call ourselves, and a number of people have been caught and killed. That does not stop us. If anything it just brings more attention to what we do. When people are seen to die for their beliefs, it touches people. For every one person that dies, there are a thousand people who are inspired. The Romans are the best way for recruiting people into this religion. Now there are some quite senior senators who are keeping quiet, but they are Christians too. It is just spreading faster and faster.

Reena: Is it only in Rome, or is it spreading outside of Rome too?

Greg: I do not know. I can only talk for Rome.

Historical scholars agree that the initial evangelizing of the teachings of Christ occurred via word of mouth, by known people. No one is going to become a follower of a person they know nothing about. People were being converted by converts, who did not witness or accompany Jesus in his ministry, but who became followers through stories and accounts told by trusted people. One person would convince another, who would convince another – by orally sharing their stories with their wives, children, neighbors, colleagues and friends. The converts' lives and behavior, as well as their experience of who they were and where they came from, changed so radically that the circle close to them was naturally curious and wished to learn more about this change. That is when the people closest to them would convert, and the stories were told and retold – in either a casual context or a more structured, weekly context. Christianity and Jesus, the miracle-working Son of God, who died for the sins of the world, and was resurrected, just spread. Everything was done orally and repeatedly to convince people.[4] This is in line with the story that is emerging from Greg's regression as Paul.

The regression continues.

Reena: OK, so what happens next?

Greg: We were introducing some of the people that are working with me and helping me with this, coming up with ideas and suggestions of how we can do things.

Reena: Are there Romans?

Greg: No, no, they're followers... who are helping do this teaching, but the subject comes up about women. I've been reminding them that their teaching about women was that all women were the same as men. And they are saying, "Yes, but everybody in Rome doesn't like that way," because in Rome there is an order of... men, or the Romans and the non-Romans – the men and the women, and then the children.

We have to really keep to that sort of order in order to get some of these ideas in. It's not all of the ideas we were taught, but at least get some of them in. So I don't know, I don't feel too comfortable about this, but I think we'll experiment and try it.

So we introduce that idea into the teaching that men are separate and that men can be the ones that can teach others about doing this type of work and not women. It seems to work reasonably well because all the other people who are working with me are men anyway, so...

Reena: Who spearheaded that whole way of thinking... about the men?

Greg: It's really come about because of where we're working in Rome and the difficulty of trying to get this message through in Rome where it's so ingrained of treating everybody in a certain order that to try to teach something too revolutionarily different just isn't getting through.

Reena: So it was a group consensus then?

Greg: Yeah, and it's basically about getting some message through that rings about the change; it may not be perfect, may not be exactly as we were taught, but at least it's getting something through. So I go along with this and everybody else agrees and of course the ones I am working with are males anyway, so we'll try to get the teachings out through males and this is what we agree. And we also agree that it's probably better that we don't get into relationships with women either.

The concern that we all have is that this is an important message and we have to go by ourselves to do this. If we have women that are with us then we either would want to come back to look after them or they would come with us and they will be put into danger. So we are thinking that maybe it is better if we go by ourselves and people feel drawn to us to do the teaching, whether they are men or women then this is their choice, and then they can take that to others however they want. It would be easier for us to work as and when and within the Roman culture.

So we do that and it's kind of not done as a forced thing but almost like an understanding. It seems to work quite well because we are getting the word out and each of the men are going to a different part of the city working with different groups. It means that they're fully focused on doing that, they are not caught up in having families or other things, so that's really helping things move forward. So I feel quite good that things are spreading within Rome quite well and it's got enough of the message for it to be powerful and to bring about a change.

Within the patriarchal Roman world in those days, it is conceivable that Paul had to adhere to some of the Roman ways for them to hear and receive his version of Jesus' message. Let's also not forget that Greg's Paul was also shocked at Jesus' Nazarene teaching of equal treatment of women, earlier in the regression. Nevertheless, Paul seemed open to treating them equally in theory, if not in practice. Despite Paul's appearance of supporting a male-dominated world, his letters made mention of his own female helpers: a servant of the church, Phoebe (Romans 16:1-2), Julia (16:15) and Priscilla the martyr (16:3-4). He also mentioned in his epistle to Timothy (3:2-5) that a bishop should be the husband of one wife and that he should have children.[5]

Reena: Do you have a lady partner, like a life partner?

Greg: No – it is too risky. By being single I can move around.

No one ever knows where I am. If I have a family, then it is possible for them [Romans] to find me. It is possible for Romans to take them and harm them. Of course, choosing to have them along with the work that I do would be my responsibility. So I choose to remain single and celibate.

Reena: Celibate as well?

Greg: It would be wrong to have a woman out of wedlock.

Reena: What would make it wrong?

Greg: There is a sacredness of marriage and of committing your body to have children. If people make that sacred decision, that's the path that they go on. Those who choose not to, choose to go on a path that does not involve family. People have to choose. All of my teacher colleagues do not have families either. They know the dangers. They were picked because they have no family. Our family is all the people we work with. They are our family. Fellow teachers are my brothers. All the women who are Christians who help us are my sisters. The new members who join us are our children. What better family can you have?

Reena: Have you been celibate all your life?

Greg: Ever since I took to the teachings after the crucifixion. Before that I had a normal life like other people do. That is when I moved from the physical world to the spiritual world. People can still have a family and be spiritual and be a Christian. We encourage it. But for me, I remain single.

Reena: How do you live? Have you got any expenses and how do you meet them?

Greg: Life is very simple. Sometimes new clothes are donated to me. Food is donated to me. I do not collect money as such. If I have a need, I state what the need is and someone finds it for me. But I am not doing anything that needs money. I am not looking to have material things. Just the basics of life – food, shelter, warmth. No shortage of people who will allow me to stay with them. They see it as a privilege.

Reena: The women who help you, your sisters as you call them... what do they do? How do they help?

Greg: Well... some of them help by talking to other women in an informal way, and drawing them in. Some of them help by educating their children with some of the things that they have heard. Some help in simple ways like distributing food, or making sure that the seating and some of the physical needs are attended to during meetings. They help in whatever practical ways they can. They help at all levels. They are just as important as the men, but the men are deliberately picked rather than women because it fits into the way that the Romans operate. It is a big enough change for them to accept the values of love that we put forward to them. To accept one God as opposed to multiple gods. To accept women as equals is just too much for them.

Reena: Do you tell them about his [Jesus'] wife?

Greg: A few people have asked, and I tell them. But the full truth of what his wife did is altered slightly. It's as I said before, we have to be very careful with how we explain women and women's roles to get things accepted here. So likewise, with Jesus' wife, we are quite honest and open when we talk about her and about how helpful she's been to him, and all the work that she does. But we don't mention that he had a family. That would be slightly difficult to explain how Jesus can have a family, and yet myself and the other teachers don't. So I just prefer to keep that part of the knowledge to one side. It's not like we are hiding the truth. It's more that we are letting enough truth out that people can handle and work with, for the purpose of growing the spiritual message as quickly as possible to as many people as possible.

The Vatican's Apostolic Constitutions claim that within the Nazarene community of Jesus, women were closely involved in the ministry. This document goes to lengths warning against the practice of women being part of the ministry. For example, it claims that "... it is wicked and impious for a woman to perform this [baptism] or any other priestly function."[6] However, where there are comments made by Paul in this document about women and the ministry, there seem to be anomalies. At times, he draws individual attention to his female helpers, praising them for their work, and on other occasions he forbids women to take any active part in ministerial duties.[7] While many theological scholars agree that Paul's words were tampered with to suit the vested interests of the bishops who compiled the Apostolic Constitution, it is clear from this regression that Paul was indeed conflicted by the involvement of women in his ministry – where on the one hand he seemed respectful of women and wanted to emulate Jesus' ways with women, and on the other wanted to keep to the patriarchal Roman culture of the time, to spread the message of Jesus as far and wide as possible. The regressions do show Paul's struggle in reconciling Jesus' view with his own personal view of women, as well as the patriarchal Roman culture he was working in.

The regression continues.

Reena: With the one God, do you still say that Jesus is the Son of God?

Greg: Yes, of course! It is really important. It is the core part of getting things over. If we said he was just a man, like you or I, people just would find it harder to accept the teachings. But when we talk about the miracles that he did, and talk about how he transcended death, and how he is halfway between God and Man, it makes him a Man God. That makes it a lot easier for his messages to be accepted. My job is simply to pass on the message in my own way.

Reena: The fact that he is a Man God, how do you talk about the family that he was born into?

Greg: Not a lot of people ask much about that. We talk about how he was divinely planted and that seems to be a slightly more helpful way of getting it accepted. Now I know that that did not happen but it seems to make it easier for people to accept it. It's like everything we do is about giving people stories to help them. The absolute truth is slightly less important than having a story that can be understood and helps people move spiritually forward in their lives... in my view. That is what I do and that is what the people who work for me do as well.

Reena: Do you talk about his siblings?

Greg: No. There is no mention about that.

Reena: What do you say happened to his wife after his crucifixion?

Greg: We do not talk about that. People are more interested in the Man God – Jesus.

One of the most important covenants of Gentile Christianity is affirming the proper belief about God and Christ. It was the development and refinement of these beliefs that established the orthodox doctrine of Christ as being fully God, and fully man, and the doctrine of the Trinity.[8] In his book *Lost Christianities*, theological scholar Bart Ehrman points out that the earliest promoter of the divinity of Christ was the Bishop of Antioch, Ignatius, who was passionate about Christ being human, with no mention of family. Many of the most prominent ancient theologians participated in this debate, including Hippolytus, and prominent Roman bishops such as Zephyrinus, Callistus and Tertullian. However, the Doctrine of Trinity that we are familiar with now was only solidified as an orthodox form of Christianity in the fourth or fifth century.[9] So, it did make sense that there was little to no talk about Jesus' "human-ness," in terms of his wife, family and siblings, during Paul's time – to perpetuate Jesus' divinity.

The regression continues.

Reena: What do you call the events that happened after the crucifixion?

Greg: The resurrection after he was dead. He rose from the dead to talk to us. I was one of the ones he spoke to and I can talk about that. That was really important because I can stand up and say that I saw him… I know he was crucified and I saw him and I saw the marks on his body. And I know he is a Man God. How else can anybody do that if they were not a Man God?

Reena: Did you see him immediately after the resurrection?

Greg: No… I saw him three days after the crucifixion.

Reena: Who else was there with you?

Greg: James, Matthew; Judas wasn't. Mary was there.

Reena: Do you tell them about Mary being there at the resurrection?

Greg: No. I do not tell who was there at the resurrection. I just talk about myself being there and seeing it. That's all they are interested in.

It is interesting that in 1 Corinthians 15, Paul cites all the witnesses of the resurrection but does not refer to any women being there, even though the Gospels do.[10] However, in this regression, Paul mentioned Mary being there but did not talk about it openly. Did Paul deliberately withhold mentioning women at the resurrection to fit into the cultural expectations of that time of not giving too much credence to women, or the fact that she was married to Jesus, to uphold his divine status?

In *Shrouded Truth*, the regressees who did see Jesus after the crucifixion did name women being there, namely Mary Magdalene. What also emerged was that there were three levels of information that were shared about the "Resurrection of Christ." Paul was privy to the second level which was disclosed to the Apostles and disciples, where they found out that Jesus was indeed crucified but nursed back to health. This is probably why Paul says nothing about the discovery of an empty tomb (1 Corinthians 15:3-5), because there was no tomb, empty or otherwise. In *Shrouded Truth,* Jesus emerged, hurt, to inform some of his disciples who were still around that he was not dead. For the safety of Jesus, they were instructed to inform everyone else, the third tier, that Jesus had died on the cross, so as to not attract attention from the Romans and the Pharisees. So Paul's accounts are consistent with the level of information he was given insight into.

In the next significant event, Paul finds himself at the arena in Rome.

Greg: I wanted to see for myself what they do to Christians that they capture in the arena. So I am on one of the highest seats right at the back. I can see these poor brave people brought out.

Reena: How are they brought out?

Greg: In chains. Four men and two women. Everybody in the crowd is shouting something along the lines of, "Kill them, kill them." It is almost like creating an animal instinct. [Sighs.] At that I turn around and leave. I really do not want to watch any more. I find the noise quite revolting. Still so much to do here in Rome.

Reena: These four men and two women – were they part of your teaching team?

Greg: No, I do not know them. I don't know all the Christians here. It is one of the things that we are carefully doing. No one knows everybody. It's all organized in small cells. If they catch some, they can't find all the other links. This was one cell that they caught. But I go away with the knowledge that their deaths are very similar to Christ's death – in going through it without fear, and forgiving everybody else. It touches them because it is something that the people can't do themselves.

Not many of them will be able to stand there for their God, and give forgiveness to those who are about to kill them, maim them and set wild animals on them. So brave. But it is such an important part of changing this whole fear-creating organization called the Romans. I am working right at the very heart of it, slowly transforming it bit by bit. I would gladly give my life in place of theirs if I thought that it would get the spiritual message out there any faster... but I fear it would have the opposite consequence. So I accept the sacrifice that they give willingly and leave.

Reena: Are you aware of what happened that made them be caught in the first place?

Greg: There are Romans and spies who pretend to be interested in Christianity. They report back and get paid money.

Reena: Do you do anything to commemorate those who gave their lives up in pursuit of this spiritual path?

Greg: We call the family members and we have a service of dedication to them. We don't have their bodies but we have their memories. I always speak at those events. We talk about their bravery, and how they have given the ultimate sacrifice just as Christ gave. Also about how they will live in heaven in the glory of being with all of those that have transcended the physical into the spiritual, and brought love into the planet.

Reena: At the service of dedication, do you just talk or are there other things that happen as well?

Greg: This particular event, we introduced the idea of drinking Christ's blood in wine, and also having a small baked crisp to represent his body. It's a symbolic event. People like it so we continue to do it. It is also a way to get people to reconfirm their faith. At times like these, when family members have lost so much, it puts on the maximum strain for them to leave Christianity. So we have this ceremony, not only to acknowledge the people who have died, but also to help those who reaffirm being part of our faith. It's worked well, so we start to do it more and more.

This part of the regression was very insightful to the structure of Gentile Christianity. Gentile Christianity authors considered this willingness to die for their faith as one of the hallmarks of their religion, and used it as a boundary marker separating "true believers" from "false heretics" whom they were concerned about.[11] Paul, commemorating their deaths with the flesh and blood of the Divine Christ, a symbol of Jesus dying for his beliefs and the salvation of all, does leave a lasting impression that martyrdom is truly the divine way to heaven and glory. This marker still exists two thousand years later, where the blood of both the believers and the non-believers has soaked the Earth in the quest for upholding the "true" proto-orthodox religion.

In the next significant event, Paul found himself with three senators. He stressed the importance of no one else being there because they needed to be especially careful. These senators had been at the arena and had seen some of the deaths of the Christians, which touched them deeply. They just wanted to know more about Christianity. With the assurance of safety and security for himself, Paul agreed to teach them.

Greg: I treat it as a service for a small group of people. So I tell stories aimed more at them – stories about having wealth, sacrifice and forgiveness. They like that it is just for them because they can discuss it amongst themselves. They like to think that they are different from everybody else. Of course they are not. Part of becoming Christians is to realize that everybody is the same. They need to do it in their own good time. So I just finished the two-hour talk with them. They want to have a think about it and come back for another meeting, to discuss the ideas and points. I say to them that they won't work it out in their heads. It has to feel right. They don't quite know what I mean but they are going off to see if they can feel it.

Reena: What is it about this service that makes it so special?

Greg: Because I am getting to the very core of what makes Rome special. There is only one level above this and that is the Emperor himself. Just getting some senators who are sympathetic at least is a big step. It just means that our tentacles are rippling through the infrastructure.

Reena: Is anything recorded at this point?

Greg: Nothing is recorded. People have to keep everything in their heads.

Reena: At what point do you start calling these events "services" as opposed to "meetings"?

Greg: They have been services all the way through and yet it's a meeting of people to discuss and learn. While everything is undercover, it does not matter what you call it.

Paul then proceeded to share a story he saved for the senators.

Paul's Parable 7: Cost of Happiness

This is a story about a king in a distant land who had enormous wealth. He had a son whom he loved dearly and no other children. For him, his life would continue through his son. Or so he wanted to believe. One day his son became ill and lay in bed close to death. So the king said to his god, "I'll give you half my fortune if I can get my son back to full health."

Would giving half the wealth you have equate to the life of your son?

Do you think giving anything would equate to the life of your son?

Do you think giving all your money that you have equates to the life of your son?

How much money would you give for your life to be one of happiness and joy?

He tells the stories differently to the senators, to make them debate and think about things that are important in life. He tells them stories that do not have an answer because they are able to work it out themselves. People who do not have quite as much education have to be given the ending. Giving senators part of the story and options, on the other hand, gets them to think about how it ends, and what they would do.

Greg: None of this is ever recorded. It is just my way of doing it. The only thing that people do start to take on is the idea with the wine and crisp bread – that is starting to get established as a common ceremony. People like to have the ceremony – I don't think much of it. For me it's more the symbolic nature that is useful. People seem to have taken to it, so I have allowed them to do that. There is not a lot fixed in the work that I do, apart from operating in complete secrecy as much as possible. For the obvious reason of trying to protect people from being taken to the arena.

Paul explains that he and the senators conducted another meeting a couple of weeks later. They met in a house of one of the senators, which was normally used for his indulgence in women and his pursuits of a hedonistic lifestyle. As it was not part of his formal residence, and was centrally located, the room they used was a convenient place for the secret meetings. The senator also had discreet servants who looked after them. So it was an ideal location.

Paul tells them another story.

Paul's Parable 8: Give Freely for Love

This one is about a king. He has a hunchback and some scars on his face – quite bad ones. He pays for women as he cannot find love because of all these physical deformities. He decides as he is the king that he can order love. One of his ministers has a young daughter. He says to the minister, "I shall marry your daughter but she has to love me. That's the condition and of course it means that you'll be elevated up to be the most senior minister because your daughter will be my wife. So it will be a great prestige for you. The children that we have will be the future kings and queens. Some of your blood will be rulers of the future. What more can I offer? But your daughter has to love me. If she does not love me then I'll have her killed. It's your choice."

If you were that minister, what would you do or say?

Is it very tempting to have all this power given that your daughter may grow to like him eventually? Is it acceptable for the daughter to do as she is told, even if she does not want to marry or love the king?

The minister said, "No – I won't do that. Love is not something that can be bought. Love is something that has to be earned."

The king draws his sword out and is about to strike his head off, when he pauses and asks, "How could she love me?"

The minister says, "You know your body is bent. She can't love that. Your face is scarred. She can't love that. But what about the inside of you – how you act and feel towards other people? Could she love that?"

The king said, "Well, what would I have to do for her to love me?"

"Well," said the minister, "perhaps you could buy her presents. Perhaps you could find out what her dreams are and see if you can meet them. Or perhaps you can make her laugh. You'll never know unless you try it. You've lived all of your life without love by acting in the way that you do – what have you got to lose? And what have you got to gain?"

The king thought about this and said, "OK. I shall try it for a little while but I think that I am going to need some help. I am not used to doing this. I am used to people doing as they are told."

So the minister said, "The first thing I must do is bring my daughter along and I'll introduce you. And you say to her… what do you dream about? And then give it to her."

So his daughter came. The king said to her, "Tell me, my dear, what do you dream about?" She said, "I dream of all the poor people that I pass coming here having enough food to eat without having to beg. That's what I dream about."

So the king says, "Royal Command: Send food out each day to the poor on the street and give them enough food to eat."

The girl was delighted at that. "Oh, thank you so much."

The king said, "Do you have any other dreams?"

She said, "There is one other dream. My brother that I love dearly is ill and I would love for someone to heal him." So the king said, "OK – send a note to all the wisest physicians in the country and see if they have the skills to heal him... and if they do, send them here to do the healing work."

So a physician was found and the brother's health came back. The girl said to the king, "You've met my dearest of wishes. Perhaps I can help you achieve one of your wishes. What's one of your wishes?"

He said, "To marry you and have love from you."

She said, "Well, I'll marry you. My love for you has grown for each thing you have done for me, and perhaps that can continue in the future."

When you give true love to people, you give them what they need when they need it and they freely give love back to you – perhaps in a completely different way.

Reena: How did the senators respond to this?

Greg: They smiled and laughed but the point was made. Of course, they want more stories. Some of them queried the beating and punishing of those who have committed crimes. This is just part of the process of them shifting and moving. There are other stories to tell at a later date. The stories can be made up – it does not really matter. It is just the power of the stories to get the message over which is the secret of this work.

Reena: How do these stories impact the senators?

Greg: Touches them deeply in their hearts. They start to come regularly to the services but they are dressed so that they are not recognized. There is a point where they can't be treated specially. They are just the same as anyone else and that is just part of being a Christian. Whether you are a servant or master or a senator – it does not make a difference. In the eyes of God they are all the same. When they are ready, they will join the other groups.

Reena: Are there other senators who join in as well or is it just these three?

Greg: This is the meeting that I am at with these three.

The regression around Paul's early establishment of the Roman Church gave great insights into how some of the more established beliefs and practices came about. Trying to break through the very fixed cultural beliefs and practices of the Romans to spread a very strange and foreign message, during a time where people were killed and persecuted for different beliefs, was an enormously difficult and dangerous task. So, Paul raised the status of Jesus to that of a divine deity that surpassed the divinity of pagan gods that were firmly entrenched in their belief system – to not only teach and spread the message, but also to enable more people to join in his ministry. In doing so, he created a Divine God that sacrificed himself on the cross for love of his people, to juxtapose against the Roman pagan gods who ruled by fear and expected people to sacrifice for divine rewards. He also ensured that those who shared in spreading the teachings were men, and not women, and diminished the roles of women closest to Jesus, so as to keep with the patriarchal culture of the Romans. He did this as a means to ensuring that the Romans will be more open and accepting of Jesus' teachings of Love.

This regression shows Paul not as an infidel who deliberately corrupted and manipulated the pure teachings of Christ for his own agenda and gain, but who ingeniously entwined the basic teachings of Jesus with the cultural conditioning of Rome at that time, to be able to reach the most number of people with Christ's word and messages.

Paul

Chapter 6

Rituals and Ceremonies

Having had a fascinating insight into how Gentile Christianity got started in Rome, this next section offers us an in-depth perspective into how some of the time-honored and fundamental Gentile Christian rituals and ceremonies came about.

Greg entered the memories of Paul's life wearing a white robe and sandals. He had been doing the work, evangelizing alone for about ten years in Rome by now, and things were well established. At this point, Paul was aware of carrying a manuscript within a scroll, which was an attempt to capture some of the things that Jesus did in writing. While Paul was the caretaker of the manuscript, it had been written by one of the most trusted scribes, who was part of his Christian meetings. He referred to the scribe as Dytham Yew, who took pains to write it as accurately as possible. At this point of entry, Paul was walking to a meeting, carrying this scroll.

Greg: Quite a big meeting – about sixty people there. It's like a courtyard but it is walled all the way around so no one can see. There are too many people to go into a room. So we have it outside but behind the wall. This is the first time we've had something written down. Have to be very careful with it. It seems to add much more power to the message as it seems really important and can be saved for the future. So I open it up and read some of the information. I have heard that others have written down Jesus' story too, but I have not read any of those accounts.

Reena: When you say others have written the story down, are the others in Rome or outside Rome?

Greg: Outside Rome. I have heard there've been several attempts to capture some of the things in writing.

Reena: What are your thoughts and feelings about these attempts?

Greg: It is understandable and is a good idea. So easy for things to get misunderstood. This is the first attempt to have something written down and used as a teaching aid. I experiment with it. People are very impressed so I am going to use it again in the future, and still give some of my stories. It's just we are finding ways to impress people. Everything about Christianity has to be different to what the Romans are doing – like having the "One God." The Romans still believe in multiple gods. However, some areas are still very similar. The aspect of having males leading this whole work is very much in tune with the way Romans think and act. So I am going through this written word and sharing it with people.

Reena: What language is it written in?

Greg: We all talk the same language here in Rome. It's too dangerous to talk in Hebrew. So we talk in the language of Rome. And the words written down here are in the language of Rome too.

It is worth pointing out here, that in *Shrouded Truth,* it was revealed that Paul was a tax collector for Rome, working in Judea, when he met Jesus. So he would have known the official language used in the government of Rome, which was Latin. As many of his writings were in fact in Greek too, it is safe to assume that Paul was extremely proficient in the Greek language, one of the more widely known languages in Rome at that time, and this was probably the language used in the manuscript.[1] He was also proficient in Aramaic, the language of Judea, and probably Hebrew, the language of the Torah, used by the Pharisees. So Paul was a highly educated man.

Reena: Please describe the manuscript and the paper?

Greg: It's like two pieces of wood. It's curled around both pieces. You unfold one and fold up the other. Move backwards and forwards. It is made of paper but the people who make this get a mixture of a few different plants and reeds, beaten up and dried. It's possible to write over it. It's quite an art to produce this. I don't know the secrets that they have. They just make it available. So we use it.

Reena: What's in this first manuscript?

Greg: Well... it starts off with the birth of Christ. It talks about how this happened – during the time when there was great activity in the sky. How he was born and had to be hidden away from the soldiers who were trying to kill him. Then it goes into the time when he started to gather his disciples together, and the miracles that he performed, and the stories that he told. And then there is the time when I joined him. It continues to the point where he was crucified, and the resurrection three days afterwards.

Reena: This first scroll – what do you call it?

Greg: The Holy Word of God.

Reena: And God meaning Jesus?

Greg: Yes.

While Paul's Christological teachings about Jesus' death and resurrection make a person right with God, he is elusive in what he says. In Philippians, the eleventh book in the New Testament, attributed to Paul's epistle to the Philippians in Greece, Christ is portrayed as becoming a human, like other humans, and Paul believed that Christ was born from a woman, and did not just appear out of nowhere. However, according to Bart Ehrman, Paul saw Christ as an angelic being – a second Adam, who reversed the sin, condemnation and death brought about by the first Adam. While it was clear that Paul portrayed Jesus as the Son of God, he did not think that Jesus was the

Father – God himself.[2]

Reena: Tell me more about this meeting. What is the purpose of the meeting?

Greg: Well – it's like all the meetings to reaffirm people's beliefs. It's not easy being a Christian in Rome. So all the people support each other and I talk about how we can do that, and about how the spirit will survive whatever happens to the physical body. People will have faith. Trust that God will always be there. Maybe we don't understand things that happen, but it is important to go with the events. Some things we just can't force. There is a wonderful mixture of people. One of them is a senator, but he is in disguise. There are a few women, a few who are just of age. Quite a lot who are wealthy enough to have fine clothes. This is more a service now rather than a meeting. We started to formalize some of the process. That makes it easier for other people to do the same thing. It started to get out of hand with different people just having short meetings or long meetings, talking about this or talking about that. Because there are more people involved, there is an attempt to get some consistency.

Reena: Before with the meetings, there wasn't any consistency?

Greg: No.

Reena: How did the lack of consistency affect the teachings?

Greg: It's hard to say because people are interested in anything on this subject. It's just my decision to try to give guidance on the most effective way of retaining the present Christians and draw in new ones. Sometimes some other teachers will try out ideas and we feed it back and everybody will go and use it. So things have started to become slightly more consistent.

In the proto-orthodox tradition that is prevalent in modern

times, there is an emphasis on church order guaranteed by a rigid church structure with one person at the top making the decisions. This was not so during Paul's time, as evident in Greg's accounts as Paul and documented evidence. It is evident in 1 Corinthians that Paul's churches were organized as communities directed by God, who gave each member a special gift to assist them to live together as a communal body.[3] However, in the time the Church was growing and developing, having no one in charge led to serious chaos. Different teachings, different interpretations of the Word of God and different belief systems were introduced. After Paul's death, an author in one of his churches wrote 1 and 2 Timothy and Titus in Paul's name to give instruction for church leaders and directives for church life together. This started the road to proto-orthodoxy church hierarchy and the Apostolic Succession, the time-honored tradition of picking the leaders of the Church.[4]

We return to the regression.

Reena: And what do you do at the service besides reading from your scroll?

Greg: We have a theme at every meeting. If the theme is about forgiveness, then we will have a story about forgiveness. Read one of Jesus' stories about forgiveness. Then myself or the teachers that work with me will explain it and give directions for what people need to do in order to grow and develop as Christians.

Reena: What else happens at a meeting?

Greg: Lots of talking. Lots of questions. Sometimes one of the people in the group will ask myself or a teacher to answer a question. Then people will be quiet and we will answer the question. Part of this whole thing is for people to meet colleagues and recognize them so that if they meet them outside, it is easier to recognize them.

Reena: The drinking of wine and eating the crisp bread that

was introduced when some followers died, what happened to that?

Greg: We still have it, but it's not done at every meeting. We save it for big important events like the celebration when Christ arises. Or we use it when we bring in new people who are joining us as Christians. We tend to use it more for that now.

In the previous chapter we saw Paul commemorating those who had died for their Christian beliefs with the offertory of wine and crisp bread. This practice has progressed to being offered at big momentous occasions – again highlighting the importance of Jesus dying for the salvation of all, and also a reminder of his resurrection during these times.

Reena: Do the senators join you at these big meetings?

Greg: Sometimes, when they think they can remain hidden. Sometimes I have small meetings for them and their families. It's been expanded out to include their families now. But now some of them have included their servants to be part of this. That is a very big step for them.

Reena: How do you feel about your work after ten years?

Greg: It's like an unstoppable force. It's too deeply entwined in the whole Roman structure to be changed. We are starting to be a little bit bolder now. These last two years we have not had any Christians taken into the arena. There's more openness now. There are more and more senators who have been converted. The present Emperor prefers not to challenge it. He is aware of it, though he won't convert himself. We have one of his cousins who is now a Christian who talks to him about it. He explains that we can settle the population to make it easier for the Emperor to manage. When people know that there is a life beyond death, they are not that fearful of the death.

The worst of their excesses are subdued. Because of that, people are happier. I don't think that the Emperor is interested in happiness. I think he just sees it as a way to give them a toy to play with. Like the arena, which is a toy they could play with. This is a religious toy. As long as it is not seen as a threat to what the Romans are doing, they are prepared to turn a blind eye to it now.

Reena: What are the Emperor's and his cousin's names?

Greg: Claudius, and his cousin is Antonio.

From a timeline perspective, this snippet is indeed interesting. While Greg has no conscious knowledge of Roman history of that time, Paul's revelation of the name of the Emperor was significant. Tiberius Claudius Caesar, more popularly known as Claudius, was indeed the Roman Emperor from 41-54CE – around the time that Paul was teaching in Rome. It was a rather tumultuous period politically, because he assumed the title of Emperor after the assassination of Caligula, his nephew, and Caligula's family. While it cannot be proven that Claudius ordered or participated in the assassination, it is said that he definitely knew about it. It was a reign filled with expansion, intrigue and coup attempts. Claudius was extraordinarily fond of games and instituted games to be held in honor of his father's birthday when he came into power.[5] This perpetuated the number of Christians killed during the games in the arena.

Religiously, Claudius had strong opinions for a proper form of state religion. He was known to have expelled Jews from Rome, probably because the Jews within the city caused continuous disturbances at the instigation of the teachings of Jesus and his followers. Claudius opposed proselytizing in any religion, even in those regions where he allowed natives to worship freely. After thirteen years of rule, Claudius was succeeded by his nephew, Emperor Nero[6] – the same Nero who allegedly ordered the beheading of Paul.

So, it does make perfect sense from a timeline perspective that Claudius was indeed the Emperor when Paul was evangelizing in Rome.

The regression continues.

Reena: These sixty people who come to your meetings… how often do they come to these meetings?

Greg: We have adopted a little bit of the Jewish idea of having it once a week. So we find that works quite well.

Reena: Is it compulsory?

Greg: No, it is up to them. People generally are thirsty for this sort of knowledge. So more often than not, it's trying to keep them away. Sometimes there can be too many for the room that we are in. If I am doing the talk, or one or two slightly more established talkers come, they all want to be there. Especially when I talk, because I was there with Jesus and I can talk about it firsthand.

Reena: Where do you hold these meetings?

Greg: Normally in a basement room. The bigger meeting I was talking about was held in a quadrangle with a wall around it and a gate. We had it in the walled area. It can take sixty people.

Reena: When you have so many people, do you conduct the meeting by yourself or with others?

Greg: I always have two or three that are with me. They are learning to do this work themselves and normally they don't talk when I am there. I do all the talking. Sometimes when there are questions or small groups, they normally go out and mingle in the small groups. People cannot really ask questions too easily in a big group so we break it into smaller groups. Sometimes I might pose a question to the big group that the smaller group asked about, and they enjoy that. They enjoy being posed with a problem and they go off and think about it.

Reena: How do they address you?
Greg: They just call me Paul.
Reena: Can you tell me roughly how old you are?
Greg: 45.

Allegedly, Paul is said to have been born around 5CE and established churches through his evangelism from the mid-30s to the mid-50s. Claudius reigned until 54CE.[7] So according to the timeline, at this point it would have been around 50CE in Rome that Paul was there, during the latter years of Claudius' reign.

In the next significant event, Paul has left Rome to go to some surrounding areas. They felt that it was safe enough to carry this work to more places, although they still had to be very careful because the Emperor could change his mind overnight. It is the middle of the day, and Paul is walking with several others. He is walking with a stick because walking is a little hard for him now.

Greg: I am coming to the conclusion that this work of going to all of the surrounding towns is going to have to be done by some of the other, younger groups of people who are teachers with me. There are several of us, and one of them has his wife with him. He is not a teacher as such because we encourage all the other teachers not to have wives. He has a merchant business and he tends to help us with money, provide goods for us, and he organizes things for us. So he helps us in that way. But the others in the group are teachers. It is almost like a parting of the ways, with them going to go off on their own ways. We are all there showing our unity. When we get to the point where the road starts to split, we sit down, have a drink and share a simple meal. Then there is hugging with not much being said. We don't need to say anything. We know that it is not an easy path to go through. They all go on their way and it's just the merchant with his wife who is left with me. We start to wander back and they are there to make sure I am looked after.

Reena: How many others were there?

Greg: Seven.

Reena: How do you address this rich man and his wife?

Greg: I call him Simon. His wife is called... Reba.

Reena: How do the seven teachers carry the information and knowledge when they go off?

Greg: There was much debate about whether to take the written word or not. We decided in the end that it would be far safer to not take anything that is written and that they will just have to remember. It simply meant that if we were caught or they were caught, there won't be anything that can be used. They wouldn't say anything when they were tortured. We are still very guarded. It is not so much that it's permitted in Rome. It's more a lull in the storm – where there was all the activity of persecution, it's now gone quiet. No one is quite sure what is going to happen in the future. We continue to grow and draw more people in, but we have to be very careful about it. We decided in the end not to do any more copies of it.

As Bart Ehrman points out in his book, *Jesus Before the Gospels*, stories about Jesus were being told in evangelism, in instruction before baptism, in teaching, worshipping services, casual conversations, in mutual exhortation and encouragement, at church gatherings, homes, and all sorts of contexts. People who had never been to Palestine, or knew anyone who had, or who had firsthand accounts of Jesus are telling these stories. So these oral teachings are rife with inaccuracies and distortions from what purportedly occurred.[8] Details get changed, episodes get invented, events get exaggerated, and there is no way to control what one person said to the next, without that written manuscript.[9] There was one instance when Paul wrote to the church of Corinth, which was wracked with problems of division, infighting, flagrant immorality, chaotic gatherings and doctrine errors, just to resolve the church's problems and adopt consistency in the teachings, services, ceremonies and rituals that they adopted.[10]

Reena: Do you carry the written word with you?

Greg: No. It's safely hidden. The people who are with me have a house. They have a place with a stone lid that slides back. We put it under there. When the lid comes on, it looks like it is a feature – not a place where something is hidden. So we thought it's a safe place to put it.

Reena: How many scrolls are there?

Greg: We could not rely on one scroll because if that was taken, it would all be taken away. So we did two copies and they are hidden away. But we have heard that there are others who have written down the word and there are some differences between how that has been written and what we have. I am not bothered about that because I was there and I knew what happened, so I could talk firsthand about it. Having things written down in some ways is more for show. When I am not around it will be very useful to have it, of course. People can say this is what I saw, and I can vouch for it. It takes a long time preparing these copies. Someone takes four months to prepare it. It has to be carefully written down, letter by letter. Getting the paper is quite difficult because it has to be produced so no one knows it's produced for this purpose. So the whole thing has to be done carefully and discreetly.

Reena: Did you add anything to the scroll or is it the same?

Greg: It's still the same information but the stories I tell are different. I do not use it very much – just a tiny bit for show. But I tell my own stories, then people have their discussions.

While there are thirteen letters that are under Paul's name in the New Testament, critical scholars are positive that Paul actually wrote seven – Romans, 1 and 2 Corinthians, Galatians, Philippians, 1 Thessalonians and Philemon. These are called the undisputed Pauline letters.[11] Even during his lifetime, Paul had occasionally warned people about fictitious letters purporting to be from him.[12] While Paul did make the first attempt to have his teachings recorded and took pains to make sure it was accurate, unfortunately he could not stop all the fraudulent writings and letters that were produced in his name, during and after his time.

The regression continues with Paul finding himself in Rome; he is now 48 years old. He just continues to do the things he has done before, but he starts to slow down. He is starting to let other people lead the talks, while he just sits, listens and chimes in with the odd anecdote. His presence supports the others doing the talks and the discussions.

Reena: Tell me about the role of women and what they do with the scroll.

Greg: We teach that everybody is equal. Everybody of both sex and any age will go to heaven. But we just use male teachers because we seem to get far more followers from within Rome who are used to males taking the lead and making decisions. The role of females is much more looking after the children and family. So we go along with that. In the discussions, the women's views are listened to just as much as the men. I personally think that the women would be far better teachers than the men. But we wouldn't grow as fast. So I just keep it this way.

Reena: How do the women serve at these meetings?

Greg: If they have come to listen then they are treated in the same way as anybody else. This was one of the messages that Christ had. Everybody from a slave to the Emperor is just the same. They will all go through to heaven if they

> ask for their sins to be forgiven. This is one thing we have started to encourage in our discussions. This is about people asking for their sins to be forgiven. Sometimes it is quite hard to do that in discussions. So some of the teachers have been seeing the Christians and saying that God forgives them. This is causing a little bit of a disagreement because some teachers have the view that this is not the role of the teachers. Only God can do this. I decided to encourage the teachers to perform the forgiveness because some of the people do not understand how to do it or say with conviction. It is a lot easier to have someone guide them through. This is something that we do outside the discussion groups, and it seems to be a growing thing. There seems to be a growth in people wanting to change the way that we do things, or they disagree with what the other teachers are doing. I say to them that it is important that we as teachers are able to lead by example and have the qualities of Christ, so people can learn from that. If we argue amongst ourselves, all of a sudden we are moving away from the very thing we teach.
>
> Some of the teachers don't like that. I think as the work that we do is more open, they are puffing themselves up with their importance and starting to take the view that whatever they say is absolutely true. If someone says something different, then they are wrong. This is not how Jesus taught us. I tried to remind them about this. But I am finding it harder to get around now and sometimes my mind isn't as clear as it was when I was younger.

This again gives us an insight into why there was chaos in the early churches that Paul started and why he wrote letters to try to bring order during this tumultuous period. Paul reinterpreted what Jesus taught to fit into the culture of where he was, and in turn, Paul's followers reinterpreted what he taught. It is a very interesting insight – and just begs the question, how much that was taught represents the pure teachings of Jesus?

The regression continues.

Reena: What is the process of people's sins being forgiven by teachers?

Greg: Well… One of the important messages that Christ had, was to take action to remove all of the sins that you had. So we set up a system where people could confess what it was that they'd done and ask forgiveness. They are doing it to God, but we act almost as a physical form for them to look at when they are doing that – and to be able to say at the end, "You are forgiven." We act almost as an intermediary between God and the person themselves. It works really well. Once we started to introduce it, we encouraged everybody to do this on a regular basis and to go along and have all of his or her sins taken away. Hopefully they continue to live a sin-free life afterwards. But of course that does not happen, but we try to help them aim for that.

There is sufficient evidence in proto-orthodoxy history that the Sacrament of Penance and practice of confession was indeed recommended and established very early on in the establishment of the Church. There is reference to confession in the alleged first-century apostolic writings known as the *Didache*, which commands Christians to gather on Sundays for the celebration of the Eucharist, "… after having confessed your transgressions," and establishes that from the very origins of the early Church, the tradition was that confession was upheld. Initially it was not mandatory, as it is now. Private confession is implied in Canon 13 of the First Council of Nicaea (325). The Council of Trent in Doctrine states that "… the Lord instituted the sacrament of penance, principally when after his Resurrection he breathed upon his disciples and said: 'Receive the Holy Spirit. If you forgive the sins of any, they are forgiven; if you retain the sins of any, they are retained.'" (John 20:22f)[13] So this is in line with Paul's accounts of establishing the practice of confession at the very inception of his teachings.

The regression continues.

Reena: Tell me more about sin. How does one acquire sin?

Greg: We take from the Jewish religion – the Commandments that Moses had. We use that as a basis for teaching people. When we do our talk, we discuss how people act in certain situations, then often say, "I've done something to upset people," or "I've hurt people," or "I have not been good enough in this area." After the discussion group, they can go through and confess those areas that we call sins. In some cases it is quite obvious, because the Ten Commandments are very simple and easy to talk about. In fact, Jesus referred to those as well, but he never talked about them the way the Jews do. The Jews take those Ten Commandments as though nothing else mattered. Jesus never did that. He only used them as a guideline, saying that these are some very virtuous things you can consider adopting. So this is the line that we took. That's why it was never written down as such. We were encouraging people, through the stories, to decide for themselves what was a sin and what was not a sin. This again has been another big debate amongst the teachers. Some of them wanted to take those Ten Commandments and some of them even wanted to add other things to it. But I tried to steer it towards allowing people to decide for themselves. Sometimes it is really obvious if someone has upset another person, or if there is a dispute, or if there is an argument, or people get emotional. It is obvious that if there is some disharmony where forgiveness needs to be found, people need guidance to help resolve it. That's another reason it is useful to have a human here, because people do not know how to talk to God. So we act and make it easier for them to have that sort of dialogue.

Reena: How do people receive this?

Greg: Very well. They enjoy it. They like to shed their sins. They like to work with love. This is the ministry of Christ and this is what we try to promote. Through everything ripples love. Love is not something you legislate for. Love comes from the core values within. This is what we try to teach, and this is why it is different from the Jewish religion. The Roman gods have got very defined rules of what you do that will be punished. We don't quite have it that way and that is another thing that attracts people to us as well.

Reena: If someone chooses not to be cleansed of the sins, or does not seek forgiveness, how would God approach that?

Greg: We don't do anything – that's their choice. Our approach is to help people discover within them what it is that they need to do. This is what makes it different. Our role is to help people discover love. This was the message of Christ. This is what we talk to people about.

Sin was a big part of the Pauline teachings. Gentile Christianity's whole premise is that Jesus died for the salvation and cleansing of the sins of all, and was resurrected again to ascend into heaven because he was the Son of God. Therefore, it was important for them, the followers of the Gentile Christianity, to be aware of their own personal sins and cleanse them as often as they could – to remain the pure beings who would themselves follow the path of Christ and ascend into Heaven. It is fascinating to witness the reasons behind the birth of the ritual of the confessional, through Greg's regression of Paul.

Reena: Have you got different ceremonies for different types of occasions?

Greg: Things have evolved over time. Initially there was nothing really fixed. Everything was really fluid. Now... we intend for new people who are brought in as Christians to have a baptism. We have the ceremony with the blood and body of Jesus where we have the reaffirmation of everybody with the ceremony of the wine and the crisp bread. We have that at least once a year for everybody. We have the opportunity for people to talk about their sins and ask for forgiveness, which is available now for everybody. Those are the only things that are fixed.

At the next event, Paul is at a baptism.

Greg: It is in one of the houses where we have our discussions and meetings. Before we have the meeting we have the baptism. There are two others as well as this particular man. We pray on some water, which is put over his head. We allow him to drink the blood of Christ and to allow the body of Christ to fill him with that energy through that ceremony. When he has done that, the members in there come round, congratulate him, and shake his hand. The next person is a repeat, and then the third person. And when all three of them have been baptized, they sit down and we go into the meeting.

Reena: What is the significance of the baptism for these people?

Greg: It allows them to make a commitment to follow Christ's messages and the word of God. Also to live a life where they can sin no more and go to heaven when they die, joined by all those others who have gone down that path. They have been saved.

Paul's interpretation of the baptism is very different from the one portrayed by both Tamar, the forgotten daughter of Jesus, and David, the hidden son of John the Baptist, in *Shrouded Truth*. There, David reveals that John the Baptist channels light into the water to heal and cleanse people who are baptized, and Tamar reveals that the light of baptism connects souls to the Oneness of creation. There was no mention of sins or reaching heaven upon death – but being connected and healing while alive. Why Paul's interpretation differed from David's or Tamar's I do not know – but it just highlights how the interpretation of stories and rituals changed and is diluted from the source, in this case, Jesus. People just flowed with what was told to them.

Paul

Chapter 7

The Evangelizer

Paul is wearing sandals and a white robe made of coarse material. It is dry and dusty, and he is about to start a talk to a group of about twenty to thirty people. They are in a large room in a house, which belongs to a cousin of one of the senators, who is a wealthy merchant and owns several houses. There are five others helping him, three on one side of him, and two on the other. These men are starting to do their own talks, so they assist Paul with his.

Greg: I am just starting to talk to them about forgiveness. That is quite a big thing here. Quite a lot of feuds go on and they are known to go over for generations... where people have been wronged or there have been grievances or they think that they own land that they do not have. So I am in the process of telling them two stories about that.

Paul's Parable 9: Forgiveness

There was once a merchant who gave some of his business to his son-in-law. One day there was a terrible storm and one of the ships was lost. The son-in-law came to the business owner and said, "I've lost the money that you've given me. Can you forgive me?"

That rich man had just lost some ships that had a lot of money tied to them.

If he can't find forgiveness, what do you think will

happen?

Some may say that the son-in-law had the responsibility of looking after that money, and lost it. So, does he really deserve forgiveness?

Who do you think will be hurt if there is no forgiveness?

Will it be the daughter? The rich man? Or the daughter's husband?

What do you think people would feel if there's a decision not to find forgiveness?

When there is no forgiveness, everybody carries some of the energy from the lack of forgiveness.

The rich man not only forgives the husband of his daughter, but has a feast to celebrate, to let go of the old business and to celebrate how they are going to work their businesses differently. There is much drinking and much laughter and the words of forgiveness are spoken. The family bond is strong. There is much happiness and joy. The loss of the ships was because of a storm and it could have happened whoever was the owner of the ships. How people related with each other will last far longer.

Paul's Parable 10: Forgiveness and Self-sacrifice

The story is about a farmer. He needed help to run his farm. One day the farmer said to the help, "I must go away for two days, and while I am away, you have to look after the farm and treat it like it's your own home."

When the farmer left, the man drank some wine and got drunk, saying to himself, "If this is my home I can do what I want, and I'll just drink." Drunk, he lay down and fell asleep. He was woken by screams outside. A barn had caught fire and was burning. Neighbors had come to see what was happening. The barn was burnt down and all the hay that was stored for the winter months had been lost.

When the farmer comes back, what do you think he should say or do, especially when this loss occurred due to the direct irresponsibility of this farmhand?

In this story, the farmer finds forgiveness and says, "You've learned something, but in future, when I am away, be vigilant. Learn from the mistake."

A few years later, the farmer goes away again, and asks the same man to look after the farm. While the farmer is away, there are some wolves that come after the sheep. The man picks up a rock and fights off the wolves. However, in the process he gets bitten. Bleeding profusely from his wounds, he lies down. When the farmer comes back, he finds all his sheep there. But the man is dying, having sacrificed his life. The man has repaid the barn that was burnt down with his life.

The power of forgiveness is the power of love.

Reena: Was this one of your stories, or one of Jesus' stories?

Greg: Very similar to Jesus' story. I adapt them slightly and I elaborate them around the people and the names that they are familiar with so that they can understand it more. The stories that Jesus told were the ones that he made up. Or maybe they were real – no one knows and it does not matter. It's the power of telling the story rather than expressing an abstract thought. With an abstract thought, people will argue and debate and not change their ways. But with a story there is always a learning. It is the power of the stories that Jesus told that are carried through. His stories are recorded just as perhaps some of mine are. But I don't encourage the recording of stories. I encourage the principles of what they are about, what the spiritual message of Jesus was to be carried forward, and for people to do it in their own way. There are some things that we have to constrain ourselves with – like the absence of women and starting to have ceremonies. I don't really like it but it seems to be an acceptable way to spread this message a lot quicker. But I do encourage all the others to tell the stories around the basic ideas of what Jesus was teaching.

Reena: How do the absence of women and having ceremonies help with this?

Greg: This is a society where women are treated as the bearers of children and the cooks of the food, and the provider of sweet words and comfort for the family. The men do the fighting or the business or make important decisions. If you fit religion within that, adjusting some of their ideas to go completely against the religion just increases the amount of resistance. In Rome, the word of Jesus is adapted to fit into the times and the Roman ways – with their ceremonies, the way the Romans have their gods with their different names, and the way they speak differently to the gods at their ceremony. So we create the ceremony of the crisp bread and the ceremony of the confession. They are just ceremonies which the people like. It was not part of Christ's way of doing things but it seems to work.

Reena: How did Christ like doing things?

Greg: He just talked about the principles of love. It is within everyone. The art is to listen to that inner message and not to judge others for the way they interpret their inner message. This causes a little tension particularly with the Jews and the Ten Commandments. His idea is that if we are truly following our heart and giving out love, there isn't

> actually a need for Commandments. You would simply follow those as part of being true to yourself. But people seem to like to have more guidance. It's almost like it's a big step from where they are to the way Christ taught. So this is why some of these adjustments have been made… simply as a short-term expediency to start moving people to where they are to change. Rome is the warrior center of the world, where everything is judged based on strength and ferocity. To shift that [center] is a bigger hill to climb than in some of the simpler villages where some of the people live spiritual lives in touch with nature. It is easier for them to adapt to all of Christ's teachings. Here in Rome, right in the center of the warrior culture, it is about phasing that in and slowly bringing about the change. By changing it in Rome, it spreads out in all the tentacles of the Empire of Rome.

This is the second time in this regression where Paul differentiates between one of the main pillars of the Jewish religion – the Ten Commandments – and the teaching of Jesus. Gentile Christianity was established on the premise that Jesus' teachings are open to everybody – not just the Jews. As Paul's teachings progressed, the vast majority of Gentile Christians had converted from paganism and saw Jews and their religion as distinct from the salvation wrought by Jesus as taught in Gentile Christianity. This in itself is ironic because Jesus and his followers, including Paul, had been Jews, and their teachings were based on the one true God, the God of the Jews. Throughout this period, the tension between Jewish Christianity and Gentile Christianity is evident as the proponents of Jewish Christianity wonder how Gentile Christians claim to know the one true way and be heirs of the Jewish scriptures when they do not keep the Jewish laws.[1]

The regression continues.

Reena: Draw your attention to the three people on one side and the two people on the other side of you. What role do these people play?

Greg: Well, I don't like to say the word "disciples" because that was a very special follower. I would say that they are people who have felt touched by God and want to be involved in the work that I am doing. They will help in whatever way, but will probably be continuing to do what I do when I can't do it anymore, or will be spreading it to other parts of Rome. This is an adjusted message of Christ but it is tuned to fit into the Roman ways of doing things.

Reena: Just tell me a little bit about each of them.

Greg: Well… on the side where there are two of them… one of them is a black-haired man… Steven. He is in his early thirties. He has been with me now for two or three years. He used to have a job as a writer. Now he has been touched by God and he is involved in all the things that I do.

Reena: How did he get touched by God?

Greg: How do any of us get touched by God? By being in the energy of the work that we do. At some point, the realization that this is the right path, and important decisions need to be made about letting go of the old sort of life. Some people do it in one big go and others continue with their jobs, but they change and they influence other people. It has to be done very carefully because we are still at a time when people of our group, if they are caught, are put to death.

The next one, next to Steven, is a slightly older man – Lionel. He is quite new. His previous job was as a blacksmith. He is well built. He still does some blacksmith work but spends more and more time with us. Enough to scare the Romans just by looking at him but he is very gentle. The other side where the three of them are… the first is Peter. Well… Peter was with me with Jesus and has joined me with some of this work in Rome.

Reena: What made him join you?

Greg: This is a difficult assignment working in Rome. There is great danger that I could be taken at any time and killed. This is seen as the biggest, most important area to bring about a change following the work that Jesus did. So, to have more support is really helpful. Of course, he can tell the stories about Jesus and some of the things that Jesus said… which reinforce my stories. He enjoys telling them. That is his preferred way. He elevates Jesus in a godlike way, which is helpful because it creates a little mystique… a little bit of a Man God, which is different from what the Romans have. Romans have either man or gods – not a Man God. I enjoy the stories that he tells because it reminds me of the stories that Jesus told and they are all powerful stories.

Reena: Was he with you when you were going to all the villages or did he join you at a different point?

Greg: He is with me right now. He joined me six months ago. I don't know whether he is going to stay in this country. We all follow wherever our calling takes us. His calling has brought him here and it is wonderful to have him. These are really difficult times. So for me it is a great joy to have him. He is an equal just as everyone here is an equal. I try to encourage Jesus' message that no one is special. We just have different knowledge to share. It's a great delight to do that so no one puts me as a Man God. I don't like that. It's not what I am teaching. It is interesting how he has his different way of communicating things. Lots of people like it. Some have even asked me if Jesus is a Man God. In a sense, Jesus was a lot different than the normal person. He healed people in an amazing way. In some ways you could almost think of him as a Man God compared with normal people. So it is interesting how Peter conveys him like that.

It's how he passes on his message, which is different from my way. It's just we convey different aspects and people can draw their own conclusions.

Peter's beliefs of what happened to Jesus, and that Jesus is in fact a Man God, is supported by Acts 2:36, where Peter is explaining the significance of Jesus to the crowd that has gathered. He speaks of Jesus' death and resurrection, stressing, "God raised this Jesus, of whom all of us are witnesses, as he was exalted to the right hand of God." Peter also made speeches indicating that God was speaking the words to Jesus whom he made the Lord and conqueror of all his enemies, by raising him from the dead.[2]

In this regression, Paul portrays a close relationship with Peter, and is rather mild-mannered towards the difference of ideologies and beliefs. However, it does not come across that way in the writings attributed to both Paul and Peter. This conflict is evidenced in Paul's writing in his letter to the Galatians (2:11-14), where Paul speaks of a public encounter with Peter in the city of Antioch over the issue of whether Gentiles who have become Christians need to observe the Jewish law. Peter, along with James, Jesus' brother, the head of the Jewish Christian Church, supports the ongoing validity of the law against Paul.[3] Maybe Paul was toning his opposition down for the regression, or his dissent grew, as he was exposed to more of Peter's teachings, or his opposition against Peter was grossly exaggerated in the writings. What is clear in both the regression and historical research is that there was a theological conflict between the two.

The regression continues.

Reena: Who are the other two men?

Greg: One of them is Brian. Brian is quite young. He is eighteen. He is so lively, so full of joy. It's almost like his whole life has been preparing for this. He is the first up in little groups when they are talking, encouraging and throwing in ideas. The last one is Steven. We call him Steven. He actually has a different name. A Roman name… He is a Roman. He adopted a Christian name – it's like saying he changed. It was his choice. But it is easier for me to call him Steven.

Reena: Is he different from the other Steven?

Greg: Yes – he used to be a Roman soldier, and he knows their ways. Roman soldiers, when they've served their time, can leave and do other things. He has served his time and now he is with us. He is going to get the message through to the soldiers. It is easier for someone who is seen as a soldier to talk to other soldiers. He can express things with his soldier stories. He has been doing some talks already. He joins us just to be with us and to keep our links.

Reena: Of all five of them, who has been with you the longest?

Greg: Some have been coming but not committed. The process of commitment can be gradual so it's hard to say that. With Jesus you could say exactly when it is because people would stop their jobs and leave it. He would be wandering around and people would follow him. So you could say definitively when they started. In Rome some people can come and go. They can keep their existing jobs to do this and it has not been as black and white as that.

Paul then reminisces about a time when Peter first joined him in Rome. Paul is at a port, where big sailing ships, with big sails and oars, are moored. Some of the ships have got slaves in them. Some are just sailing ships with sailors. Some are anchored in the water. Some of them are against the quayside, unloading both people and goods. Although he had received a letter that says when Peter will arrive, it is not clear how long the journey takes or when Peter set off. Paul had to estimate a range of dates that Peter could arrive, and they had some of their colleagues going along to the port looking for him during that period. Paul picked four dates that he himself went to port, and it is quite coincidental that on one of those days, Paul saw Peter coming ashore, from a small boat, which carried him from the main ship to the dockside.

Greg: I recognize him right away, and he recognizes me. We embrace. There is much laughter, hilarity and humor. I think he is coming from a place called Syria but I am not entirely sure. I just know that he has travelled a lot since our time together with Jesus. He had known about my intentions to go to Rome because it's been part of the planned discussions that we have had when we were together with Jesus. He sent a letter through a colleague who was a Christian who passed it to me. So we knew he was coming. Now he's arrived and we are wandering back to the house where I am staying, to spend the rest of the day and evening drinking and eating. People come in to meet him, and go out. We have to be careful with people coming in and out, because we try to organize our groups in little cells so that if people are found and tortured then they only know people in the immediate cells. But news has spread about him through the other cells so we have some of the other people coming to meet him. They are so keen that some of the security has broken down a little.

According to Paul, Peter spent about five years with him, in Rome. In that time, the number of followers had grown quite large. There were about ten different cells, with a few thousand people who were followers of Jesus.

Greg: Peter tells me that he is feeling a yearning to move on. He is younger than I am and I feel a longing to stay here. I ask him where he is feeling drawn to go. He is talking about going to a land north of Syria. He has arranged with one of the owners of a boat, who is also a follower of Jesus, to go on the trip. It's all organized.

Reena: What's calling him there?

Greg: Things are growing really fast here, and there are other places where there isn't anybody doing any work.

Reena: What are some of Peter's biggest contributions whilst he has been with you?

Greg: Peter has got a passionate and charismatic way of talking and engaging people. They love him and they can almost follow him like he was the Christ. He's just got a yearning to go to another place. There isn't a need for him now, because there are so many people now who have learned the art of conveying Christ's message. So we see it as a time of sadness but also as a time of great excitement for him to go off and continue to spread the messages. So we have one last night talking about the old stories and in the morning, he goes to the port and continues to make his farewells.

In 1831, theological scholar FC Baur put forth a hypothesis that the two patron saints of the Christian Church, Paul and Peter, were more like feuding cousins than brothers in faith.[4] Baur's theory has been criticized for portraying too simplistically a bipolar rivalry between Jewish and Gentile Christianity,[5] as this regression shows. In fact, this shows that while there were two varying points of view, the two worked together quite nicely. Scholarly research would not take it that far, but this regression shows just how much respect and affection Paul had for Peter, even if their views differed.

The next significant event sees Paul writing letters to James, the brother of Jesus, and telling him of the things that he has been doing. Paul writes to James because he has always seen James as being Jesus' most senior disciple. Even though Paul is doing the things himself, he just double checks with James to make sure that he is not going astray.

Greg: There are not very many people I check with, but James is very good. He tells me about the other disciples and how important it is that we carry the work ourselves, as Jesus is not here. I put details about the things that I think are important to say, and how open people are to the information. I go into great lengths about the interpretation of all the things that Jesus has said – not so much the telling of his stories or the people that he has healed and the metaphors and stories he told, but much more about the important messages that people need to get. I talk about all this in a whole series of letters that I write to him. I get encouragement coming back from him but most of the flow of information is from me.

At this point, Paul reminisces about his first meeting with James, after Paul left his trappings of being a tax collector and joined the Brotherhood of Disciples with Jesus. He found James to be an inspirational figure even then, full of ideas and energy. He saw his bond with James to be a close one then, and a close one now, after all the disciples spread to the different parts of the world, to carry out the teachings. Although it was never formalized who was going to stay at the center, where they had all come from, Paul had always and still respected James as the most important disciple.

This is an interesting revelation from Paul's regression. Although common perceptions and knowledge holds that Peter was the "Rock" whom Jesus entrusted with his church, via the Vatican's Apostolic Succession, other writings, including the Gospel of Thomas, the earliest Gospel that has been proven authentic by scholars, makes it perfectly clear that Jesus bequeathed his personal leadership to his own brother, James. "Jesus said to them, wherever you are, you are to go to James the

Just." Therefore it is through a direct edict that James became the head of the Jewish Church, Bishop of Jerusalem. Even Bishop Clement of Rome had written that Jesus' brother James was, "The Lord of the Holy Church and the bishop of bishops."[6] So it makes sense that Jesus would pass his church on to his blood relative, and it is why Paul would respect James as the most important disciple. We shall see how this evolved with James in Part Two of this book.

The regression with Paul continues.

Greg: I am writing the letters. Sometimes I get more than one letter arriving at the same time, when a ship comes into port. I look forward to the letters. James is such an inspiring person. He has been doing it for longer than we have. He always has advice or hints or tips. The role of women is one of the big ones that we talk about. We talk about the Romans and how we should treat all of their gods. We have to be very careful talking about Roman gods... even if we do not believe in them.

Reena: What are his views about the Roman gods and how you are working with that?

Greg: The idea is to try to incorporate some of the ceremonies – to keep that part. To keep the part of women having a lesser role in things because that fits into the way that the Roman gods are looked at.

Reena: How about the Jewish God – does this fit into that as well?

Greg: That's not a problem at all. The Jews who understand that Jesus is the Messiah will follow quite easily. The Jewish religion is a very straightforward step to move from one to the other. It is the Roman that is particularly difficult. But importantly we have to get them to believe in the one God. And to do that, James is advising that we really make a big thing about Jesus surviving the crucifixion. In order to get the Romans starting to accept the importance of Christianity, and the teachings of Jesus, finding a way for it to be more acceptable is quite important. I include it in my teachings.

Jesus did survive the crucifixion because he was substituted on the cross. This came out very strongly in *Shrouded Truth*. The focus on the one God is also a deeply-held Jewish belief, that Jesus used as a foundation for his teachings, as did Paul, in his attempt to convert the Gentiles from their pagan religion.

The Epistle of Barnabas (though which Barnabas is not agreed on) argues that it is Christians, and not Jews, who are the heirs of the covenantal promises made to Israel, and that the Old Testament is a Christian and not Jewish book. Claiming to have received knowledge directly from God, Barnabas discounts the understanding of aspects of the Jews' own religion including the covenant, fasting, sacrifices, circumcision, kosher food laws, the Sabbath and so on. The author is adamant that the Jews have always adhered to a false religion.[7] However, this regression is especially insightful because, despite later arguments that tried to separate and nullify the Jewish faith from the Christian, here Paul openly acknowledges that the Jews are the earliest followers of Christ, and shows an inordinate amount of reverence to James as the most inspiring person.

Reena: In your stories and teachings, what do you tell people about what happened after Jesus survived his death?

Greg: I tell them that he died for people. I tell them that he was not a human but he was God in a human form. That makes it easier for the Romans to accept him. To accept a Jew telling them what to do is just too much. But to say that Jesus just happened to emerge from that part of the world, that he is God in a human form, and convey some of the stories of the miracles that he did, that helps convince

> them that they need to let go of the old gods and move on to this new God. And in doing that, then the other ideas of a more loving way of life can be slowly slipped in.

This just highlights the difference between the teachings of Gentile Christianity, which focuses on the death, resurrection and salvation of Jesus, and those of Jewish Christianity, which focuses on Jesus being the Messiah on Earth, and that it is a different, more liberal, practice of Judaism, of upholding the Judaic law and the worshipping of the one God. However, it is especially pertinent because this is the first time in this regression that Paul refers to Jesus as being a Jew, and he gives his reasons as to why he changed some of the teachings to fit into the Roman culture and belief systems.

Reena: Do James and you talk about rituals for people who adopt their beliefs from their gods – like baptism or circumcision?

Greg: [taken aback] Circumcision?! I never did any circumcision. This was the tradition of the Jews. Some of the Christians who were Jews before were circumcised. This was nothing I was involved in. Baptism is an important part. It was what John did and this is a way of allowing people to move from the old to the new. Very important. So yes, we keep that.

The subject of circumcision is an important distinguishing factor between the Jewish Christians and the Gentile Christians. Certain believers in Jerusalem, who were of the Pharisaic sect, believed strongly that circumcision and adherence to the Jewish law was a strict requirement for Gentile converts. Jesus and his earliest followers were thoroughly Jewish in their beliefs and practices, and believed strongly that Jesus was the Messiah of Israel. Paul and Peter gave testimony to how God had been at work through the Holy Spirit, converting so many Gentile believers, which seemed to fulfil the biblical prophecies that at the end of the age, the nations would acknowledge the one God, culminating in the establishment of the Kingdom of God on Earth with Jesus as the eternal Davidic King.[8] Yet the Jews thought it was unclean to share meals, break bread or share any religious practices with the "unclean" Gentiles who did not circumcise.

While Peter withdrew his support of Paul for "fear of the circumcision faction," Paul stood firm in his rhetoric that everyone needed to be able to access and worship Jesus' teachings, whether or not they were Jews and followed the Judaic laws. Hence the divide between the Jewish Christians and Gentile Christians widened due to circumcision. According to the account in Acts, it was not Peter, but James who made the final call on this issue, which speaks volumes about James' leadership, and Paul's and Peter's regard for him. James did decide that the Gentiles need not convert or circumcise to be a true follower, but needed to keep to the purity of some laws including what they ate, refraining from idols and from wanton sexual practices.[9]

Reena: What rituals do you use that you did not agree with James about?

Greg: Well, James had the view of a softer, more loving God. I portrayed it as more of an almighty powerful God. Otherwise the Romans just would not convert. But I explained why I did that. I think he understands.

Reena: Is there anything else of significance with your dealings and relationship with James at this point?

Greg: Only on the subject of Mary Magdalene. Because the role of women was being downplayed, I don't talk about Mary Magdalene at all in the work that I do. And James does. It's not that we disagree about it, it's just that I chose not to talk about it because it did not fit into the ideas that

I had.

Reena: What was his response?

Greg: He understood.

Reena: When you were writing the letters, were you in Rome?

Greg: Yes.

Reena: Where were you sending it to James?

Greg: Some went to the islands. Some went to the big area of land near Greece. He went to different places. When he wrote, he left messages so that when things came for him, people knew how to forward it on. Sometimes I did not entirely know. I had the names of the people, a network, to send it to. It was more important to know the names of the people than the names of places.

In the next significant event, Paul went forward to the time when he wrote his last letter to James.

Greg: I am getting rather old now. I have been having dreams of what would happen after the work of the disciples has finished. So I write a bit about my dreams to him. This is about wars, conflict and how the Christian messages get hidden. I talk about how all things rise and then fall and that we are at the very beginning of the rise. Over many hundreds of years, it will rise, stretch out and touch people. Then it will decrease. Almost like breathing in and out.

Reena: What was his response to that?

Greg: He does not really understand it. It is not something I am rationally trying to work out. It is just what came to me. Maybe this is a long time off. Sometimes you have to let go of the old to move to the new, just like the Romans having to let go of all of their gods. There will be a time when something new comes through and people have to let go of all that we are teaching them. There are truths

> within truths – right now we need the truth of the one God. We need the truth of treating people in a loving, compassionate way. At some point we will have to move on.

What is really interesting here is that Greg's Paul does not recall any meetings with James in Antioch or Jerusalem, which are widely written about in Acts. According to Acts, Paul specifically went to Jerusalem to see the Church elders, particularly James, because he was straying from the centralized teachings of the Church in Jerusalem, and he was not demonstrating the Law of Moses. The events described in Acts were quite dramatic as they did seize Paul, and dragged him out of the temple.[10] Curiously, this did not show up in the regressions. When directed to the last time Paul met James, he went to the time that he, James and some other disciples accompanied Jesus on a donkey into Jerusalem. All he does recall is the understanding and philosophies that he and James agreed upon. Perhaps the events were too traumatic and got pushed out of his psyche. No one can really know.

Although prompted, Paul was not aware of James' death either – which is also curious because James was thought to have died in 62CE, in Jerusalem,[11] whereas, Paul died in 67CE in Rome.[12] Perhaps after the events in Antioch and Jerusalem, Paul broke away totally from contact with James and the Jewish Church, and therefore did not know that James had died just five years earlier. It is a secret that Paul still holds close to his chest.

Paul

Chapter 8

The Passing

In the next event Paul finds himself at the point close to his death.

Greg: I've had a feeling that it is my time. And it is not going to be very pleasant either. The followers of Christ are still being killed, persecuted and eaten alive by lions. But because there are so many people who are desperate for something new, there's no shortage of people coming.

It's almost like the more brutal the Romans are, the more people that come who want to know about what we're doing, particularly the ones who die holding the faith. Even some of the Romans are starting to come and secretly getting involved with what we're doing. Yes, it's a good job we kept males doing the work, it's a lot easier to draw the Romans in for that, they kind of understand.

Women come in and they listen to our teachings and they go off and work. And so, you know, we have people of both sexes, we even have some children that come and that's OK. So we have now about ten or eleven parts of Rome where we're working and now we're planning to take this to other parts of the Empire.

We'll keep this structure because it works really well, and as people are trained they take this consistent message and we've got enough of the stories of Jesus and I'm going to take this to the other parts... of the country and the Empire. People are going out with this and getting the message out there and it is spreading.

This is consistent with Paul evangelizing and taking Christianity to Asia Minor and all of Europe – which was, at that time, predominantly under Roman rule.

In the next event, Paul is sitting on a chair in a room, aged, with whitish hair and a bit of a cough. Even though followers of Christ are still being killed, and persecuted, which weighs on him, he still feels quite content with everything that he had achieved in his life. There is a knock on the door, and when he opens it some soldiers barge in and grab him. He catches a glimpse of one of the followers by the door, skulking in the shadows. Elema, he called him – the follower who betrayed him.

> Greg: Rope is pulled around my neck, pulled tight and garroted, coughing and spluttering. The worst part of it is that I can still see in the distance the person who betrayed me. I can't feel anger towards him – just disappointed. Then my life is over. I feel myself coming out of the body. Looking down, I can see one of the Romans lift up a sword, [he] takes off my head, and wraps it in sack-like material. My body is just left there and my head is taken away. I just go on my way.

Historical tradition claims that Nero, Claudius' successor, had Paul beheaded. As we mentioned earlier, Paul identified Claudius as the Emperor when he was at the apex of his teaching in Rome. So, it is fully historically feasible, as Claudius was only Emperor for thirteen years, after which Nero took over and ordered the death of Paul. While tradition commonly holds that Paul died via public beheading as opposed to the private garroting that this version reveals, it could be that tradition chose to glamorize his death to be in line with the treatment and accolades of those martyred for the Gentile Christian cause.

Paul dies with emotions of disappointment that the structure was too rigid and that they could not do more work with women, as Jesus had with Mary Magdalene. Paul also died with guilt: the message that Jesus had given was distorted when they got to Rome and Paul regretted changing the message and method to get it accepted. The more people that got involved, the harder Paul felt it was to change it, and it took on a life of its own.

To help him get closure, he moves to the "Kingdom of Heaven" as he called it, where he meets the spirit of Jesus and his Spirit Guide. He apologizes for letting Jesus down by distorting the message. The response he gets is that there is no *one* message. People have to see the message behind the words; however it is expressed is fine. Everything he did was to carry the message into the very heart of where there was an absence of love, and Paul was embraced for that.

Greg: They review some of that life of mine so I am able to see just what happened to Jesus. They go through the crucifixion and show how another person was substituted and how Christ was looked after and how he went to other parts of the known world quietly without others knowing.

Reena: How does this make you feel?

Greg: Well, well, well… I never spotted that. It was explained why it was important to do so. One of the major ways of drawing people into the Church was the story of Jesus' resurrection. I needed to witness that resurrection to tell people about it. It is all part of a plan. There is a remembrance of that. It's a lot easier to remember that where I am now, than when I was in human form. You can tune into any knowledge that you need to. There isn't, like in the human body, judgement of what's good or what's bad; this is sin or that is sin. I found it quite interesting because we did say a lot about sins. Yet up here no one seems to be too concerned about it.

Reena: What was the importance of spreading the message about sin?

Greg: People needed to have very simple guidelines to work

with. It was almost like the Christians were given a level of truth beyond what some of the non-Christians had. This was just a different way. Quite a lot of the other religions were quite tied up with war. It was quite difficult to untangle the real spiritual message from it. Whereas what we were doing, what Jesus did to start with, and what I did afterwards, was to untangle the warrior part from the spiritual part. It just made it easier for people to start working it out from themselves. The Jewish religion was very prescriptive and the serious Jews would follow it almost to the letter. It took away the whole purpose of what the spiritual message was. This was why Jesus got so upset with some of the Pharisees. They turned it [religion] into a business and they looked after their own interest. They'd forgotten that the whole spiritual message was about what was happening and there needed to be something entirely new rather than change something that was so corrupt. It still serves its purpose and still has a lot of value with it. But something new was needed and this is what Christ tried to do. Then the souls had a choice. They can grow spiritually in one type of religion or they can grow with the ideas and messages that he put out. It's not that one is right or one is wrong. They both need a different type of environment to grow. This is what the different religions do.

Reena: What was the plan around spreading the message of God in the way you taught it versus the different messages other followers of Jesus were talking about in other parts of the world?

Greg: All of them interpreted it slightly differently. Having seen how the ideas that I started became solidified and almost as fixed in their ways as the Jewish religion, it filled me with a sadness that the core message of Christ got lost on the way. I changed a few small things just to fit in with the conditions in Rome. But others took it and it progressively became more and more distant from what the original message was. I feel quite a lot of regret with the fact that I started to allow it to move – like the use of only male teachers, and introducing some of the ceremonies we had, and emphasizing what is and is not a sin. But the others up there say that what I did was to help to bring in an entirely new spiritual message and how the others wish to use it or change it is their responsibility. I don't need to accept responsibility for how things developed over time. I am being reminded that there is no right or wrong. It is something that I participated in. I understand and accept that. Still filled with sadness though. Over time the true spiritual message just got lost. It got hijacked – the same way the Jewish religion got hijacked. The same way the other religions got hijacked. By people using it to either inflate their own egos or their own greed and corruption, or they have excessive fears. They use it to try to reduce the fears that they have.

Reena: What was the plan for Paul's teachings after you passed away?

Greg: I was not privy to the larger plan. People are given free will in situations to respond to it. So how the teachings were put together and how it was grown had flexibility. I only got involved with the part of the plan that was my job of taking Christ's work into Rome and growing it into Rome. That was my plan and that's what I did. I am being reminded up there that I achieved all of the things that I had contracts with to do that.

Greg's regressions into Paul's memories are important and eye-opening because we can see how and why he evolved the pure teachings of Jesus, and how his teachings evolved to the generally-held beliefs to this day. Paul comes across as a soul who genuinely wanted to spread the word of God as purely as he received it from Jesus. However, he had to modify some of the fundamentals of the story to have it be relevant, fit into and be accepted by the Roman culture that he was operating in.

Laurence Gardner sums up Paul's teachings of Jesus quite well in saying that, "Through Paul's imaginative teachings, a whole new concept of Jesus arose. No longer was he simply the long-awaited Messiah who would reinstate the Davidic line and free the Jews from Roman oppression. He was the heavenly savior of the whole new world. For Paul, the veneration and worship of Jesus was sufficient to ensure the entry into the Kingdom of Heaven. All the social values professed by Jesus were cast aside in his attempt to compete with a variety of pagan beliefs."[1]

Much that we know about Paul has been gleaned from his numerous writings and letters. However, theological research and scholars have authenticated only seven of the thirteen writings attributed to Paul as actually from him – and these seven are known as the undisputed letters. Laurence Gardner stresses in *The Magdalene Legacy* that, "even during his lifetime, Paul had occasion to warn people about fictitious letters purporting to be from him."[2] So some of the letters that are in the New Testament were possibly forged by others at a later point, to interfere with the pure teachings of Christ and Paul, and to further the agenda of the proto-orthodox church.

The relationship that comes across about Paul, James and Peter is a prime example of this. In this account, Paul showed that, while they had small disagreements, he and Peter worked closely with one another. Both James and Paul focused on the main message of love. They just had different ways of teaching and delivering. It is a pity that the discussions about the method of delivery has taken away the importance of the message that both of them focused on – which is love. Sure, there were disagreements between the three. This is just part of where and how they were working, and of course their egoic selves.

However, all of them devoted their lives to getting this message out.

Paul had a difficult job to do – the hardest of all the disciples. Laurence Gardner, in his book, *The Magdalene Legacy*, also agrees that Paul had a tough job to do. His allotted task was to progress the Christian message in the Greek-speaking countries and the heartland of Rome. According to Gardner, the prevailing religion of Imperial Rome at the time of Paul was polytheistic and emanated from the worship of natural deities. Religion in the first century was a hotchpotch of glued-together cults and creeds, and a complex set of beliefs.[3]

In doing so, Paul had to compete with a variety of pagan beliefs and gods that were all of supernatural origin and had astounding powers over ordinary mortals. Paul encountered problems that the original Apostles never faced in their native environment. His route to success against such odds was to present Jesus in a way that would transcend these paranormal idols – leading to the Divine Jesus of orthodox Christianity.[4] He did it the best way he knew how. Peter was a lot closer to James and the way he had been writing about the events was closer because he was addressing different types of people in different cultures. He was addressing the wider population who were not under the control of the Romans.

Paul also kept many of the meetings quiet, choosing to teach small groups in secrecy. Laurence Gardner mentions in *The Grail Enigma* that Christianity was among these diverse movements, but where other religious proponents flaunted their faith, the Christians kept to themselves and held their meetings in private. A Roman report from the second century reads, "They exclude from their fellowship the wise and good, and consort only with the ignorant and sinful." All this engendered a deep suspicion and fear of their separatist motives and gained them a reputation of being menacing and subversive.[5]

With the methods Paul employed and the way he described

it, the teachings and stories grew far quicker. There are a lot of people who were expecting something special to look up to – they were used to having leaders, masters or emperors that told them to do this or that. So they expected to have someone external telling them what to do. Paul delivered this to them – Jesus – a Divine Being – a Man God. Paul found the middle road between the teachings of Christ and the existing religion at the time.

The fact of the matter is, Paul's teaching of Gentile Christianity evolved tremendously after his death. Due to the lack of consistency of the teachings during his time, there were plenty of "internal" conflicts that occurred within the Christian community. Every church became embroiled in turmoil, for which his letters were supposed to solve the problem.[6] Scholars argued that the early Christian Church did not consist of a single orthodoxy, but a number of divergent forms.[7] So the earliest Church leaders, including Tertullian, Ignatius and Clement, developed a church hierarchy, through the Apostolic Succession, which was invested with an authority that was used to determine what was to be believed, how church affairs, including rituals and ceremonies, were to be conducted and which books and teachings were accepted as scriptural authorities.[8] This process took hundreds of years, and included the development of polemical treatises with stereotyped and harsh attacks on the views of others, forged documents in the names of apostolic authors, and a group of texts were collected into a canon of scripture that was invested with the sacred authority as having come from God. This gave us the New Testament, the 27 books accepted by Christians since the fourth century, down to the present day as canonical scripture.[9]

It cannot be denied that Paul's efforts were the start of what is now one of the biggest religions in the world. However, we have reached a point in time where what was widely accepted as "truth" needs to be examined deeper. It is time for the evolution of the teachings because of the change of the Age, and the shift in the Consciousness, where people are now able to understand the deeper truth and will be able to resonate far more from the transition of Christianity to the true teaching of Christ.

With this in mind, it would be prudent to learn more about the other prevalent Church that was evolving at the beginning – the Judeo-Christian Church – led by James, the brother of Jesus.

Part Two

Judeo-Christian Church

Oneness can be instant or it can take much discipline. It can be fleeting or it can be maintained. The choice is ours.

James

Chapter 9

The Brother

Mia went back to a memory of being a man in his early twenties with straight, dark-brown hair and beard, dusty, strappy sandals on his dusty feet. A long beige robe draped his chest with a strappy belt that hung down in tassels. The belt held his purse containing silver coins.

Mia: I'm a merchant… Mm. It's part of the family business.

Reena: What sort of merchant are you?

Mia: We trade metals. And silks. And spices. The metals are new. This is something I want to trade.

Reena: Did you introduce this to the family business?

Mia: Mm. I introduced it.

Reena: And is it doing well?

Mia: We're only just starting. But the rest of it does very well.

Reena: Tell me about your family.

Mia: We are a wealthy merchant family. We are a high-placed, Jewish trading family… We are traders that trade in various goods from across the land and it's made us very wealthy. And given us certain political influence.

Reena: Who is the main networker of this political influence, in your family?

Mia: Our father.

Reena: Is your dad in the business with you?

Mia: Mm.

Reena: And what does he do?

Mia: He's the head of the family.

Reena: And how about your mum?

Mia: My mother is very special. Like an angel.

Reena: Are you the only child? Or are there others?

He went on to explain that he was the third child – with two older brothers, and a younger sister. He then went on to say that while both his mother and sister were never exactly involved in the family business, his two brothers were. At that point of the memory, they had stopped being involved.

Reena: What do they do now, your two brothers?
Mia: [pause] My brother's a holy man.
Reena: Both of them or one of them?
Mia: Both. One follows the other.
Reena: How do you address them?
Mia: Jesus and Mark.
Reena: OK. So Mark follows Jesus? [Mia nods.] And do you follow them? [Mia shakes head.]
Reena: OK. What happens next?
Mia: My father needs me.
Reena: How do you refer to your father?
Mia: He is my lord and master.
Reena: What is his name?
Mia: Joseph.

By this point, we had gathered accounts that Jesus' father was not a poor carpenter as is popularly believed. He was a merchant, whose reach stretched far and wide if he was trading silks and spices. Jesus, according to the Gospels of Matthew and Luke, was of the royal lineage of King David, via the generational descent in the male line through his father, Joseph.[1] It does make more sense for Jesus' family to have had some status within the community. So how did the tradition of Joseph being a carpenter start?

According to Laurence Gardner, in his book, *The Magdalene Legacy*, the true meaning of this tradition was lost in translation, when the Gospels were translated into English in the seventeenth century. The term used to describe Joseph, the ancient Greek term of *ho tekton* (which has been misconstrued as being a "carpenter"), really defines him as a learned man and one who is the "master of the craft." Joseph, being a successful merchant in this regression, is in line with Gardner's thesis as well as being part of the Davidic bloodline.[2] The regression continues.

Reena: How was Joseph when Jesus and Mark left the business?

Mia: Cross.

Reena: Shall we go back to the time when Jesus left the business then? And just tell me what it is you are aware of?

Mia: I am younger. The first son was to go into the priesthood. This is our way. [Pause.] He had a calling. God called to him… Our mother knew this would be the case. He just upped and left. He renounced everything he was… I felt angry. He had a duty to his family, to us, but he said he had a bigger family.

Reena: Are you still angry with him?

Mia: No. You cannot stay angry with him. He is love. He is just… it was what he was meant for.

Reena: Is it your family way or a cultural way or…?

Mia: Cultural. We are Jewish. But we are not traditional Jews. We are part of a sect.

Reena: And what is the name of the sect?

Mia: I think we are Essenes. Joseph is proud of this. My father is very proud. And proud his son will join the priesthood. He goes at puberty. Jesus goes at puberty to be trained in the priesthood.

According to historians, the Essenes of Qumran were to whom the Dead Sea Scrolls are attributed. They are also known as the Keepers of the Covenant. This related to their renouncing property and wealth in order to ascend to the Way.[3] This could potentially be why the term Ebionite is derived from the Hebrew term *ebyon*, which means poor.[4]

According to Gardner, this Ebionite confirmation that Nazarene Christianity was born from Essene Judaism is further emphasized by a Qumran scroll fragment called *Aramaic Apocalypse*, and Jesus' teachings were based on the Qumran model.[5] So it is perfectly feasible that Jesus was sent to be trained in the ways of the priests of the Essenes when he reached puberty.

While, regretfully, there does not seem to be any primary source material for this group, one thing that is known is that there was a specific Ebionite group, the Nazarenes, or Nazarites, who renounced all their worldly possessions and lived as ascetics.[6] If Jesus did renounce everything he had, as James claimed he'd done, this could mean that he became a Nazarite, adopting the ascetic lifestyle of this very strict religious order, that observed practices such as fasting, abstaining from alcohol and rigorously upholding the Jewish law.[7] As Laurence Gardner states, "Jesus was a Nazarene Jew and did not follow the rule of Rome."[8]

The regression continues.

Reena: And how old are you?

Mia: Five or six. I am sad… [Mia's voice gets softer and trails off.]

Reena: What's making you sad?

Mia: He is my big brother. I love him.

Reena: Are you close to Jesus?

Mia: I really look up to him. He's got big eyes. He is so gentle. My other brother is a bit tougher. We fight.

Reena: You and Mark?

Mia: Mm. Jesus never fights. He's like my mother. [Big sigh.]

Reena: How about your sister? Does she fight?

Mia: No.
Reena: What is your sister like?
Mia: She is very sweet but very naughty. She is rebellious.
Reena: How do you address your sister?
Mia: Sarah.
Reena: And what is your mother's name?
Mia: Mary.

The next significant event takes us forward to the time when Mark wanted to leave the family business.

Mia: I'm older. This is where Mark wants to leave. He wants to follow Jesus.
Reena: He wants to go into the priesthood?
Mia: No. Jesus has left the priesthood.
Reena: And what does your dad say to Mark?
Mia: He says that's not the way. He is supposed to come into the business.
Reena: How old are you at this point?
Mia: Seventeen. Mark has been in the business, as have I. But now he wants to leave. He wants to become a disciple.
Reena: A disciple of Jesus?
Mia: Mm. He is saying this is the way and my father is saying this is not the way. But he is going to go anyway.
Reena: How are you feeling about all this?
Mia: A bit scared.
Reena: What is scaring you?
Mia: Now it's up to me. My father is old. It's up to me to run the business. Without any help apart from my father, who is very old now.
Reena: What does your father say to you? Do you assume that you have to run the business or does your father tell you?
Mia: He tells me but I know.
Reena: How does your father address you?

Mia: "You are my only son."

Reena: "You are my *only* son," he says?

Mia: This is what he says now.

Reena: Is he unhappy with Jesus or…?

Mia: No. But he gave his son to God. So he is no longer his son.

Reena: And with Mark walking away, did Joseph kind of disown Mark, then?

Mia: He has left. He has chosen a path.

In the next significant event, Mia finds her past-life name.

Mia: I am James. I have found my identity now.

Reena: How did you find your identity?

Mia: I became a man.

Reena: Oh? Is that like a naming ceremony or did you just find your identity internally?

Mia: We do have a ceremony but it took some time for me to feel myself.

Reena: OK. So what's happening in this significant event, James?

Mia: I have gone to see my brothers. And my mother and my sister are there.

Reena: Did they go with Jesus as well?

Mia: Mm.

Reena: So the only ones left in the business are you and your father?

Mia: My father is now dead.

Reena: How old are you now?

Mia: I am in my early twenties.

Reena: How long has your father been dead for?

Mia: Not long.

Historical speculation is that Joseph died in 29CE, before Jesus started his ministry.[9] By Mia's account, this would mean that James was born sometime between 6-8CE, and Jesus around 7BCE, which is in line with historical records.[10]

When asked about his emotions around the death of his father, James said that he was sad but free of his father's expectations of always doing as he was told.

Reena: So you go off and see your brothers and your mum and your sister. What's happening?

Mia: There is a huge crowd. I haven't seen him for a long time. He looks older.

Reena: Jesus?

Mia: Mm. But still so kind.

Reena: And what happens next?

Mia: [sighs deeply after a long pause] I just weep at his feet.

Reena: What's made you do that?

Mia: I don't know – it's so strange. [Sighs.] I just felt so lost and now I feel found.

Reena: Is this the first time you have seen your brother since he left?

Mia: Not since he left but for a long time.

Reena: What happens next?

Mia: I'm talking to my brothers... We're talking about his [Jesus'] beliefs... He left our more traditional priests. He's got his own ideas. And he's quite vocal and forthcoming with them.

Reena: What happens next?

Mia: He lifts me and hugs me and calls me his brother... He says, "Come be my brother now in life – not just with past ties."

Reena: And what do you say in response?

Mia: I feel I have obligations but [sighs] – oh, gosh – in my heart I have to... I have to be with him... I say I'll join but I need to continue to work. My mother is pleased. She is with my sister and she says this is how it's meant to be. This is how it's meant to be now.

Reena: So what happens to your business?

Mia: I can take time and run part of it. There are ways. My position is to also be in the world, not to be with Jesus all of the time. And to travel. I travel on business and also then, within the travelling… There's a network, it's to carry messages within that network.

Reena: Tell us more about this network and what sort of messages are being carried.

Mia: Part of it is about freedom for the Jews, for the Jewish people. This is a turbulent time. It's to carry messages of uprisings.

Reena: How are you feeling now?

Mia: I wonder what I've got myself involved with. [Sighs deeply.] … This is a freedom movement. It's a mass freedom movement. But Jesus is different. While others call for war and violence, Jesus says that freedom comes from a freedom of the heart and through love and that's how we gain our freedom. It's different. Very different. He's talking really about, it's very different, the spiritual freeness from the priests as well that are very revolutionary. Being true to God. Being closer to God and that it's God's love and God is the only master, not the Romans and not the priests.

When asked if James understood the essence of the message, he replied: "Much of it. But I feel I don't understand all of it. Certainly not in the way Jesus does. Jesus has an understanding that I don't think any of us truly grasp, apart from maybe my mother."

When asked how the message is received in the wider public he gave a big sigh. "Many don't want to fight but they want to feel a respect for themselves. They want a new message: they are thirsty for it, thirsty for change. They are fed up with being dictated to by the Romans and by the priests. It's received well because of who he is. Because of the love, the energy. The love is... He just settles everybody. And in his presence there is a knowing that all will be well. Just to sit in his presence..."

James then went on to describe a little of their lifestyle. According to him, he, Jesus and his followers travelled together often. Sometimes they were joined by their mother Mary and sister Sarah. Sometimes they stayed in James' and Jesus' family home, but when they travelled, they relied on the generosity of their supporters for shelter and lodging.

When asked for a name or title for the people who follow Jesus' teachings, James responds: "He calls them his children. And his family. They are his brothers and sisters, his children, his family. They are his family. It's a very big family."

James is then asked about the political environment around him. "It's more the priests. The priests are not happy – not happy at all. [They] are afraid of an uprising. They are afraid they will lose their power. They are afraid they will lose their power by the Romans smashing all the Jewish establishments. All the infrastructure. And they are afraid they'll lose their power from beneath. From the people. That people will no longer respect them. So they are being squeezed by the power above and the power below. And they are not happy... So, they spread rumors. They are very angry. They have meetings and are very angry. I have said Jesus is not the troublemaker. He talks of peace. But he is the most charismatic. He is the one they are most afraid of, even though there are others. The Romans are more unhappy with others. But the priests..."

When asked how Jesus responded to the priests' unhappiness and their rumors, James laughs and responds, "We are all children of God," and then, "God is my Father and when it's my time, He will receive me. I will return to Him."

Reena: Are these the same priests that Jesus went to when he was a teenage boy, when he hit puberty?

Mia: Some of them, yes. They feel betrayed.

Reena: What are they betrayed by?

Mia: Because Jesus is cleverer than them and he is teaching things different to how they taught it to him. And he has a different understanding of their teachings. Different meanings that they have never seen before and they don't want to accept this. They don't want to change from the old ways.

This account is consistent with not just that of the New Testament but also historical accounts of the environment of Judea during the days of Christ. The first century CE saw Judea in heaving political turmoil and religious unrest. From 150BCE to 100CE, Galilee, the birthplace of Jesus, was also the birthplace of revolts against the Romans, and their crushing taxes and land regulations.[11]

The most highly acclaimed Romano-Jewish historian of the first century, Flavius Josephus, wrote three major works: *The Jewish War* (78CE), *Jewish Antiquities* (94CE) and *Against Apion* (97CE),[12] which are widely referred to by historians and academics because his writings and records are the earliest historical references that are available for the biblical period. In them, Josephus regularly differentiates between three main sects or schools of Judaism that existed in this time: Pharisees, Sadducees and Essenes.[13]

- The Pharisees – devoutly orthodox, they were keen on maintaining the rigorous Jewish faith that Jesus was against.
- The Sadducees – predominantly the Jewish aristocrats, wealthy and in collaboration with Roman rule – they had some theological differences with the Pharisees.

- The Essenes – who saw that Judea was getting corrupt and who withdrew into the caves and the wilderness and were spearheading the change in regime. Ascetic in outlook, they were reputed to be the most cultured and learned religious order.

Elsewhere Josephus also seems to refer to a fourth movement as the "Zealots," which refers to those who participated in the first revolt against Rome.

It is interesting to note that though Jesus was sent to study with the Pharisees, he disagreed with their teachings and held on to the ideologies that the Essene community had. The Essenes were free of the contamination of politics or orthodox religion, and wanted a change for Judea.[14] Again, this is in line with what Mia was recounting.

The next significant event found James eating with a group of people, who he identified as Jesus' disciples and wife.

Reena: Who is his wife?
Mia: Mary.
Reena: Isn't Mary the mother?
Mia: Yes.
Reena: It's a different Mary then?
Mia: Mm.
[Later, in the debrief, Mia says that during the regression, she was sure that this was Mary Magdalene, although she was not known or addressed as "Mary Magdalene" during that time.]
Reena: And where is Sarah?
Mia: Sarah is helping to prepare the food.
Reena: How many disciples are there?
Mia: Many disciples.
Reena: How many are there at the meal?
Mia: Fifteen.

Reena: Is Mark there? [Mia nods.]

Reena: Are you a disciple?

Mia: I am a disciple but my role is different. I am not with the Master all the time.

Reena: What is your role?

Mia: I go between the inner circle and the outer world.

Reena: So who are the fifteen who are there? Mark…

Mia: Jesus, John, Sarah, my mother, Mary, James…

Reena: Aren't you James?

Mia: There's another James. [Long pause.] Peter. I don't like Peter.

Reena: What about Peter don't you like?

Mia: I don't trust him. He loves Jesus but he cannot see… He just cannot see the truth. He still has anger in his heart.

Reena: Can Jesus see this?

Mia: Mm. Jesus loves him, though. He laughs. Jesus laughs and tells me not to worry. [Pause.] I really don't like him.

Reena: Have you told Jesus your feelings?

Mia: Mm. He [Peter] is rude.

Reena: Who else is there?

Mia: … The rest of his inner circle. I don't spend so much time with them. The time I spend, I spend with Jesus and then I continue with my work outside. I am not really part of their circle. And this is the problem. This is where Peter thinks he's the boss of the circle. This is what I do not like.

Reena: Who do *you* think is the boss of the circle? Or is there a boss of the circle?

Mia: Jesus is the Master.

Josephus Flavius mentions three key figures in rising early Christianity – John the Baptist, Jesus and James, the brother of Jesus, though he never labels the group or movement/s to which they belonged. The reason being, apparently, that the earliest followers of Jesus did not use a self-identifying label but preferred a variety of descriptive terms.

However, through a reference in the book of Acts, we get a clue, a glimmer of the Hebrew name for the movement Jesus was active in. Paul, on trial before the Roman governor Felix, is referred to as being "the ringleader of the sect of the Nazarenes" (Acts 24:5). Associated with the term "Nazarenes" is a second Hebrew designation, namely Ebionites, that was also apparently used for the earliest, mostly Jewish followers of Jesus.[15]

It is worth pointing out here that there is historical speculation that the term "Jesus of Nazareth" is not a reference to the town that Jesus was born in. In the Old Testament, Nazareth was not listed as a town in Jerusalem. Instead "Jesus of Nazareth" could be a misinterpretation of "Yesus Nazarene" from the New Testament. Nazarene is the term given to the spiritual leadership of the Essenes.[16]

So Jesus was quite possibly a leader of the Essene movement. In fact, he was considered to be of the royal lineage of King David, of the House of Judah,[17] and so he was the Messiah, the King of the Jews. His teachings, which are now referred to as Christianity, were based on the Qumran model of the Essene sect, which disagreed with the Pharisees and Sadducees.

These accounts of Jesus being the Master fit in quite nicely with the speculation of biblical historical scholars.

The regression continues.

> Reena: Does Peter think he is the Master as opposed to Jesus?
> Mia: No, but he sees that Jesus is concerned with spiritual things and that he must run the more mundane.

James relays a memory of arguing with Peter before the meal, thinking that Peter is trying to take over and enforce his will – which, in James' opinion, is not the will of God. In response, Peter tells James patronizingly to stop being a spoilt child.

Then James talks about sitting down to eat and describes

the meal. He sits as far away from Peter as possible. They dine on stew, with goat meat. They also have olives, fruit and dates, cuisine that is consistent with what was commonly eaten during that time in that part of the world. Goat's meat was the most common meat, and stewed meat was considered to be a dish given to honored guests. Olives, dates and fruit are also recorded to be an important source of food consumed by Israelites in those times.[18]

At the mention of the fruit, James smiles.

Mia: Mm. I like sweet things. And we have wine. And a type of bread. It's a very special occasion.

Reena: What's special about it?

Mia: Jesus is explaining the planning. He's explaining that he must leave and go into hiding and how things should be run in his absence.

Reena: What's makes Jesus want to go into hiding?

Mia: That it's getting too dangerous for him. We aim to continue his teachings there... But he is fighting with this idea. Fighting with the idea of going into hiding or facing the priests and so there is a discussion. [Pause.] He now decides he wants to face the priests... He decides he wants to travel... to where the priests are holding a meeting. He wants to face them.

Reena: How do you feel about this?

Mia: I'm not happy. I think it's too dangerous.

Reena: How do the others feel about this? Your mum, Mary, Peter, Sarah, Mark?

Mia: Everyone feels it's too dangerous. But his mind is made up. He prepares to travel... I go on ahead of them... I have to do some business and sort some things. And so I arrive later.

It is interesting to note that this could be an account of the Last

Supper. In the next scene, James says that he is always on the outside – not part of the inner circle.

Reena: And how does that make you feel?
Mia: It's OK. This is my position.

Then he explains that he is not with Jesus, but in the capital that he eventually identifies as the Holy City. James is with Mary, his mother, Sarah, his sister, and Mary, Jesus' wife. Due to religious reasons, the ladies are unable to have contact with Jesus and the rest of the priests during the time of the meeting. So James stays with them to protect them. A little later, James gets a message from Mark that Jesus has been arrested.

Reena: How does this make you feel?
Mia: I knew. I knew something would happen.
Reena: What happens next?
Mia: My mother is quite calm but the other women are wailing. Mm. I ask my brother to stay. I must go and try and bargain for him.

At this point, James did not know what the charges were for Jesus' arrest. Calmly but urgently, James decides to see Jesus and the city governor, as the next course of action, to offer a bribe for Jesus' release.

Reena: How do you address the city governor? Do you address him by name?
Mia: Pontius Pilate.
Reena: And what does Pontius Pilate say when you offer him a bribe?
Mia: He will accept but he will put it to the people and offer to free one of the prisoners. This is the best he can do.
Reena: How many prisoners are there besides Jesus?

Mia: There's many but they will execute three.

Reena: Tell me what happens next.

Mia: I go to the guards and I offer a bribe to the guards. They say they will accept the bribe but they must have someone in his place... [Sighs heavily.] I accept this. I tell them I must find someone that looks like Jesus and that it will be OK because he will be released. The people are bound to want Jesus... One of the followers [sighs heavily] offers to take Jesus' place. Jesus is nearly dead anyway. They've tortured him. He is unconscious. We take him and we hide him.

Reena: [referring to the heavy sighs] Are you feeling emotional? [Mia nods.] Are you feeling emotional that Jesus is nearly dead or that someone has offered to replace him?

Mia: The whole thing. And someone must take his place.

Reena: And you take Jesus and hide him...

Mia: We hide him in a cave, a burial cave where he won't be disturbed. But we have to heal him. [Sighs heavily.] Oh, gosh!

It was clear through this entire exchange that the weight of what James had orchestrated weighed heavily on him.

Reena: What happened to this other person that is taking his place?

Mia: There's only me, my brother and the women that know this. It must be so secret. We leave the person that takes his place. [Sighs heavily... pause.] Jesus is safe. [Long pause.] And then we go to the trial and Pontius Pilate keeps his word. He offers it to the people and the people do not choose Jesus. And an innocent man will die. Is it right that it's a different innocent man? [Sighs heavily.]

Reena: Does Jesus know that this is happening?

Mia: No. Jesus is still too ill. [Sighs.] The only ones that know are me, my mother, Jesus' wife and my brother.

Reena: Does your sister know?

Mia: [shakes head] People will realize, though. His [the substitute's] face has had to be bloodied. He looks beaten. [Long pause... softly.] And I did that to him – I asked him to do that.

Reena: Did you ask or did he volunteer to do it?

Mia: He volunteered. But it was at my request.

Reena: This person... do you know him?

Mia: Yes. [Long pause.]

Reena: Can you tell us his name?

Mia: No.

During the account of the next few memories, Mia became increasingly distressed, holding her face and head in her hands, sighing repeatedly and even pulling on her hair.

Mia: He (the substitute) is killed.

Reena: How is he killed?

Mia: On the cross. We have to take his body, we have to dispose of the body, because it will be realized it's not Jesus. Oh, gosh, what a mess! What a mess! [Sighs heavily.] We take the body and we bury it. We must remove it [from the cross] so that when people come, they do not see the difference. I think some people have already guessed.

Reena: How did you get access to the body?

Mia: We are allowed to take it because we are the family. [Sighs heavily.] ... Terrible. I feel sick.

Reena: Do you think it's your fault?

Mia: It's not my fault but I've played a part. And as [to] the part I have played, was it correct?

James went on to explain that the substitute was a follower who looked just like Jesus, though not an exact doppelgänger. The substitute had known exactly what he needed to do, and gave his life willingly for Jesus to survive.

While most Western scholars and Christians believe that it was Jesus who died, most Muslims believe he was raised to Heaven without being put on the cross and God transformed another person to appear exactly like Jesus, who was crucified instead of Jesus. The Koran has a verse that mentions a substitute – Surah An-Nisa' number 157 that says (interpreted), "And (because of) their saying: 'Surely we have killed the Massih – son of Maryam,' the messenger of Allah, and they could not kill him nor could they crucify him, even though a likeness of that was made for them."[19]

There are also Gnostic Gospels, like the Gospel of Basilides, that mention that Jesus survived the crucifixion and specifically say that Simon of Cyrene was the substitute. "Thus he himself did not suffer. Rather, a certain Simon of Cyrene was compelled to carry his cross for him. It was he who was ignorantly and erroneously crucified, being transfigured by him, so that he might be thought to be Jesus."[20]

This account of the crucifixion is also found in two second- and third-century Gnostic texts in the Nag Hammadi Library: the Apocalypse of Peter[21] and the Second Treatise of the Great Seth, in which Simon of Cyrene is also identified as being one of a succession of bodily substitutes for the spiritual Christ.[22]

The regression continues.

Mia: So we take the body [to dispose of] and when the rest of the disciples come, the body's gone. They are all proclaiming it's a miracle and I know… [pause]. I tell Jesus.

Reena: What is Jesus' reaction?

Mia: Angry. He is angry with me. He said that no one should die in his place. [I said] I did what I felt was right. Nobody should have died. He should have been released. Jesus kisses me and tells me he knows. He says he has to see his disciples one last time… to explain his message. He has to explain his message so it doesn't get misinterpreted…

James elaborated that, in his understanding, Jesus' message was one of love. Of equality. All men and women are equal in the eyes of God. We are all brothers and sisters. We are all family. We are all children of God.

Reena: And tell me what happens next.
Mia: I am preparing. We're going to leave. He must leave. He must recuperate in the mountains for some time before [sic], because it will be a very long journey.
Reena: His wounds are quite extensive, then?
Mia: Mm. He was beaten very badly.
Reena: Who beat him?
Mia: The guards. The guards were paid by the priests to beat him. [Sighs heavily.] He has many wounds. They marked him when they held him. They marked him as if he had been crucified. He was stabbed. And they tortured him.

This piece of detail is quite significant in the regression because even though Jesus was not crucified, he was marked as though he was. This would account for all the subsequent witnesses of Jesus feeling distraught at seeing his wounds, including the marks of crucifixion.

Next, James talks about Jesus meeting his disciples, telling them that he is not dead, and that he has to leave.

Reena: Does he tell only the fifteen that were at the dinner?
Mia: Not the fifteen. No, the fifteen had left. The fifteen was made up of me, his mother, his wife. He tells the remaining ones.

Reena: What is their reaction?

Mia: Disbelief. They are confused. I am waiting for him. He wanted to talk to them alone, though.

Next, James gives the account of travelling to a safe place, in hiding. At first, only James and Jesus went to the safe place – for Jesus to heal. Then, they continued on, with many travelling with them.

Eventually James left them to travel on by himself.

Mia: I need to go back and make sure everything is OK. I need to make sure they will not be followed.

Reena: It seems to me that you are taking care of all the mundane things in all this. Where is Peter in all this?

Mia: Peter is… [sighs]. He takes some of the disciples and he teaches. They must all split up. They must all go in different directions. This is a very dangerous time.

The next significant event that James remembered was when he next met Jesus.

Mia: I travel. Yeah. He's in France. My mother's old now. It's her time.

Reena: Is she in France as well?

Mia: Mm. With Mary [his wife].

This is a fascinating account. Little is known of what happened to Mother Mary after the crucifixion. However, some historians claim that Mother Mary travelled with Disciple John after the crucifixion and died in Ephesus, after having lived there for nine years, not in France as Mia claims. Why there is this contradiction, I cannot say. Another intriguing question to ponder on.

The regression continues.

Mia: They have a child. They have two children now.
Reena: Jesus and Mary?
Mia: Mm. Jesus wants to travel. He says he must carry his message. He wants me to go with him. He must leave Mary. He needs to travel. He wants to go south.
Reena: South to where?
Mia: I think Crete.

Laurence Gardner also names Crete as one of the islands in Jesus' destinations.[23]

Reena: Do you go?
Mia: [nods] He wants to travel with me because I travel and… I have the ship! [Laughs.] So we travel. And Jesus tells me he's afraid his time is coming. And he says his time has come to travel and carry [on] spreading his Gospel. He is afraid that on these travels he may not get back to Mary, his wife, and he makes me promise to look after his son, to help his son, and I promise that whatever happens I will take care of his family.

I then asked a series of questions about his own family. James said he did have a wife in Jerusalem and that it was a marriage of convenience. She passed away while he was not around. They did not have any children.

We drew this session to an end. What struck me while I was conducting this regression was that by James' account, Jesus was not the only son of Joseph, the poor carpenter. In fact, it seemed that Joseph was a merchant, and was fairly well-to-do by the standards of the civilization that they lived in. A handful of biblical historians are in agreement that Jesus was a true lineal descendant of the Shepherd King, David.[24] As such, this family would have had both means and some influence in the community in those times.

According to Laurence Gardner, by historical accounts, Jesus was the heir to the throne of David, the dynastic House of Judah. In this kingly line, the patriarchal title of "Joseph" was applied to the next in succession. According to Mia, James' second brother seemed to be disowned because he chose to discard his cultural familial role of assuming the responsibilities of head of the family including the running of the business. So the duties of the second son fell on James' shoulders. Hence, James would have assumed the title Joseph.

Furthermore, despite his mother Mary's reputation as being a virgin, the New Testament makes it clear that Jesus is not the only son. Matthew 13:55 clarifies that Jesus had brothers, and in the New Testament epistles, St. Paul refers to his meeting in Jerusalem with "James, the Lord's brother." First-century historian Flavius Josephus refers to, "James, the brother of Jesus, who was called Christ."[25]

Another point to note is the role Mia's James played in making arrangements with the Romans about the crucifixion, and taking Jesus' body from the cross. Tradition holds that it was Joseph of Arimathea, a wealthy, influential relation, who did this. The fact that Pontius Pilate accepted his involvement in Jesus' affairs without question, and also accepted a rather large bribe from him, shows that Joseph of Arimathea did have familial ties with Jesus, and was rather well-to-do. However, records show that there was no such place called "Arimathea." "Arimathea" is actually another title representing high status. So Joseph of Arimathea is in fact a title, not a name. Outside the scriptures he is presumed to be Jesus' mother's uncle. However, if he were, sources say he died in either 63CE or 82CE, which would put him at between 100 and 125 years of age.[26] So, he could not be Jesus' granduncle, but someone younger.

Historically, it is much more feasible that the person who interceded on Jesus' behalf was his own brother, as Mia claims. James took on the role as the head of the family business, making him an influential merchant. He had familial ties with Jesus, therefore enabling him to intercede as and when he did. He would have been between 58 to 75 years of age, if he had died between 63CE and 82CE.

This therefore could mean that James, Jesus' brother and Joseph of Arimathea, are indeed one and the same. This connection strengthens as the regression continues.

Chapter 10

Britannia

The following week, we picked up from where we left off at the previous session. James described the landscape as being different, green with trees, and colder. He states that he is in France, and gives an account of getting here by boat. His companions in the boat were Jesus, Mary, the wife of Jesus, Sarah, Mary's sister and two of Jesus' followers who were there to protect them.

In the recollections of Clement, there is mention of Joseph of Arimathea being the leader of a band of people, including Martha, the three Marys, Salome, Lazarus, Zacharius and his servants.[1] While there is no mention of Jesus, it makes sense that if the existence of Jesus was to be kept quiet, great pains must have been taken to write him out of history post-crucifixion – for his safety and the safety of the spiritual mission he had.

Reena: Who made the decision to go to France? Was it you? [Mia nods.] And what drew you to France?

Mia: It's far and out of the way.

Reena: Do you know anyone there?

Mia: I know of a settlement there. It's not just Jewish but there are friends of Jews. They're not hostile. There are some Jews but they are open in their thinking.

To the north of Marseille was Vienne, which at that time housed the Herodian estate in Gaul – used as a place of exile by Herod Archelaus (brother of Herod Antipas).[2] Being of the Sanhedrin Council, which was the Supreme Court made up of seventy of the most influential men in ancient Israel, Joseph of Arimathea, or

James, would have had knowledge of, and ties to, this potential safe refuge, and may have made arrangements to send his family members and their entourage there, which would tie up with what Mia is claiming.

There are also records, one especially from Cardinal Baronius a curator of the Vatican Library, that mentioned that they sailed along the Mediterranean towards the coast of Gaul and landed at Marseille. From there, Joseph of Arimathea travelled to Britain in 36CE.[3]

The regression continues. The next significant event saw James landing and letting everyone else off. However, James stayed long enough only to put more supplies on the boat. He felt an urgent need to go back to Jerusalem to continue trading, but more importantly to make sure that people thought that Jesus was dead.

Reena: What's so important about people thinking Jesus is dead?

Mia: Because Rome stretches throughout Europe.

Reena: And what does that have to do with everyone knowing Jesus is dead?

Mia: To protect him so they don't come after him. They see him as a troublemaker.

Reena: What happens next?

Mia: His disciples are confused. They're confused about... that he's still alive and they want to tell everyone. I tell them they can't and they want to spread the message. I tell them they can't [desperately, emphatically]. They want to take his teachings... He tells them to take his teachings and go into the world. And also they must go to the outer edges of the Roman Empire. All of them have to move to the edges to be safe.

In order to keep the charade going, James places urgency in

getting back to his life as a merchant – to act as normally as possible. So he busies himself by working with the Romans in extending his trade routes throughout the Roman Empire. Though this keeps him safe, he is constantly asked about rumors surrounding his brother Jesus, which he denies.

At the next significant event, James is wearing sandals with ties, and a long, dirty, dusty robe. He is loosely holding a rope with both hands coming off a boat, on a small island. He is not very well having just completed a long voyage, from Britannia, and had stopped over on an island that he identified as perhaps being Cyprus, on his way to Jerusalem.

Reena: Who are there with you?

Mia: My crew and my cousin. He's younger than me.

Reena: Is he part of the crew?

Mia: No. We hire the ship… and the crew come with the ship.

Reena: Tell me more about your cousin being on the ship.

Mia: He's learning to trade… From me.

Reena: Mmm. Travelling to Britannia, is that for trade purposes?

Mia: Yes. I like it there. Plus, we get metal from there… We take the metal ores and we travel through the Roman Empire for trade.

Reena: What do you trade for metal ore from Britannia?

Mia: Different ports, they work the metal in different ways and they have different goods. We buy and sell and barter and then take it to the next port. Then finally we have a fine array of pieces from across the kingdom to bring back to Jerusalem.

Reena: What do you do with it in Jerusalem?

Mia: We sell it. We trade it. This is the family business.

Reena: What happened to Mark?

[Long pause.]

Mia: He travelled south. He couldn't stay with Jesus. It was too risky.

Reena: Did you see Mark again after he went south?

Mia: No, I haven't seen him.

Reena: So you extended your trade routes. Where did you extend them to? What are the two furthest points?

Mia: We wanted the ore. We went to England. That was the furthest. The first time, we knew there was good metal coming from England because of what was being traded. And so we took goods. We took spices and different things.

Reena: Have you got a fleet [of boats]?

Mia: Maybe not a fleet but we have some boats.

According to Isabel Hill Elder, in her book *Joseph of Arimathea*, by the eleventh century BCE the tribe of Asher, seafaring men from Israel, under the name Phoenicians, had coasted along Spain and Gaul, establishing a trade with the "tin islands" – the Scilly Isles and Cornwall. Camden's *Britannia* Volume 1 chronicles that the merchants of Asher worked or farmed the tin mines, not as slaves, but as masters and exporters. There is some evidence of their cultural residue left in Cornwall, namely the practice of burying their dead, as opposed to burning like the Romans; as well as the similarity of Welsh and Cornish words and whole sentences with the Hebrew language.[4]

Sir ES Creasy, in his *History of England*, writes, "The British mines mainly supplied the glorious adornment of Solomon's temple," thereby giving us another recorded anecdote of the tin being used by the Israelites.[5]

So, it is not far-fetched to think that James had a commercial network and a small fleet of trading boats that travelled to England. Although the area was not called "England" during the biblical period, the memories were being filtered through Mia's current-life vocabulary, hence her use of terms from the current times. As is mentioned by Isabel Hill Elder, "It is not by mere chance that Arimathean Joseph became acquainted with Cornish tin and Somerset lead mining, for as a Prince of the House of David, Joseph was aware that his kinsmen of the tribe of Asher had made Cornwall famous for the prized metal." Again, this implies that the family of Jesus was an important, well-to-do family.[6]

The regression continues.

Reena: So you took your spices and other things and sailed to England...

Mia: We met the king. A kind of tribal king.

Reena: What was your reception like in England?

Mia: I took an English person with me. There were people in France who were English. I took a trader and he spoke. They were very... [long pause]. They were very loud and... they were friendly. They liked what we brought because they hadn't seen it before. But they were very different... Not as refined as the Romans.

Then we went on to the topic of gifts. James rather smugly mentioned that the tribal king, whom he addressed as "My Lord," wanted to bestow upon James his pretty daughter as a gift. James insisted that it would have been rude to have refused.

Mia: [smiles coyly] Work must be done to form trade routes!

Reena: And what happened next?

Mia: I explained I'd have to travel. And he's agreed sometimes she would come with me and sometimes she would stay.

Reena: Where did you and she stay? Did you take her back to Jerusalem or were you staying in England or somewhere else?

Mia: I took her with me... to France.

Reena: Did she meet Jesus? And his family?

Mia: Yes. And I took her to... outside of Rome. To trade. It wasn't Rome. It was near. I don't like going to Rome.

Reena: What don't you like about it?
Mia: Too many Romans.

There is record of James (under the name of Joseph of Arimathea) being the guest of the Silurian King Caractacus and his brother Arviragus around the Isle of Avalon, known as Somerset in current times. It was recorded in the Domesday Book that Arviragus gifted James twelve hides of land, tax-free, each hide representing 160 acres.[7]

Laurence Gardner independently concluded that because James the Just first visited Siluria in 35CE, his wife would appear to have been the daughter of King Cymbeline and the sister of Arviragus, Enygus, thus justifying the generous gift of the twelve hides of land to him.[8] Again, this is consistent with Mia's account.

Mia: I settle in Britannia. I settle far away from where the Romans have their capital, so it is a haven. We can say and do and practice how we want to. There is a freedom here.

It is fascinating to note the change in Mia's language here, where she uses "Britannia" instead of "England." The deeper she goes into the memory and more familiar it becomes, the more associated she is with the memory and the more she accesses and switches to using the language from that time.

Reena: Where is your brother?
Mia: My brother is in hiding… from the Romans and from the Jews. They didn't like his teachings. They see it as heresy. My brother embraces all and, like myself, I embrace all with our teachings. I have brought it to Britannia and we have our own belief here. We practice and live with the pagans. And we embrace all. He embraced all, but the Jewish Pharisees and the priests do not like this. They

> do not want outsiders. No Gentiles. Nobody who is not Jewish. We should not be passing this knowledge on to those who want salvation. We are here for God's salvation for all. God's love and God's teaching.

This claim is in line with the historical difference between Jesus' views and the views of the conservative Pharisees and Sadducees of the Jewish religion. Jesus' views stemmed from the Essene traditions, as referenced in the Dead Sea Scrolls. Jesus openly criticized the Pharisee rabbis and the Sadducee priests, advising his disciples not to follow their examples of advocating one thing and doing another.[9]

Reena: Where in Britannia are you?

Mia: West.

Reena: Did Jesus and Mary and the kids ever come to see you here?

Mia: I came to them. Most people don't travel.

Reena: Did Jesus' children ever come to Britannia?

Mia: Not when they were young.

At this point, James recalled that Jesus had three children: a daughter called Sarah, a son called Jesus Jr., or "Yesoo", and another son whose name James could not recall.

The regression continues with James wearing a light-blue smock over a white tunic. He hears the ocean in the distance and he can smell salt in the air. He is standing on very green grass, under blue skies. It is very cold, colder than he is used to. The grass is different to what he is used to as well.

Mia: It's like all these differences are more familiar to me, and I feel more comfortable and safer than our home [in Jerusalem]. [Sigh.] Our people have come after a hard day, weary at work, and they wish to hear from me more. They wish to hear stories from home – our home. I am able to go back and forth whereas these men are not. These women are not either.

James proceeds to tell them about the conditions in their homeland.

Mia: The conditions at home are very treacherous. The Roman conquerors think that they can boss us around but we say that they cannot. We try to fight. There are some that work with the Romans. It is like in order to preserve a crumb they give the bread. But when we want to fight, we say no. This is not our Way. Our Way is being taken away by the Romans [sigh].

These accounts are in line with documented research. The Ebionites were opposed to the corrupt Sadducee priests in Jerusalem, to the ruling family of Herod, and even to the Pharisees whom they saw as compromising with that establishment to get power and influence from the Hellenistic/Roman powers.[10] They claimed to be the remnants of the original Jerusalem church, and revered James, the brother of Jesus, for his outstanding righteousness under the law and considered him to be the leader of the Apostles after the death of Jesus.[11]

The regression continues. James' workers are worried for their families, and so James tries to get as much news about their families as they can when he goes back. It keeps his bond with his workers strong for they are so far away from home, and James is the only way they can get messages from whom and about what they are familiar with.

Mia: We talk about preserving our Way. Our Way is about staying true to our… to Yahweh. Staying true to the One Spirit that holds us all. For we are all connected to this

One Spirit. We need to, as much as we can, stay true to the laws of Yahweh. But we are able to mold and change it slightly – just a little bit.

James, when talking about the rules, the laws of Yahweh or the Jewish law, is referring to the collective body of Jewish religious laws derived from the written and oral Torah. The Hebrew term for Jewish law is *Halakha,* which literally translates to "the way to behave" or "the way of walking."[12] It is what the Sadducees and Pharisees insisted on following in Jerusalem.

Reena: Just give me an example of bits that you have adapted and changed.

Mia: It's not about my personal adaptation and change. It is what suits the workers to be here. Cleanliness and hygiene are the most important things. That has to be maintained at all times predominantly for health reasons. The cleaner we are, the healthier we are. Better quality of life. Back in the old home, it was a very dry, dusty, hot place. So we take frequent ablutions, frequent washes. Clothes have to be washed frequently as well. Whereas in this land, it is colder. But just because it is colder, does not mean that we have to let our hygiene standards lapse. These workers work very hard and so they need to maintain these ablutions. It is just being clean to be healthy.

Reena: And what else are you communicating to these workers?

Mia: Nutrition. We are communicating about how it is best to eat food that is rich in nutrition that will help their muscles grow – the body become healthy. It is very difficult to observe the kosher rules while here. Food is not prepared in the same way.

Reena: Can you give us some examples of the food that is rich in nutrition that you are suggesting they have?

Mia: Cheese and milk are aplenty here. And it helps keep them going and strong whilst they do the work. Meats… if they can afford it. But they eat predominantly fish because of what they are able to afford. On special days they have meat. [Sigh.] Then there is the Sabbath. The Sabbath is very strict back home. But here I say to them, Sabbath is not about the rules of just thinking and paying homage to God. It is about resting, and what you do on your rest day, as long as it falls within some of the rules, is OK. Do not hurt, do not kill, do not gamble… do not consume alcohol. But if you wish to walk in a park, that is OK. If you wish to contemplate the Lord, that's OK. If you just wish to be in companionship with your fellow colleagues, that is fine. It's a lot more relaxed than the Sabbath that they used to observe. A part of it is to help with the integration with the locals but a big part of it is just to break them from the rules and to make them accountable – to make all of us accountable – without being told and without being controlled. This is the way that Jesus wanted. This is also why we wish to oppose the Roman rule. But then some of our kind take it a bit further and they wish to fight.

Reena: This wishing to oppose Roman law – is that something that Jesus taught? Or is this something that you teach?

Mia: It's not a teaching. It's a principled belief that we hold. Our group – and what Jesus wishes for. The opposition stems from the observation of the Romans suppressing our ways and controlling us, imposing high taxes, not being merciful or compassionate to those who have to toil to pay those high taxes, which leaves very little for themselves. Not understanding that the land is not consistent and will not consistently give the same amount of yield all the time; yet imposing higher taxes, and punishing when the yield is not as much. We, the people, cannot help when trade is not good or when the land does not yield as much

> or when the fishing diminishes – which causes us a lot of suffering and hurt and tension when we are unable to pay those taxes. Here in this land [Britannia] they are away from the Roman rule – the oppressive Roman rule of our land. Here they work for my partners and I, and we give them wages. So it is a lot freer here. However, we also prefer this way of life here because we can implement our principles without being controlled by the Romans and the Pharisees and the Sadducees. Between the religious control imposed by the Pharisees and the Sadducees, and the administrative, economic control, and sometimes cultural control imposed by the Romans, it is unbearable. There is very little freedom over there at home. We oppose the Roman rule, and to a certain extent, we wish to shift and change the Pharisees and the Sadducees and what they teach religiously to give more freedom to the people.

In the next significant event, James feels a burden. Jesus has told James that he needs to step in to lead his teachings… to be responsible for his flock.

> Mia: I am with my brother. He is telling me that God has told him I should start the church in his name in Britannia. This is not my way. I am not supposed to be the spiritual leader. That was him. Not me. I feel a burden, a responsibility – far greater than that of taking over my family's business. But I acquiesce to lead a small flock in Britannia. And so I start my teachings here.

James' accounts were totally in line with academic research. In 1502, Polidoro Virgilio, a scholar from Italy, was sent to England as a tax gatherer for Pope Alexander VI. He became the deacon of the Somerset diocese of Bath and Wells, which includes Glastonbury, and wrote 26 books about the history of Britain. In it, he wrote about Arviragus being the principal chief in Britain during the time of Nero (54-68CE). He writes that Joseph of Arimathea came to Britain with followers, where he preached the Gospel and the teachings of Christ. By this, many men were baptized and assured of the Holy Spirit. He goes on to talk about how they were given a gift of a plot of land four miles from the town of Wells, in Glastonbury, where they laid the first foundations of the new religion.[13]

Joseph of Arimathea had settled in Avalon and built not just a community of believers in Jesus, but also the Wattle Church, on the grounds of which Glastonbury Abbey stands today. The Wattle Church is considered to be the first Christian church erected in Britain, and is chronicled in *The Christian Church, in These Islands Before the Coming of Augustine*, written by Rev. GF Browne, former Bishop of Bristol. The more researchers study Celtic Druidic religion, the more similarities they find with old Israel – and this is credited to Joseph of Arimathea and the integration of the first Christian communities with the Druidic tradition in Britain.[14]

From manuscripts in the Vatican collection, Vatican librarians maintained that Britons had indeed embraced Christianity as early as 35CE, just a couple of years after the alleged crucifixion of Christ, and more than two decades before Paul was martyred in Rome. They also mention how Mary Magdalene, Martha and others sailed to Gaul (Marseille, France, in their words), and Joseph of Arimathea and his company voyaged towards Britain.[15]

The regression continues.

Reena: Is this before or after your brother went into hiding?

Mia: After.

Reena: And how do you feel about that?

Mia: He says his church is safer on the outer rim of the Roman Empire, so this is where we must establish it. He also says his teaching school would become corrupted. He says we must maintain the purity.

Reena: Just tell me what are the aspects of purity.

Mia: My brother is a revolutionary. He is a bit different from other revolutionaries. He is in peace and in God's love, but he knows how dangerous his ideas are. He says that they will be taken and transformed to control as all ideas are, and as all teachings are. He says that we must establish beacons of hope and God's love. So we are taking his message; me to Britannia, Mary in France.

Many historians do acknowledge that Jesus indeed was a revolutionary or a rebel against the suppression of Roman rule in Jerusalem. However, they do differ on what type of revolutionary Jesus was – was he part of the militant freedom fighters known as the Zealots?[16] Or was Jesus a spiritual soldier of love and peace, the deemed Messiah of the Essenes?

Some historians hypothesized that Qumran, where the Essenes lived, was an outpost for the Zealots, fighting to free Judea from the Roman occupation, and not the haven for the spiritual, ascetic pacifists known as the Essenes. If this was so, they hypothesized that Jesus was not the radical rabbi with a message of love, but a political rebel.[17] However, James' comment disputes this hypothesis entirely when he confirms that while Jesus is indeed a revolutionary, he is a Prince of Peace and God's love, thereby making him different from other revolutionaries, who were the Zealots.

Reena: Where is he taking his message?

Mia: North Africa. But he travels. He keeps travelling and carrying his message across the periphery of the Roman Empire.

Reena: Does he do this in partnership with other disciples, or does he do it by himself?

Mia: He sends his disciples out to carry his message.

Reena: So they all have contact with him.

Mia: No. Only a few. Many do not know of his survival.

Reena: Does Paul know of his survival?

Mia: Not to the level of where he is now. He met him and saw him but does not understand. So he does know of his survival, but not in the way that those closer to him do.

Reena: That's understandable. So, if a lot of these disciples do not keep in touch with Jesus, who is making sure that their message is kept on track?

Mia: Their hearts! Each disciple can take the message and spread the word in many different directions. The messages of God's love to all men and women.

James starts his teachings by leading an informal gathering for those who work and mine the metal in Britannia. There is a mixture of those who have come with him from Jerusalem, and the locals who are curious and interested and want to hear what he has to say about the rules, compassion and love. He starts his teaching by talking about hygiene and nourishment.

James' Teaching 1: Hygiene and Nourishment

We are accountable for our health and hygiene. But our health and hygiene are not just limited to our physical bodies. Our physical bodies hold our soul and so we need to maintain the health and hygiene of our soul, as we maintain the health and hygiene of our physical bodies.

Just as we take care with the ablutions of our physical body, just as we nourish our physical body, we need to cleanse our soul and nourish our soul. This is because what is inside is reflected on the outside, and what is outside is reflected on the inside.

How do we nourish the soul? When we look for food,

we choose what works for our physical body, and what doesn't. We choose. We will not eat a poisonous plant that would make us quite sick. But we will find food that is healthy, that makes us feel good.

It is the same for the soul. Look for and seek things that make our soul feel healthy, that make us happy, that make us feel fulfilled. Whether it is work, whether it is in companions, whether it is how we spend our free time. Look for things that enhance our soul – whether it is new knowledge that excites us, whether it is new experiences that entice us, whether it is exploring new places.

When we can discern what is healthy and what nourishes our soul versus what is unhealthy for our soul, we can step away from what makes our soul feel sick. Just like we step away from what makes our body feel sick.

What's really important here is that we have the choice. That it is not being imposed on us. It's having freedom. But with freedom comes great responsibility. With freedom – we are accountable. We are all individually accountable for every single action and consequence of that action.

When we get paid for some work that we have done, do our employers impose on us how we have to spend that money? No, they do not. It is up to us to make the decisions of how we spend our wages. We can choose to spend it on food or we can choose to spend it at a brothel. And the consequences are ours to bear.

In the same way, what we do with our lives, we bear the consequences. But we have the freedom to do whatever it is that nourishes our soul. Feeds our soul.

Reena: Is there anything else communicated to them with this teaching?

Mia: We keep – or I try as much as possible to keep it to one subject per time. So that people get the maximum absorption of what I try to tell them. But also for me at this point, it makes me feel comfortable just disseminating it one by one. I am a bit more of a practical man compared to Jesus – I have had to be. So I always link my talks to practical matters. Jesus did as well, but Jesus had a higher innate wisdom that I do not have.

Reena: What are the people's responses to this teaching?

Mia: For the locals, they have had that freedom but they have not thought about how to use that freedom to nourish their souls. So they mull and think about it and ponder it. They are open to it because it is not such a big step from where they are. Whereas those who work with me, for me, who have come from our homeland… they find it very difficult to break away from feeling that they can be free to do as they decide what's best for them, as opposed to doing what they are told. And so for them, each step is more tentative. But these are people who have met Jesus, been with Jesus, heard Jesus. They are the people who follow what we do, our teachings. So they are open to making that change. It is a bit more scary for them, but they do. Especially here in this land where there is so much freedom – much more freedom than in the homeland.

Reena: Are any of the people at this teaching of the Jewish religion or have they other religious beliefs?

Mia: Those who have come with me follow the law. The locals, they have their own religion.

Though not widely known and talked about, James' time in Britannia was clearly the impetus in spreading Jesus' teachings and messages in this region. Having a tight relationship with the leaders of the region played a big part, not only for his trade, but also for the locals being open to receiving his message and his expertise. It was while being in Britannia that James started to be a little more open to the adaptation of the Jewish laws, so that his employees were not confined to the strict practices that might inhibit them while they were in a foreign land. It also helped them with adapting to and integrating with the local cultures, and assimilating seamlessly with the local people.

James was emphatic that Jesus' teachings are about a way of life. They are about adding value to the way of life. It is not about imposing rules and rituals as Jesus was not about rules and rituals. This is different from how the Pharisees and Sadducees taught – where strict rules and adherences played a prominent role in their teachings. James' way opened up Jesus' teachings to more people and made them easier to be absorbed by the local people, and the local traditions of Britannia.

James

Chapter 11

Leading the Flock

The next significant event saw James visiting his brother and his family. Jesus was not there, however. He'd gone south to Greece to see some disciples. James received an astonishing proposition from Mary, the wife of Jesus.

Mia: Mary wants me to take young Jesus… take him back to England.
Reena: Did Mary tell you why she wanted young Jesus to go to England with you?
Mia: We have a community there. And maybe for marriage.

So James takes Jesus Jr., or "Yesoo," back to Britain with him and proposes that he marries his cousin Sarah – James' daughter. I ask what happened then, and James replied, "Jesus [Jr.] settled in Britain. We have a community there. So I could go home to Jerusalem."

Tradition in Britain holds that while Jesus was a boy, his mother Mary entrusted him to Joseph of Arimathea, her uncle, to travel to some major trading ports and ended up in Glastonbury and the Mendips. William Blake, a famous English poet and artist, was so moved by this tradition he wrote a poem about it – *Prelude to Milton*, better known as the hymn *Jerusalem*.[1]

However, our regression is consistent with Laurence Gardner's version that actually it was Jesus *Jr.* who travelled to Britain with *his* uncle, James aka Joseph of Arimathea, sent by Jesus' wife, Mary. Laurence Gardner goes on to give an account that the feet that walked "upon England's mountains green" were indeed those of the son of Jesus, who consecrated

St. Mary's chapel, in the Wattle Church, in what's now known as Glastonbury Abbey, to his mother, Mary Magdalene.[2]

Gardner also mentions that while Jesus Sr. was referred to as Yeshua, Jesus Jr. was referred to as Gais or Gesu.[3] I find it interesting that within the strong Druidic priesthood, the name "Yesu" was incorporated in the Druidic Trinity as a godhead.[4] The use of the term "Yesu" is consistent with Mia's account and Laurence Gardner's independent finding that it was Jesus Jr. who made the trip to Britain, and that eventually he does marry – but to whom is hazy.

The regression continues. In the next significant event, James progressed on to a time when he was growing more confident with leading the flock in Britannia.

Mia: I have Yesoo with me, the eldest boy of Jesus and his wife. We have more set times for the teachings – set times for these meetings, these teachings, and the group has grown. More and more of the locals wish to be part of it. There is some talk – conflict – between those who work with me and for me, and the locals. Initially when the groups were small, there was no conflict because the locals and those who work for me were friends, colleagues. So they went together in groups. But now, as more and more people are coming, there is no personal familiarity. So those who work with me and for me are questioning some of the locals who have come to hear the teachings, the discourses, yet who don't apply the rules to themselves.

Reena: Can you explain what you mean by the rules?

Mia: There are some rules that are quite strict within the old religion. Rules such as circumcision. Rules such as observing the Sabbath. Rules in the food that we consume. These sorts of rules. But some rules are quite relaxed, as I mentioned, like how we observe the Sabbath here and how we maintain our hygiene here and how we cook and eat foods here. But circumcision is something that has been ingrained within us – how important it is, especially for hygiene reasons. But the locals do not wish it.

So James proceeds to give a teaching on freedom of choice and acceptance.

James' Teaching 2: Freedom of Choice and Acceptance

Choice and being accountable – as long as we respect one another's freedoms to make those choices, we can observe tolerance. If we can tolerate one another then that is the key for loving one another.

Tolerance is not just about tolerating what we agree with. It's being able to tolerate what we do not agree with – like lack of circumcision and some of their ways of life that we do not agree with.

Love is not about being sanctimonious. Love is about openly embracing all the beliefs and all the culture and all the behavior, even if we do not agree with it. Even if we cannot embrace it.

Can we embrace their not wanting to be circumcised even though we choose to? They can also choose to not be circumcised and God's words or Jesus' words are not just limited to those who are circumcised.

The words are for all because love is for all. I turn to the man who is the angriest about the uncircumcised who have come to the teachings and say to him, "Do you only love those who are circumcised?"

The man spluttered and muttered and said, "No."

Then I ask, "Do you only tolerate those who are

circumcised?"

The man looks at me and says, "But this is the old way. This is the way I've been brought up."

I say, "Yes… That is *our* way. But it is not the locals' way. They do not tell you to be uncircumcised. But yet they welcome you to their lands, and they embrace you and you work with them and they share with you."

The man agrees and I continue, "It is the same way. Just because they are uncircumcised does not mean that we cannot talk to them or share. If they are interested, we are not forcing our words on them. We are not asking them to come against their will. They choose to come and we welcome them. And we share with them, the same way that they share with us."

Mia: Again it's very hard to break the tight bonds of the laws – the rules – the tight bindings of those that came up believing in the laws and the rules. But slowly they are integrating more and sharing more and understanding more of these teachings. And Yesoo is with me. And he is listening to me… he is just part of the group now.

According to the Nazarenes or the Essenes, anyone who embraced the teachings of Jesus the Messiah would be accepted and included as students of these teachings. While the Nazarites upheld the Jewish law rigorously for themselves, they did not expect all the converts to do the same, with the same rigor. This is in line with James' teaching of tolerance. We will see this as the regression progresses, around the topics of rituals and circumcision. The Nazarenes, under the leadership of James, also embraced anyone into their faith, including those who were not Jewish. On the other hand, some of the believers in Jesus who had been part of the Pharisaic movement, who were the more conservative Jews, believed strongly in the adherence to the law and Jewish rituals, and upheld a strong hierarchy, therefore demanding the conversion to Judaism before embracing the teachings of Jesus.[5]

The regression continues.

Reena: Is there anything else of significance at this point?

Mia: With the local group, there is a mixture of men and women. They are integrated. However, with our group there are predominantly men. This is something I wish to change. And I wish for the people who have come from the homeland to be open to bring their spouses and daughters and cousins and female relations, but they are not ready yet. It is a bit difficult for our men to see and to accept and welcome the women. But the more I talk about tolerance and compassion and love for all, the more their resistance is weakening, which is good. It's also interesting because the local women mix with the womenfolk from our homeland and the local women share what they have heard with the womenfolk from our homeland. And so the messages are also slowly getting to the womenfolk of our homeland, which makes me happy. After all, within my group, men and women were never equal, but Jesus always talked about equality and he treated Mary as an equal. So it is something I keep teaching.

The next event saw James at his most significant time teaching in Britannia.

Mia: I am teaching the children, the young, and we are teaching them to write. There was not the written language. We are teaching the love of God.

Reena: The children: they are both male and female?

Mia: Yes!

Reena: Oh, so you are teaching females as well.

Mia: Oh yes! But we teach them separately.

Reena: What makes you teach them separately?

Mia: They concentrate better. They concentrate on God, and their writing. It's God's language.

Reena: How do you address God's language?

Mia: We have the scriptures. We are writing the scriptures. We also write the history. We write all things. We teach so that they may know themselves and know God. And we write the stories. The stories of Jesus. Mmm. We write his teaching. Loving one another and that we are all children of God and that it is not for one to have the right over one another. Here we have no slaves.

Reena: Tell me more about these teachings. What else do he and you teach?

Mia: We teach harmony. This is a way of living in harmony and then dying in peace, and harmony to achieve heaven here on Earth and in the afterlife. It is a teaching of love and cooperation and of joy amongst all.

Reena: Can you please expand a bit more?

Mia: I come from a place where there was hierarchy and strict ethnic division and one could not step outside of this. One could not step outside of one's preordained role from birth. There was a restriction. There was no room for spiritual direction and Jesus broke this. He threw it away and allowed God's love to enter one's soul through baptism and through his teaching and the baptism into the Light of God. Any person that desired God's love could achieve it. So we have to renounce our past and be reborn through the baptism in God's love. We're all brothers and sisters.

This account is especially interesting because James illustrates one of the ways that the Ebionite/Nazarene Jews differentiated themselves from the more conservative Pharisees and Sadducees. All a person needs to do to embrace the love of God is to be baptized – a ritual that John the Baptist introduced. In *Shrouded Truth,* it was revealed that baptism is a sort of initiation that believers undergo to be awakened to the Light of the Oneness, or in James' words, the Light of God. Once this happens, there is camaraderie with their fellow believers. In contrast, with the Pharisees, they impose strict rules and rituals that the converts have to comply with to be invited into their faith.

Reena: Do you teach the children this or do you baptize them?

Mia: We teach the children and then when they reach an age of decision, when they decide whether to join and be baptized or they can leave – they can. This is a personal choice, that each person must make for themselves. It's not forced upon them, but every child is christened into the love of God.

Reena: Tell me more about being "christened into the love of God."

Mia: When a child is born, we christen the child in Christ's name. We take the child, so that every child is given the love of God so that it may stay with them and guard them until they have reached an age where they can decide for themselves.

Reena: I understand. So if they choose not to be baptized, what happens to the love of God?

Mia: God's love is always with us, even if we reject it. This is what we choose and this is what we teach. God's love is for everyone. This is not what the [Sadducee and Pharisee] priests teach.

Again, this account highlights the difference between the Ebionites' methods and the traditional Pharisaic way of conveying the old religion of Judaism. The Pharisees emphasized temples and following the priests' teachings to the letter. The only way to get to God was through them – the priests and rabbis. However, Jesus' views on the matters of baptism, wealth and marriage were in no way commensurate with the first-century Hebrew culture of the Pharisees and Sadducees, nor were they in agreement with the scribes of the Temple law.[6] The Nazarene/ Ebionite way is to believe that everyone is able to receive God's love, and they do not need a mediator in the form of a priest to access that love. They could have a direct relationship.

The Ebionite/Nazarene interpretation of baptism is also very different to Paul's version, as seen from Paul's regression. Paul claimed that baptism allows a person to follow Christ's message and live a life where they stop sinning and go to heaven upon death. Baptism is a way of saving a person. Whereas from James' perspective, baptism is about receiving the love of God. It is interesting here to see how the Judeo-Christian Church teachings started to differ from the Gentile Christian Church, where the former was softer and more open, and with the latter being more severe.

James' interpretation of baptism is a lot closer to what was portrayed by both Tamar, the forgotten daughter of Jesus, and David, the hidden son of John the Baptist, in *Shrouded Truth*, where baptism was more about healing and connection to the Oneness. Both Jesus and John the Baptist were Nazarene, so it just makes sense that their interpretations of baptism are aligned.[7]

Reena: Go through the christening ritual for me.

Mia: The child is brought… as a baby. The mother and the father and the aunties and uncles and those from the community are there and the child is held and then blessed with sacred water and granted the love of God. This love will protect the child, and grant it God's love and a pathway to heaven until the child is old enough to decide for themselves.

Reena: How did the practicing pagans take to this teaching? Did they embrace it or is it very different from their own beliefs?

Mia: Some embraced it and some did not. We are not here to force it on people. Some still hold their ways and celebrate the festivals of the seasons, but they also hold God's love. And we can embrace all.

I find it interesting again about how different James' Nazarene perspective towards pagans is when compared with Paul's Gentile perspective. Paul went out of his way to modify his teachings to compete with and exclude the pagan religion, whereas James was more inclusive with his teachings. However, to be fair, the environments in which the two operated could not have been more different. In Rome, where Paul concentrated his teachings, the pagans persecuted and executed members of the fledgling Christian Church. In Britannia, where James was, the pagans were accepting and collaborative. So it makes sense why the two took the stances that they did.

Reena: Tell me more about the place where you teach. Is it indoors or outdoors?

Mia: When the weather is good, we teach outdoors, and then in the winter we teach indoors.

Reena: How many teachers are there?

Mia: I am the main and we have many teachers… we teach each person so then they can teach another. So when somebody has the love of God passed to them, they are then able to teach one another. They are able to pass it on. But there are then structural teachers that teach the younger ones and are like, I suppose, the headteachers, and there are three women and five men.

Again, there is another stark difference here between Paul's teachings and James' teachings. Paul was very careful, though conflicted, to not include women in teaching or leadership positions within his ministry, predominantly because he did not want to go against the patriarchal cultural beliefs of the Romans. Jesus' ministry, on the other hand, included female helpers like his mother and sisters. There was Mary Magdalene and Martha, and Luke 8:3 also mentions, "Joanna, the wife of Chuza... and Susanna, and many others which ministered to him of their substance."[8] So James followed Jesus' lead in including both men and women within the Jewish Christian ministry that he led.

There is also a stark difference between James' ministry and the strictly patriarchal conservative Jewish Pharisees and Sadducee ministries as well. One Pharisee, Hillel, known for his moderation on many issues, once said: "The more women the more witchcrafts." (Avot 2:7) Another Pharisee, Ben Sirach, declared: "From a woman sin had its beginning, and because of her we all die. Allow no outlet to water, and no boldness of speech in an evil wife. If she does not go as you direct, separate her from yourself." Another instance of Pharisaic disdain for women is in the Outside Writings: "For from garments comes the moth, and from a woman comes woman's wickedness. Better is the wickedness of man than a woman who does good; and it is a woman who brings shame and disgrace." (Ecclesiasticus 25:24-26; 42:13-14)[9]

The Gospels indicate that Jesus held a far different position. Luke, in particular, demonstrates the Messiah's high regard for women just by virtue of the fact that he spent time in their company. Jesus stressed that women had worth. He even came to the defense of a woman caught in the act of adultery, charging her accusers to cast their stones only if they themselves were without sin (John 8:7). Women were a part of the band of disciples, both as ministers and as students of the Messiah (Mark 15:40-41;

Luke 8:1-3; 10:42; John 4:7-27).[10] According to Gnostic traditions as well, Jesus knew and honored the truth of womanhood and the great power that is in it. He loved and honored women.[11] So James just followed his brother's lead in choosing both males and females to lead his ministry.

The regression continues.

Reena: These three women and five men, did they come with you from somewhere else?

Mia: One of the men was with me.

Reena: Tell me about this man.

Mia: He was my friend and my servant, and he stayed with me and is now my equal.

Reena: Did he learn from you as well?

Mia: Mmm.

Reena: Did he used to follow your brother?

Mia: He followed his teaching, but he was not a disciple. I was not really a disciple in the way of the others, as I was not with my brother all the time. There were many that stayed with him all the time and there are some that still do.

Reena: Do you keep in touch with them, with any other disciples?

Mia: No. I have contact with my brother and with Mary, his wife. When I travelled, I would travel and see them, but now I do not. I am now settled here.

Reena: Do you trade at all at this point or do you just teach?

Mia: I live peacefully and teach.

Reena: What made you decide to stop trading?

Mia: God spoke to me and told me to settle here.

At the next event, James became very solemn and quiet and started to feel anxious. His anxiety was contagious and reverberated through his flock, when James got word that Jesus had passed away. James had a feeling that he would be called to Jerusalem to lead the flock there. But he did not want to go back. He wanted to stay in Britannia.

Mia: My congregation – they are sad. They are upset that Jesus has passed away. But they are happy that he has passed away in the arms of his family – his wife, and his daughter. So I try to put the impending summons back home out of my mind. But I am still feeling the anxiety and I weep with my flock here at the loss of my brother. Although we spent quite a lot of time apart, and it's been quite hard. We were always very close. So I talked to them about brotherly love.

James' Teaching 3: Brotherly Love

I talk about Jesus – the love Jesus had for me and the love that Jesus had for all those around him – about how pure it was. Jesus loved a tax collector as much as he loved me, his brother. How Jesus' love was unconditional and how, as the recipient of that love, myself, the tax collector, and everyone else around him, thought it was like a gift – all this love that Jesus gave.

Jesus' love did not see the tax collector as being the "Tax Collector." In Jerusalem, tax collectors were reviled and considered terrible, terrible people. And they were hated. But Jesus never saw that. He saw the tax collector's soul, and he saw my soul and everyone who came to him, he saw their soul. He did not see the external trappings. He did not care how physically beautiful or how physically ugly someone was. It did not matter. He did not care if someone was a Roman soldier or a beggar or someone with leprosy. It did not matter.

He saw everyone's soul and he loved everyone equally. That was the love he showed everyone. That is what I call brotherly love.

We can just love the external. We can love the relationship.But this is not love from the deepest part of our soul. The love from the deepest part of our soul is to love another soul. It does not matter if they are rich or poor or sick or healthy. Conditional love comes not from the soul. Conditional love comes from the outside – the head. It's not heartfelt. It is not the deeper soul love to be able to love everybody equally and unconditionally.

When we say unconditionally, we mean without the condition of the external trappings. So we do not see how powerful they are. We do not see how disempowered they are. We do not see how rich they are. We do not see any of that. Those do not matter. We see how their soul is. Even if sometimes we do not agree with what they say, or what they do, the minute we stop loving them because of what they say and what they do, it becomes conditional love. It is an intolerant love. Or it is the love for intolerance.

We just love wholly the soul. Even if they do something we disagree with, we can still love them. We love unconditionally, whilst preserving our boundaries, so that we maintain our freedom to be our authentic selves.

Mia: This is a very powerful teaching I teach at this time to my flock. And I teach this by using Jesus as an example. Of how he did it.

While James' teaching of brotherly love is beautiful, historically his use of the word "brotherly" is pertinent. The Nazarenes/

Ebionites believed they were the final generation and would live to see the end and the coming of the Messiah. They saw themselves as the remnant core of God's faithful people – preparing the way for the return of the One God. They considered themselves the brotherhood or community, and they referred to themselves as brother and sister.[12] So showing one another "brotherly love" is important to establish Oneness and familiarity within this community.

Reena: How do you communicate this to people? What teaching methods do you use?
Mia: We use stories and rituals.

It is heartening to note here that both James and Paul use the same methodology in their ministries. The only thing that changed was the interpretation of the rituals, and some content of their stories.

Reena: Just go through those rituals for me.
Mia: We have the ritual, the breaking of bread and giving of God's sustenance, the holy bread and the holy blood of God to take into us, to nourish and sustain us on this earthly plane.
Reena: Who started this ritual? Was it Jesus?
Mia: Mmm.
Reena: When did he start it?
Mia: He started it in Jerusalem. Feeding the many, so he took the Jewish ritual and gave it to all who wished to receive God's love, and this is receiving the Holy Spirit through the sustenance of the body and the blood, and taking God into our bodies.

One of the scrolls found within the Dead Sea Scrolls, the *Scroll of the Rule,* describes the ritual observance for the annual Messianic

Banquet. In 33CE, this coincided with the scriptural tradition known as the Last Supper.[13] It was at the Last Supper when Jesus passed the cup of wine to the Apostles saying, "This is my blood," as opposed to "fruit of the vine," in reference to his ancestry from King David, which was what was traditionally said and upheld. In Isaiah 5:7, Israel and the Royal House of David are described as the Lord's "cherished plant" and in John 15:1, Jesus referred to his ancestry from King David with the claim: "I am the true vine." By claiming that the cup of wine was his blood, Jesus solidified his position as the true heir of King David, the long-awaited Messiah.[14] Hence, James was accurate in claiming that Jesus started this tradition, as Jesus did modify this Nazarene tradition. The Pauline Gentile Christianity also adopted this modification.

Reena: I understand. What other ritual is there to illustrate God's love?

Mia: We take the ritual of marriage. The pagans would handfast. We take that and we join the man and the woman in the ritual of marriage... Many of the pagans, they enjoy sex... they enjoy much of this. We feel, as part of the Jewish teaching, there were times to withhold from sexual desire and there were times for contemplation. And so, we try and teach time of contemplation without sexual desire. For some this is very good and for some this is not. [Laughs.] But we include it in the teaching. We teach chastity. So there is time of contemplation, without the lust of the body. These are times when men and women can be separate from each other, so they may contemplate the spiritual presence of God without distraction.

Reena: And these are significant distractions?

Mia: For some very significant.

In the next significant event, James finds out that his wife in

Britannia has died.

Mia: My wife has died.
Reena: How does that make you feel?
Mia: Sad. She was a very good woman. It's time for me to go home. I'm getting old.

James gets the call that he has to leave Britannia for Jerusalem. His time in Britannia is up.

Mia: They have called for my return.
Reena: Who are they?
Mia: I was sent a messenger. A boat came and told of what was happening in Jerusalem. There was fighting. Fighting within the church. Jesus' teachings and efforts are being twisted and convoluted. But even more, those who stayed back can't agree on what to teach. What the principles are. There is a lot of infighting and a lot of pressure by the Sadducees and the Pharisees to impose their will on our Church. With the threat of the Romans, everyone is scared. There is a lot of chaos and confusion. I have to go.
Reena: Who was leading the church in Jerusalem when you were in Britannia?
Mia: There are several factions. Many people trying to say, "This is The Way."
Reena: So it was all a bit chaotic?
Mia: Mmm. Also it is safer there now. From the Romans.

During that period, biblical historians agree that there were four schools of Judaism:

a. Pharisees – considered the spiritual fathers of modern Judaism, who were in a sense blue-collar Jews who adhered to the tenets developed after the first destruction of the Temple of Solomon; such things as individual prayer and assembly in synagogues. Their main distinguishing characteristic was a belief in an oral law that God gave to Moses at Sinai along with the Torah. The Pharisees believed that God also gave Moses the knowledge of what these laws meant and how they should be applied. This oral tradition was codified and written down roughly three centuries later in what is known as the Talmud. The Pharisees also maintained that an afterlife existed and that God punished the wicked and rewarded the righteous in the world to come. They also believed in a Messiah who would herald an era of world peace.[15]

b. The Sadducees – considered elitists who wanted to maintain the priestly caste, but they were also liberal in their willingness to incorporate Hellenism into their lives, something the conservative Pharisees opposed. The Sadducees rejected the idea of the oral law and insisted on a literal interpretation of the written law. Consequently, they did not believe in an afterlife, since it is not mentioned in the Torah. The main focus of Sadducee life was rituals associated with the Temple. The Sadducees disappeared around 70CE, and none of their writings have survived, so the little we know about them comes from their Pharisaic opponents.

   Both the Pharisees and Sadducees served in the Great Sanhedrin, a Jewish Supreme Court made up of 71 members whose responsibility was to interpret civil and religious laws.[16]

c. The Essenes – considered to have believed that the Sadducees and Pharisees had corrupted the city and the Temple. They moved out of Jerusalem and lived a monastic life in the desert, adopting strict dietary laws and a commitment to celibacy. This is allegedly the same group as the Nazarenes or the Ebionites.[17]

d. The Zealots – a political movement in the first century which sought to incite the people of Judea Province to rebel against the Roman Empire and expel it from the Holy Land by force of arms, most notably during the First Jewish-Roman War (66-70CE). The Zealots were founded by Judas of Galilee in the year 6CE against an invasive tax reform, shortly after the Roman Empire declared what had most recently been a Jewish tetrarchy to be a Roman province. The Zealots agree with the Pharisaic notions; but they were fierce defenders of liberty, and said that God was to be their only ruler and Lord.[18]

Due to the fact that there were different schools of Judaism, adhering to different types of beliefs, there was a lot of pulling and tugging, trying to establish each sect's individual beliefs and ideologies as the absolute for the whole. This did lead to chaos and confusion.

The regression continues.

Reena: So, what is it that made them call for you as opposed to any of the other disciples?

Mia: I am his blood relative.

During the first to the fourth centuries, there were references in historical literature to certain dynastic offspring recorded by the chroniclers as being the "Heirs of the Lord" or *Desposyni*. This distinction was reserved only for the blood relatives of Jesus, through his mother.[19] The regressions in *Shrouded Truth* and biblical historians concur that James was the blood brother of Jesus. Although the term Desposyni did not appear until after the lifetime of Jesus, it is claimed that Jesus was the royal heir to the House of David. Forty years after the alleged crucifixion of Jesus, in 70CE, the Roman Emperor Vespasian, in crushing the last Jewish revolt, commanded that, "the family of David to be sought, that no one might be left among the Jews who was of the royal stock." Why? Because during the first to the third centuries, the Jewish-Christian Church (the Ebionite/Nazarene branch) was dynastically governed by hereditary leaders of the Desposyni. The Gospel of Thomas, from the Nag Hammadi Library, makes it perfectly clear that Jesus bequeathed his personal leadership to his own brother, James: "Jesus said to them, wherever you are, you are to go to James the Just." Even Bishop Clement of Rome had written that Jesus' brother James was "the Lord of the Holy Church and the bishop of bishops."[20] Also, Acts and the regression with Greg in this book show that Paul did respect the authority held by James. This regression thus corroborates this claim.

The regression continues.

Mia: So, I give one last teaching to my flock here in Britannia. They are all sad to see me go but I am very happy to see that there is a lot more integration here – between the locals and those who came with me to work here. There's more integration between the men and the women here. There are children who are born through these teachings who just maintain the teachings. They did not know the difference. They never knew the conflict. I see all this and I feel very happy because this was a blank canvas and this was my ground to learn and to be a spiritual leader. Before, I was more a political leader, an economic leader, a business leader, but this was a big step for me to acquiesce to Jesus' wishes to take on being the head of the church.

I thank them all for being open to me, to what I have to say, to accepting what I have to say. For teaching me to be a better leader for the spirit. And I tell them that I am so happy to see so much integration and it makes my heart light up because as a business leader and economic leader,

> I used to see how we can thrive materially. But here, I am seeing how they are thriving spiritually and how their lives changed and shifted and how they are working together. It's just given them a much better quality of life. When I was a business leader we just paid them wages so that they could live, whereas here, they are alive and living. It is special to me and I can understand why Jesus and everyone else thrive on it. I can also understand Jesus' vision for our homeland because I can see how it changed here in Britannia – with the pagan locals and those who followed our law working together and being together in a community and being tolerant, and being compassionate, yet being free to embrace what they want to embrace. That can happen back home as well. It's just that back home, the Romans and the Pharisees and Sadducees are a lot more strict for control. But I want to help my people so that they can grow and bloom and be like my flock here. So I thank them [Britannia flock] for showing what can happen. And I ask them to continue to just spread the word, spread the message. And so they do. But they are sad to see me go. They ask me if I am going to come back and I say I would like to, but I do not know if I am able to. And then I get on my ship and I go.

James' ministry of Jewish Christianity in Britannia marked his transformation from a business leader to a spiritual leader. It was fascinating to note the difference between his Ebionite Jewish Christian ministry, Pauline Gentile Christianity, Pharisee and Sadducee Judaic teachings. Where the Pharisaic and Sadducee teachings were the most conservative and controlled, Jewish Ebionite Christianity took a more liberal and inclusive view of the Jewish teachings and the laws, while emphasizing personal freedom. Similarly, while Pauline Christianity was more controlled and strict than Jewish Christianity, it moved the furthest away from Jewish teachings and the law than Jewish Christianity.

Moving forward, we will see just how this ministry was applied in Jerusalem, where James is called back to head the church.

Chapter 12

Jerusalem

The next significant events see James having just returned to Jerusalem. He is aware of having been away from his homeland for twenty years. The air is heavy with the stench of fear and sweat, and it is very cloying. There is a feeling of oppression and burden in the air. It is very heavy.

Mia: Well, I am in my homeland. And – ugh! – it is such a different feeling. I do not feel free. I feel very constrained. But, as Jesus says, it is in this sort of environment where you can make the biggest difference. It is in such darkness where the light of love is desperately needed. It is well and good where I was – where there was light – to be light. Whereas it is just so heavy here. It is more challenging but much more rewarding to be a light here.

James is aware that some people, who have come to meet him, are very pleased to see him, and some not.

Mia: Well, there is Peter. And there are a few more followers of Jesus who have stayed. My sister is there and her son. I left Yesoo back in Britannia to continue being part of the flock in Britannia and I so wish that my sister's son could go and join him instead of being part of this mess.

James mentioning his sister and her son is very interesting indeed. Laurence Gardner, in his book *The Grail Enigma,* mentions that the Gospel of John relates that Jesus' sister was married to Cleopas, and the second-century Palestinian chronicler

Hegesippus recorded that they had a son called Symeon. The acclaimed historian Eusebius wrote that Symeon remained in Judea to become a bishop in Jerusalem, and was martyred under Emperor Trajan (98-117CE).[1] This is in line not only with this account, but also in a later regression when James touches briefly on his nephew's ascension in the Judeo-Church.

Back to the regression, James is also aware of much that has changed, and much that has stayed the same. He senses that there is more acceptance of a limited level of diversity within the wider Jerusalem. But there is fighting in the church.

Mia: I am taken to the outskirts to the building where we…

Reena: Where exactly are you at this moment? Do you have a name for this particular place?

Mia: [pause] No. It's an unknown small little village because we want to keep a lower profile from both the Romans and the ruling class. I am met and greeted in the church, by those who are currently running it in the building. And we… [sigh]. It is such a mess. It is such a mess.

The physical church, he describes, is made of stone, with three floors and an open roof on the top. There is also an area for many to meet. It is located halfway between the center and the periphery – the outskirts – of Jerusalem. So this clearly was not the legendary Temple of Solomon that was built the second time after its destruction in 587BCE, which was located in the middle of Jerusalem. Nor was it in the Qumran Caves, where the Dead Sea Scrolls were found, and where the Essenes were said to have lived.

Mia: There is infighting within the church. There is fighting between those who wish to follow Jesus' teachings through his bloodline and those who have taken his teaching and created a political structure around it. They are from the different groups within our movement. As I've said to you... we oppose the Romans. But there are those who want to fight them. And those who want to remain in more strict accordance to the law. Without Jesus, everyone's own beliefs and philosophies of what best to do are emerging. And so I have to listen and I have to understand where each person is coming from and how he fits into Jesus' vision for this movement.

Reena: Do you recognize any disciples in the different sides?

Mia: There is John, who stands by the political structure.

Reena: OK. And who else?

Mia: Peter – he is here and he seems torn. There are about eight including myself.

Reena: Mmm. And is Mary there?

Mia: No. These are men that did not like women. Women should not even be allowed within the church. They must stay on a separate floor... Or a separate area, but in our church there is a separate floor. They must not come on the ground floor of the sacred church.

This sounded like the more traditional Jewish way of worship, in a traditionally patriarchal society, where there was segregation between men and women. This was not how Jesus led his ministry, nor how James did, as he claimed, while he was in Britannia.

Reena: Who is leading this church?

Mia: I am coming to lead it now.

Reena: Who was leading it before? Was it Jesus?

Mia: No. Peter was leading it, but he is not sure of his way.

Reena: And so who called you to come and lead it.

Mia: My sister... She was very upset at what was being done in Jesus' name.

Reena: What was being done in Jesus' name that upsets her?

Mia: They were not allowing the women to play any role in the church, and they were creating a structure where those in their favor took positions of power, so the righteous were not allowed to speak their truth.

Reena: And what were they doing to Jesus' teachings? Were they being true to the teachings, or did they change it slightly?

Mia: Some of it was true to his teachings, but some of it is not!

Reena: So which areas of the teachings did they change?

Mia: They wanted to create more structure and authority.

This was an interesting account because the Pharisees and Sadducees were a structured and hierarchical religious sect. Jesus was a rabbi who did not oppose the Pharisees as a whole, but opposed Pharisees who took advantage of their positions of authority to exploit and suppress the Jewish masses.[2] So it was interesting to see that his eventual ministry in Jerusalem wanted to implement the same elements that Jesus stood against in the first place. James, who was a follower of Jesus' ministry, and who was given the responsibility to lead the Jerusalem Christians, was called in to restore Jesus' teachings and methods that were true to the Ebionite/Nazarene movement.

Reena: So tell me what it is that is communicated to you.

Mia: I just listened to each belief. Why we need to embrace the laws more. Why we need to fight. Why we need to totally break away. I, just at this point, am listening.

Reena: Are there any thoughts that you have as you are listening to this?

Mia: I wish I was in Britannia [chuckles]. These men are loyal to Jesus, not to me. They are loyal to me only through Jesus. They know of me, and they know me, but their loyalties are for Jesus. So they listen to him more. He inspires them. They don't carry the same reverence for me, although they do respect me.

Next, James is aware of a scuffle in the church between two men who are members of the church.

Mia: My sister was right in calling me. Leadership was definitely needed here. I gather all the information that these other men have given to me and I retire to my private rooms to ponder. And then I decide to give a talk on tolerance to the entire congregation. I ask the seven men to round everyone up. The seven men look rather suspiciously at me [chuckles]. It's only men that come. Here in Jerusalem, it is a very male-oriented society. The women stay far away from these meetings. I think the congregation don't know how to receive me. The Romans are established in their ways. The Pharisees and Sadducees are established in their ways. The Nazarenes/Ebionite are old and new at the same time. They are not very established. There are so many different factions within that movement.

James' Teaching 4: Tolerance and Balance

I ask the Zealots who wish to fight, "Why is it you wish to fight these Romans? Why is it you wish to fight to get our way established?"

The Zealots talk about the history and they talk about being patriotic and they talk about not wanting to embrace the Romans' ways.

Then I ask them, "What is it that makes you think that it is more important for us to establish our ways instead of adopting the Roman ways?"

The Zealots talk about how cruel the Romans are and

how much suffering they bring to them, the people.

Then I ask, "Do you think that fighting them will cause less suffering to our people?"

The Zealots go a bit quiet.

I tell the Zealots that I agree with them. They are opposing the Romans, their way of doing things, their morals and their values to a certain extent. But can they not do it in a way where they are respectful and tolerant of them, instead of fighting them? This guerilla fighting is not necessary.

The Zealots keep quiet. They consider what I say. Then I look at the faction that wants to remain within the law more stringently and I talk to them about how there are some of the followers who are taking Jesus' messages outside and if they adhere too strictly to the law, then these people are unable to be part of their movement.

"Isn't it important to have Jesus' messages be spread to as many people as possible as opposed to just limiting it to those who believe in and practice the law?" I ask. "The law is important. It is not about breaking any of the laws, or disrespecting the laws. It's about adaptation."

I address both the Zealots and those who want to adhere to the law about being too extreme. When people hold such extreme beliefs and values, they become very intolerant. However, when people are open and understanding and are both faithful to their own beliefs yet are compassionate and understanding to another, then they become tolerant.

Extremism begets intolerance. Balance begets tolerance. Isn't tolerance about understanding everyone and loving everyone. That's Jesus' message – to love.

Ultimately the Romans, the Sadducees and the Pharisees practice extreme ways of Being – extreme controls, extreme fundamentalist-type belief systems and ideologies. I wish to impart a way of Being that is tolerant.

A way of Being that is in balance.

Mia: Initially my congregation were fidgety and disturbed. But then I see the majority of them start to settle as I speak and talk about tolerance. And the majority of them understand where I am coming from. But there will always be those who hold extreme values. I see this not as a task to be fulfilled immediately. It is a mountain to be climbed. As long as I keep it at these consistent reminders, then I think we can move forward in peace and harmony where we can embrace both our versions of the law, we can embrace new souls into the congregation and we can oppose anybody who threatens our way of Being.

Reena: What happens next?

Mia: The seven men who are with me, the main leaders, listen to me and nod. They see the wisdom of my words. Because I have not been here in so long, the congregation respects these seven men. When they see the seven men agreeing with me, they are more open to agreeing with me as well. I talk to the seven men about the possibility of inviting more women to the congregation but the seven men were resistant to it. They say it is not time yet. The flock are still very much ingrained in the old ways. They did not want the womenfolk to be in danger with the Romans. They wanted the womenfolk to be safe. So at this point, I agree. But I have secret meetings with my sister and her son. We just stay together and she asks me what happens, and I tell her. I take her counsel, she heeds my advice. I do suggest to her that what we could do is have small meetings with women who are interested, who wish to hear and wish to learn separately. Not in that building, in the church. In homes. It is not compulsory or necessary. But I say to her that it is important to impart the fact that it is more about them practicing a way of Being – practicing the Way – as opposed to listening about it.

This shows how dedicated James was to honoring Jesus' way of including women in the teachings. He was prepared to break with the ingrained Jewish patriarchal culture for women to have access to the teachings. Although it was not in the open, it was a first step. This is just customary of James constantly upholding the Way, in thought and behavior, and in practicing what he was taught.

The regression continues with James moving to a point when he feels sad. One of his friends in Britannia has passed away.

Mia: He was one of the leaders of the tribes. We went into partnership to mine [metal]. He owned the lands. Or the lands belonged to the tribes of which he was the leader. His son takes over. And that's OK. We are good – the son and I. He was one of the locals who came to the talks in Britannia and was very open to it. His son joined the little schools that we started, and now he is attending the congregation there, the flock. So it is going well. I am sad because I miss them. And I am sad because I could not see my friend one last time. I am so saddled with the responsibility of this Church here.

Earlier in the regression, James revealed that he had a wife in Britannia, who had sadly died early on while he was still there. His wife is supposed to have been a daughter of King Cymbeline, the sister of Caractacus and Arviragus, who were both chieftains in their own right. Such a link would explain why Arviragus granted James land in Glastonbury and subsequent marriages between their families.[3] Furthermore, to have obtained metal mining rights for trade, it would make sense that he has a close relationship with land or tribal chieftains. So, it would also make sense that he would mourn them dying in Britannia, while he was so far away in Jerusalem.

The regression continues.

Mia: It is tough. It's a tough responsibility because the Sadducees and Pharisees look at us suspiciously, and the Romans consider us to be rebels and inciters of violence. So we cannot do anything too much in the open. Everything is done undercover. It is hard to manage the extremists' way of thinking, their beliefs. But I persevere. In Britannia, when I started to talk and teach, it was very straightforward. It was about putting the focus on inspiring people and putting the focus on the message. Here it's become a more political thing of constant mediation and reminders and just being cautious and aware. There is no freedom. In Britannia there was so much freedom. Here everything is done covertly. That is why our church is in one of the outskirt villages where nobody would think it's a church, a movement. A lot of the work is done in the caves, not here. It's all about safety.

We constantly have Zealots who are caught. At least every other day, one of our movement is caught. And it is hard consoling the family, managing the family. It is hard convincing them that our God is a fair and a just God when they have lost their sons and when their sons are tortured. And then on the other side, we have got the extreme views that we are being punished because we are not following the laws. It's a matter of appeasing those fears as well and just persevering and moving through the teachings of Jesus. It is tough. I don't know how Jesus did it when he was living so far away from them. I don't know how he did it, or whether he did do it. Maybe people just listened to him. [Chuckles.] He was very inspiring. But I am finding it difficult. But I have skills. I have mediation skills, and negotiation skills from being the merchant. I just never thought I'd have to apply it here.

At the next significant event, one of James' flock has been captured, tortured and killed by the Romans. James calls a special congregation in remembrance of the deceased. It is the only time when women are allowed in the congregation. His family and the village and those who knew him were invited.

Mia: We say how brave this person was. We sing him praises and accolades. And we talk about how he is now at peace. We talk about how he pursued his passion and how his life had meaning. Then, we talk about how Jesus was also tortured for his way of Being – for sticking to the Way. He was crucified, but he was healed, I say to them. And I say to them that he left in exile and he died whilst he was in exile.

Reena: What do they say?

Mia: The thing is, this is not news to the brethren, who were closest to him – who stayed behind. They all knew that he was healed and that he was exiled and everything had to be quiet. It's fine now to talk about it a little bit more because he has passed away, and his life is no longer in danger. The congregation and the followers, they understand. It's not like it's a big surprise, a special surprise. Those who would stay home to maintain this church did keep in regular contact with Jesus somehow. But they did not mention his whereabouts to anybody else. His whereabouts were only known to one or two. Nobody else knew.

James then went on to talk about how Jesus was tortured and of all he went through to stay true and authentic to the Way, to the teachings… to his way of life. James also talks to them about the difference between the spirit and the physical body.

James' Teaching 5: Balance and Authenticity of Spirit

The spirit is always strong as long as we keep feeding the spirit with truth and authenticity, sometimes maybe to the detriment of our physical body.

In a world of judgement, oppression, intolerance and control, authenticity is not readily accepted. If our beliefs are different, we are condemned for speaking our beliefs. We are judged for feeling a particular emotion that is incongruent with the mass conditioning. And so, if we choose to feed our spirit, our spirit will remain strong, sometimes at the expense of the physical.

However, if we choose to be inauthentic and feed the physical, the flames of our spirit will slowly diminish until all we are is a follower of something that we do not believe is true, that we do not subscribe to. This is very disempowering.

I emphasize the strength of Jesus' spirit, and the strength of this particular Zealot's spirit – this follower's spirit is to remain true.

Then, I talk to them about balance. It is about speaking our truth but not forcing it down someone else's throat – or forcing it on someone else. It is about staying within our truth but being open to consider another person's opinion. This is where balance comes in. But it is hard to talk about balance in a world that is so imbalanced. And there is so much extremism.

Mia: The flock, the congregation, they understand what I am saying, and they get it. The most important thing is that the family has got some peace from it. I can never bring him back to them, but I can bring them peace.

It is interesting how James viewed dying for the Way differently to how Paul viewed it. While both men were sensitive to how the deaths impacted the families and the immediate community, James went on to talk about staying authentic to one's principles and voice, yet staying in balance in being true to the Way, and not forcing their views onto someone else. Paul commemorated the deaths of his followers with the flesh and blood of the Divine Christ as a symbol of Jesus dying for his beliefs and the salvation of all. While James still had Zealots dying for the cause, he did not totally embrace and welcome it into the heart of his Church and teachings. He always strived for balance. Paul, on the other hand, used the persecution and death of his followers as a lasting impression that martyrdom is truly the divine way to heaven and glory, and became a marker for the later followers of Gentile Christianity, separating the so-called true believers and the non-believers. This was another difference between the Gentile and Judeo-Christian churches.

At the next significant event, dawn was just breaking over the horizon. James took some new followers, who wished to be cleansed, down to the river.

Reena: What is this cleansing that you are talking about?

Ritual: The Cleansing (or Baptism)

It's a ritual where we cleanse them of the past. It's symbolic. We cleanse them of past belief systems, past ideologies, past conditioning, to embrace the Way. It's symbolic. Once they have been cleansed, it's about bringing down the Light into them, via the sun, the rest of the congregation who volunteer and myself. We encircle, hold hands and encircle them, as we transmit the Light from our heart, our thoughts and our hands.

Once this cleansing and the bringing of the Light is complete, they become members of the flock. We keep the circle to embrace them like they are newborn. We do this so everyone comes equal. Not one soul has come in more or less.

We can have a Pharisee and a farmer, and they are equal in our congregation, in our church. No one is more special than the other. They both contribute equally as much as they can. We don't force contribution.

Reena: And these that are going through the cleansing, are they all of the Jewish faith or are some of them of other faiths?

Mia: They are predominantly of the old faith, the Jewish faith. There are some, a handful of pagans from the Romans, but the Romans are notorious for punishing dissenters. And they are notorious for punishing those who come to our movement because we threaten them – our movement threatens them. Jesus threatened them by being the Messiah – the King of the Jews. So it is considered treasonous, dangerous, for dissenters of the Romans to come to our movement. So we have only got a handful – not many.

Reena: And these pagans that come in, are they taught the Jewish ways as well as the new ways you've been teaching?

Mia: We just teach them our way – which does include the Jewish ways. We have a more liberal way of adopting the Jewish faith, but we focus a lot on love. We want to show the congregation as opposed to enforcing controls onto them. We wish for them to embrace a way of life as opposed to following strict protocols and rituals. It's not about obeying. It's about Being.

Reena: Are there any rules that they [pagans] have to follow?

Mia: We believe in the one God, but we also talk about the God within. We talk about hygiene. It's incredibly important, especially here, the desert, where it is so hot. I am still very relaxed about the food, whereas there are those who wish to follow strictly the old ways. They wish to keep the kosher rules.

Reena: And circumcision?

Mia: They wish to keep the circumcision. Yes. But I am relaxed about it because I say that it is up to the pagans if they wish to be circumcised. They are not brought up in a culture where circumcision is even thought about. I push for a little bit more liberal, more open way of thinking, to encourage more souls to follow the message. But at the same time, I need to keep the laws, because that is of my belief, my faith. It's a fine balance.

Reena: And the laws that have been passed down from Moses – are those the ones that you have to follow?

Mia: Yes.

Reena: Are any of those relaxed or are those law –

Mia: No… they are set in stone. That is our way, our teachings. And those who join us in Jerusalem, they have to adhere to the laws of Moses. Even in Britannia, I talked about the laws of Moses, to enforce them strongly.

The Ebionite/Nazarene movement in Jerusalem was indeed made up of mostly Jewish followers of John the Baptist and later Jesus, who were concentrated in Palestine and surrounding regions and flourished between the years 30-80CE. Non-Jews were certainly part of the mix but the dominant ethos of the group was an adherence to live according to Jewish law (Galatians 2:14). They were zealous for the Torah, and continued to observe the commandments as enlightened by their rabbi and teacher, Jesus. The non-Jews in their midst were apparently expected to follow some version of these laws (Acts 15:28-29).[4] So James' accounts are totally in line with historical accounts.

The regression continues with James progressing forward to when he is a bit older. He is more established in the Church. People respect him more. He perceives himself to not be inspiring, but being able to mediate skillfully and get people's agreement.

> Mia: Jesus was very charismatic. He would have a presence about him. He would glow as he talked and people would flock to him. He would do all these incredible things. Mary did the same thing. She was very inspiring in her own way as well. She just had a presence about her and the women would flock to her. She would be very nurturing. Together they were a very charismatic couple. I don't have that presence. I am a businessman. I have skills. I mediate. I negotiate. I can find common grounds. I can read people and their needs and find ways to meet it. I am a businessman and that is how I lead this Church. I do not lead via presence and inspiration. Sometimes I do give talks but that wisdom comes from Jesus. My skill is keeping the Church together during these hard times, with different factions within and a very tough climate outside. But what is important to me is to be true to Jesus' vision, spirit, words and teachings. To be true to the Way. People see that. People respect me because I am true. Even though it is hard, I maintain the original, authentic message, which I totally believe in and I practice. So people respect me because I am not one of those who says one thing and does another. In fact I live an ascetic life. Even though I

> am wealthy, I live a simple life now. I don't indulge in luxuries or hedonism. I work hard. It is not easy leading this Church. There is always a part of me that craves the freedom that I found in Britannia, but I know my role and my responsibility is here.

What struck me most in this chapter is how very different the conditions were in Jerusalem to Britannia for James. While his teaching and messages were the same, the environment in which he taught could not have been more different between Britannia and Jerusalem. While his role in Britannia as a spiritual leader was predominantly to teach, in Jerusalem his same role was more about negotiating the political quagmire to be able to teach and keep Jesus' message pure, while keeping the peace. Fortunately, he did seem to have the skills necessary to hold it together.

The next chapter sees what became of the Judeo-Church in the later years of his leadership in Jerusalem.

Chapter 13

The End

In the next event, James finds himself within the church. It is a cool relief in the hot and dusty Jerusalem. He has been here for a while now, and is acting in the capacity as the Advisor of the Church.

Reena: How has the Church changed under your advisement?

Mia: It's getting harder and harder to help the flock keep the faith, because the promise was that Jesus is the Messiah to take us into the new world, into a new land. But yet, as time goes by, the Romans get stronger, the Pharisees get tougher, and people are being persecuted, prosecuted. They are being heavily taxed. Our people don't see the Golden Age. So we get word that there are other groups, other movements outside ours who are feeling fed up and there are murmurings that there are other people who are calling themselves the Messiahs. So the Romans are getting more and more fearful, and therefore, they are controlling more and more. We never had much freedom before, with our movement and our Church, but it is getting harder these days.

But I am getting word in Britannia that it is easier [there]. More and more people are flocking, which I feel really good about. I hear stories from others who have gone away. I hear Paul is in a very dangerous place but he is preaching the message of Jesus, though he has changed it all. I don't like how he has changed it because it has taken Jesus' authentic message away [sigh]. I wonder about Mary and how she is doing. I am sure that she'll be fine. The Romans are not so active where she is. My sister is getting older and her son is playing a more prominent role in the Church. He sees my vision. But I worry… I worry about the future of our message and of our Church. It's so fractured.

We hear that Paul is bringing more and more Roman pagans into the faith, which is great. [Sigh.] But I wrestle with myself because in one way, yes, it is great, but in another, it is almost like twisting tales to entice people to come in. I am a businessman. I know we do this in business to sell our wares, but I struggle with this in the role of being a spiritual leader. For me, it is about authenticity and truth. [Sigh.] But the more Paul works at getting people within Rome to accept the faith, the easier, hopefully, it will be for our people to practice the faith openly with the Romans here. I can't do much. So I am pushed in a corner. He constantly asks for us to completely discard the Jewish laws and rituals that we are so used to. So, it is another form of extremism that I have to manage. There is just so much anger and fighting and I do not see so much love within the Church and the structure that is building up around it.

Reena: And who is building the structure?

Mia: Paul. Paul sees his way and his way alone – a strict hierarchy of carrying the message to be passed down through his anointed servants. There was a joy and a love in the heart of Jesus. I do not see that in this man. To carry God's love, one must love. To show love to one's fellow man.

Reena: How much contact do you have with him?

Mia: A little… I am leading the Church in Jerusalem, but only here in Jerusalem.

Reena: And how about him? What capacity does he play?

Mia: He travels and he is creating churches from here to

Rome.

Reena: Does he discuss anything with you? Does he communicate with you?

Mia: Yes. In letters. He tells me how he believes it should be done.

Reena: Do you respond at all?

Mia: [shakes head] No.

Reena: What stops you from responding?

Mia: I have my flock here to look after and to work here. I am too old to get caught up in the anger and ego of this man.

Reena: Tell me about the anger. What is he angry with, do you know?

Mia: I do not know. He has anger in his heart.

While the history of the Jewish Christian literature remains in dispute, these same writings provide firm evidence that the early Jewish Christian community was firmly opposed to Paul and his theology. All of the earliest followers of Jesus, up to the commencement of Paul's mission, thought of themselves as Jews – regardless of being a Pharisee, Sadducee or Essene/Nazarene.[1]

The Ebionite/Nazarene Christians believed that Jesus was the Jewish Messiah sent from the Jewish God to the Jewish people in fulfilment of the Jewish Scriptures. Their belief hinges on the fact that in order to belong to the people of God, one needed to be Jewish and observe the Jewish traditions and rituals. The Ebionite did not subscribe to the notion of Jesus' preexistence or his virgin birth. They believed that Jesus was a real flesh-and-blood human, born as the eldest son of the sexual union of his parents, Joseph and Mary. What sets Jesus apart from all other people was that he kept God's law perfectly.[2]

In the eyes of Jesus' original followers, any Gentile who wanted to become a follower of Jesus was to become a follower of Judaism. However, as Paul's evangelism brought in ever-larger numbers of Gentile converts, the issue of just how far these converts had to go in order to become followers became very difficult.[3]

Gentile Christians were not all inclined to adopt the ways of Judaism. The vast majority of Gentile Christians had converted from paganism and saw Jews and their religion as something distinct from the salvation wrought by Jesus. While they knew that Jesus was Jewish, who adhered to the Jewish law, and the revelation of the one true God is the God of the Jews, the Gentile Christians were not open to following the laws of Judaism and become Jews.[4] For many of the Ebionites, on the other hand, Paul was considered a heretic and they rejected his writings that were considered to have led many astray by insisting that a person is made right with God separate from keeping the law, and forbade circumcision.[5]

However, as Gentile Christianity gained popularity, the Gentile Christians took matters into their own hands with the Epistle of Barnabas. While it is written anonymously, it is attributed to Barnabas, the travelling companion of Paul. This epistle, according to Bart Ehrman, is "most virulently anti-Jewish in its message, arguing that it is Christians and not Jews, who are heirs of the covenantal promises made to the patriarch of Israel. It also claimed that the 'Old Testament' is a Christian and not a Jewish book, and as a result the Jews have adhered to a false religion." Contrarily, the Epistle of Barnabas does not spurn but embraces the Jewish Scriptures, and provides a "true" interpretation of key passages, in order to discount the Jewish understanding of significant aspects of their own religion, including the covenant, fasting, sacrifices, circumcision, kosher food laws and Sabbath, to name a few.[6] This animosity between the two factions of Christianity probably helped fuel the discord between James and Paul.

In the next event, James is in Jerusalem where he is meeting Paul.

Mia: We are sitting eating and there are many people. Some people are with us. He is telling me how the Church should be run. I just sit and listen. Mmm. I find it very difficult to like this man.

Reena: Based on what he is saying? How ought the Church be run, according to Paul?

Mia: That there are priests that tell the congregation – the followers – they are just followers. Not that each individual gains God's spiritual grace through the baptism, as Jesus did. Jesus granted the baptism, which created the spiritual connection. Whereas Paul teaches that spiritual connection is through the priests, through his servants, through the hierarchy. This was not Jesus' message.

Reena: What about the laws and rules?

Mia: That we don't have to be hygienic. That they are able to eat anything and everything. I was relaxed about food but to a certain degree. He just wants to obliterate all that law. He does not speak to his flock about our family… Jesus' family – be it Mary and the children or be it ourselves. But at the same time he is getting so many new members. I struggle. I struggle with it. But it is also managing him, his enthusiasm and his fervor. It's like a raging fire. It's really difficult to communicate the Way to him, our Way to him. So the people within the Church, those who want us to adopt more of the old laws, just want Paul and all his followers, his flock, out of our movement because they are disrespecting the laws that they hold so dear.

Reena: What do you say to them?

Mia: I tell all of them, including Paul, to be more tolerant of each other's views. To not be so ingrained in their own belief systems and their own views. To just be compassionate. Our whole movement is about love. It's not about hanging on to our own belief systems. There is an element of pride there. This inflexibility. This "I am right" and "I am going to prove to you I am right" behavior. [Sigh.] And then you've got the Zealots who don't understand why Paul is going to Rome where the enemies are, to carry the message of Jesus, and then to twist it. So it is hard. It's so hard to mediate. I am also getting older so I don't have the fire and the veracity anymore.

Reena: What are his and your beliefs about circumcision?

Mia: I lived in Britannia for a long time and they did not practice this as such, but I believe this is a clean way. Paul believes circumcision should not be any practice of the Church.

Reena: And what do you say to that?

Mia: I believe circumcision is a cleaner way… and cleanliness is closer to godliness. So it is better, but it is not necessary for all. However, for those wanting to be priests, I feel it is.

In the first century, Gentile and Jewish Christianity were very loosely defined and developed into some subgroups. The different takes on circumcision, which was seen as necessary for salvation under strict Jewish law, was a barometer that symbolized the adherence to the Mosaic law and the faith in Jewish rituals and beliefs.

In fact, the Roman Catholic scholar Raymond Brown posits four distinguishable groups:[7]

a. Jewish Christians and their Gentile converts who practiced the full observance of the Mosaic law, including circumcision necessary for salvation.
b. Jewish Christians and Gentile converts who did not insist on circumcision as salvation for Gentile Christians but did require them to keep some purity laws. Brown believed that James and Peter belonged to this group, and this is consistent with the regression of James.
c. Jewish Christians who did not insist on circumcision as

salvation for Gentile Christians and did not require their observing Jewish purity laws. This group did not entail a break with the practices of Judaism nor did it impel Jewish Christians to abandon circumcision and the law. This is where Brown suspects that Paul seemed to take his stance on the issue.

d. Gentile Christians who saw no significance in the old law and the Jerusalem temple and lost all lingering connections to parent Judaism.

So, determining where both James and Paul stood on the issue of circumcision helped us assess their stance towards the old law, and thus highlights yet another difference between their teachings and ideologies.

In Luke's account of the first Jerusalem Conference, in Acts 15, it is evident that members of the Pharisaic party believed strongly that circumcision and the adherence to the law was a strict requirement for Gentile converts. Peter, Paul and Barnabas gave testimony to how God worked through the Holy Spirit among the Gentiles. The conversion of so many Gentile believers was seen by many as fulfilling the prophecies that at the end of the age nations would come streaming into Jerusalem acknowledging the Jewish God, establishing the Kingdom of God on Earth with Jesus as the eternal Davidic King. However, during this time, Paul pushed the question if circumcision was a necessary requirement for Gentiles to be part of Jesus' Kingdom. According to Acts 15, it was James who made the final decision on this crucial issue, showing without a shadow of a doubt his leadership role in the Jerusalem Church. James decided that it was not a requirement for the Gentiles to be circumcised, but asked that they abstained from food offered to idols, from fornicating, from eating rare meat and animals that have been strangled – ancient regulations found in the law of Moses.[8]

Reena: What else do you discuss besides structure and circumcision?

Mia: The right of women in the church to speak. He does not want women in the church to speak. Women should be silent and should obey.

In Paul's regression, he did outline his reasons for not giving the same opportunities to women as men. The main reason was that Paul was trying to spread a very different spiritual message in Rome, which had a culture that had established social practices and spiritual beliefs. He was very cognizant about what aspects of the cultural boundaries to push, and which aspects not to, in order for his message to have widest reach and the greatest impact in Rome. Paul decided that having women to spread the message was pushing this very patriarchal Roman culture too far, and would shut people down to the message.

James, on the other hand, followed Jesus' method and ministry and included both women and men as teachers and active participants in his teachings in Britannia. Although he wanted to adopt this method in Jerusalem, he was advised not to, because those around him felt that the Church was not ready. However, he did include women, albeit surreptitiously in their homes, through his sister. This claim is confirmed by the Vatican's Apostolic Constitutions, which claim that within the Nazarene community of Jesus, women were closely involved in the ministry.[9]

The differences continue.

Reena: Did he also hold the belief that Jesus was going to return to establish the Kingdom of Heaven?

Mia: Yes.

Reena: And what was your belief about that?

Mia: We must create the Kingdom of Heaven within ourselves with God's love. And within the community we live.

Reena: Did you share this with him?

Mia: Mmm. [Yes.]

Reena: What was his reaction?

Mia: He became angry. He insists that Jesus' resurrection creates the Kingdom of Heaven.

Reena: How did you respond?

Mia: I told him Jesus' resurrection was a trick, so Jesus could escape.

Reena: How did he respond to that?

Mia: He told me I was lying... He looked at me in a way. It chilled me. Told me I should not spread this lie. The man is setting up a mythology.

Reena: How does that make you feel?

Mia: Sad. But Romans love myths.

James' regressions claimed that it was he who concocted a plan to save Jesus from being crucified. Being a Pharisee himself, and carrying the familial title of "Joseph of Arimathea," James was able to use his influence to prevent Jesus from being executed on the cross. Instead, a substitute was crucified and died in Jesus' place.

In order to keep Jesus' survival quiet for his own safety to appease the Romans and Jewish Sanhedrin Council, they decided that there were three levels of information that were to be shared about the "Resurrection of Christ." The first level of what really happened was known only to a close-knit circle comprised of James, Mary Magdalene and Mother Mary. The second level was that disclosed to the Apostles and disciples, where they found out that Jesus was indeed crucified but nursed back to health. Paul was included in this tier. The third level was to the general public, including the Romans, Pharisees and the Sanhedrin council who had sentenced him, that Jesus had died on the cross, resurrected and ascended to heaven.

Having different levels of knowledge also explains the

difference in teachings in Paul's and James' ministries. James knew that Jesus was a flesh-and-blood ordinary human, who did extraordinary things. He also knew that though Jesus endured torture by the Romans, he was not crucified. He also followed the Nazarenes' teachings of "The Way," to create the Kingdom of Heaven within the followers, here on Earth. James also took over the leadership of Jesus' ministry, whose followers were well aware of and understood the teachings that had come from Jesus.

Paul, on the other hand, thought that Jesus was crucified and was later miraculously healed. Compounded with Paul's task of spreading Jesus' message in Rome, one of the toughest areas in Europe, where he had to almost compete with the pagan beliefs of immortal gods, Paul chose to carve Jesus into a mythical divine figure, in order to establish a ministry and convince them to embrace his teachings. He also perpetuated the belief in Jesus' crucifixion and resurrection for people's salvation to strengthen his story that Jesus was godlike, who was just as powerful as their pagan gods. The difference is that the Divine Jesus offered a gift through his sacrifice that was motivated by love, versus the pagan gods, who were motivated by power and greed to demand sacrifice for themselves to grant favors. So Paul spun this myth.

Ultimately, both Paul and James were trying to pass the message of love through their respective ministries. Their methods, stories and rituals were different due to their individual pasts, perceptions of what had happened and the environments in which they were teaching. What unfortunately occurred was that people chose to focus more on the divisive factors of methods, stories and rituals, instead of the unifying essence of what they were both teaching – love. In my opinion, this is the biggest tragedy of this story.

The regression continues.

Reena: And when he gave you that look that chilled you, that first time, how did that whole meeting conclude?

Mia: We could not reconcile these differences... We did not see each other for some time.

Reena: Did he leave?

Mia: Mmm... He was causing problems. And I forced him from Jerusalem.

Reena: And how did you force him? You used the people?

Mia: Mmm. They told him they did not want his Roman ways.

Reena: When he came to the church to see you, did you call him in or did he come voluntarily?

Mia: I called him to try and create peace between us, to reconcile the differences between our views.

This account of James' meeting with Paul is in line with the Jerusalem Conference, a meeting of all the key leaders of the early Church, described in Acts 15. Paul's description of this meeting in Galatians 2 is in line with this regression, and Jeffrey Butz hypothesizes that Paul harbored some resentment toward the Apostles in Jerusalem. While Paul saw James, Cephas (Peter) and John as the acknowledged pillars, acknowledging their leadership role in the Church, he also refers to them as "those supposed to be acknowledged leaders (what they actually were makes no difference to me; God shows no partiality) – those leaders continued nothing to me." (Galatians 2:6-10) Some scholars have seen Paul's sarcastic tone as evidence of a deep rift between Paul and the pillar Apostles of the first church, which is concurrent with James' account.[10]

James then went to the event when he met Paul for the second and last time, in Jerusalem.

Mia: Paul's come to see me. He needs my blessing, as the head of the Church in Jerusalem, for his teachings.

Reena: Do you give it to him?

Mia: No. He has not welcomed the love of God into his heart, and his teachings reflect that.

Reena: What is his reaction when you do not give him your blessing?

Mia: He is very angry.

Reena: How does he express his anger?

Mia: He goes very red. [Laughs.] He threatens. He threatens to destroy me and to… there is no need for Jesus' bloodline and he denounces it. It is not necessary to him.

Reena: How do you react to that?

Mia: How can one react to a man in anger? I must stand true to my integrity and to Jesus' message… I stand firm and I do not react.

Reena: Are John and Peter with you and Paul, or is this private?

Mia: It was a private discussion but they are at the periphery. They are in the surrounding area.

Paul's last visit to Jerusalem is generally dated around the year 56CE, and is documented in Acts 21.[11] Jeffrey Butz claims that the reason for this visit was to deliver a rather large amount of money that he had gone out of his way to collect for "the poor" in Jerusalem. Ebionite, the sect led by James, translates to "the poor" in Hebrew, so could Paul have been collecting for the Ebionite Church? Jeffrey Butz hypothesized that Paul hoped that delivering the collection would unite the Jewish and Gentile wings of the Church. However, according to biblical scholars, this collection, and his Gentile ministry, were rejected by James and the leaders of the Jerusalem Church, possibly because James and the Jewish community followed the law to establish a vanguard of the new eschatological community that God was establishing, and Paul did not fit into that.[12]

Reena: How does it come to a close between you and Paul?

Mia: The last thing that Paul said to me was that he will crush

> me, and crush the message I carry. He storms out and he mobilizes a rebellion within the church. There are people from outside the church as well. They are angry and they storm the church. The Zealots, those who believe in the old law, those who are followers of Paul – it's too much. [Sigh.] It's become a bit violent. They don't believe in me as their leader anymore. [Sigh.] They just don't know how hard it is to hold it all together.

This is interesting because while James claims that Paul mobilized a rebellion against him, Acts 21 claims that the rebellion was mobilized by the "Jews of Asia" against Paul. While they were trying to kill Paul, the Roman tribune takes Paul into protective custody.[13]

Mia: I'm too old for all this.
Reena: What is "all this"?
Mia: All this nonsense. All these silly people.
Reena: Who are these people? Are you talking about the Romans?
Mia: Some. Most of them are the Jews. They are so silly. They want me to shut up but I am too old for that. It's not just the Jews but really it's the Jewish elders, which is funny because I am as old as some of them, or older.

When asked to elaborate on what he was telling the Jewish elders that they did not like, James responded, "I am telling them about Jesus and his message. And just that the world's a bigger place than just Jerusalem. They are so small… they are so small-minded. I am just an old man but they can't tell me what I should be saying. It doesn't matter to me. All they can do is kill me and I am going to die soon anyway. A body can only last so long. So I will just keep on saying what I am saying and if they don't like it…"

Reena: How old are you roughly?

Mia: Three score years and ten [seventy]? I'm not quite there...

Reena: And what happens next?

Mia: I have a place of worship and they want me to shut it. I tell them I won't. We are arguing. And because I have money, I have a good building. This annoys them that I have the money and so I also have the power and, I like to think, the charisma. Well, I like to think so. I am arguing with the elders and with other people who are higher up. And we're pushing each other. [Emphatically.] I won't take their nonsense!

Reena: Are you physically pushing each other?

Mia: Physically pushing each other. They are shouting. They are shouting at me and they lift me and carry me... to the top of the church and they throw me from the top. One man pushes me and I fall.

Reena: Where do you fall?

Mia: I fall down to the ground. I'm still alive but I'm hurt. The building was not so high but I'm old. They threw stones on me.

Reena: Where were you when they pushed you off?

Mia: We were all on the roof of the building, where we often go for meetings. I was shouting. I was shouting to the people below. I don't know if it was an accident or if I was pushed on purpose. I like to think it was an accident.

Reena: During this time, was Paul there?

Mia: Not that I am aware of.

James' heart stops beating.

Then, I navigated the soul of James/Mia to go the point just after his death, where Mia reported that she was floating above the physical body and was still aware of everything that was happening around her.

Mia: There's my people there and the other people. And I was badly hurt. And so one of them says they should stop the pain and beat me on the head.

Reena: Did they?

Mia: Yeah. [Pause.] They're all arguing and there's a fight.

Reena: What's the fight about?

Mia: Because of what's happened to me. Some are saying it's an accident and some are saying it was on purpose. It's all a bit chaotic. It was time, though.

This account of James' death is in line with records of James the Just, the brother of Jesus, being hurled from the pinnacle of the temple to his death and being stoned to death in Jerusalem by the Jews in 62CE,[14] while contradicting the many accounts of Joseph of Arimathea being laid to rest in 82CE and his remains being in the Isle of Avalon.[15]

The acclaimed first-century Judea-Romano historian, Josephus, in Jewish Antiquities, claimed that upon learning of the death of Festus, the Roman governor of Judea, Nero sent Albinus to Judea as procurator, and removed Joseph from the high priesthood. In his place, he instated the son of High Priest Ananus the Elder. Ananus the Elder (known in the Gospels as Annas) was high priest from 6-15CE, and was the father-in-law of Joseph Caiaphas, the high priest from 18-36CE, who tried Jesus.[16]

Ananus the Elder's son was similarly called Ananus too. The younger Ananus was a Sadducee. After Festus' death, and before the arrival of Albinus in Judea, the younger Ananus took the opportunity to convene the judges of the Sanhedrin and "brought before them a man named James, the brother of Jesus called Christ and certain others." James was accused of having transgressed the law and was sentenced to be stoned. However, the local Jewish inhabitants, who adhered by the law strictly, were offended by this execution of James, given that he was considered to the head of the Temple of Jerusalem, and was considered most just, therefore earning the name "James the Just" – and convinced King Agrippa II to intervene and order the younger Ananus to desist from further actions. Three months later, the younger Ananus was deposed from the high priesthood.[17]

Eusebius, while quoting the account of Josephus, also records otherwise lost passages from Hegesippus and Clement of Alexandria (*Historia Ecclesiae,* 2.23). Hegesippus' account varies somewhat from what Josephus reports. According to Hegesippus, the scribes and Pharisees came to James for help in putting down Christian beliefs. However, James refused and testified that, "Christ himself sitteth in heaven, at the right hand of the Great Power, and shall come on the clouds of heaven." The scribes and Pharisees, failing to obtain the desired testimony from James, decided to throw James from the temple, so that his followers and believers in Jesus would be afraid and not believe James' teachings. Because James did not die from the fall, he was stoned.[18]

While Mia's James' account of James' method of death corresponds with the historical account (of being stoned), this account has also alluded to the trial in front of the Sanhedrin or Pharisaic council, when she spoke about arguing with the Jewish Elders. Mia's James though did not mention that the younger Ananus was a party to his death. The Church Father Origen, who consulted the works of Josephus in around 248CE, related that the execution and death of James gave cause to the Roman siege of Jerusalem by the Emperor Vespasian.[19]

The siege of Jerusalem by the Romans in 70CE resulted in the dissolution of the Jerusalem Church and the scattering of those who upheld Jewish Christian belief into the Diaspora. As Gentile Christianity gained popularity, it severed any lingering ties with Judaism and Jewish Christianity, and based its theology completely on Paul's teaching of faith in Christ as the replacement for the law. Without its Jewish roots, the Pauline teachings came to understand the new covenant through Jesus as a complete replacement for the "old" covenant that God had made with the Jews.[20]

As the new Gentile Christianity teachings and rituals gained popularity, the Jewish Christians faced a backlash from both fellow Jews and Gentile Christians and were declared heretics and banned from synagogues and Christian meetings. As Jeffrey Butz says, "This was a double indignity for the descendants of the original Jewish Christians (including Jesus' own family), to be branded as heretics by both religious orders, when they carried the original teachings of Jesus."[21]

Although the Jewish Christians were splintered and persecuted after 70CE, scattered groups such as the Nazarenes, Ebionites and Elkesaites managed to hang on in areas such as Syria, Egypt and parts of Arabia, even influencing the rise of Islam. The Christians that Muhammad encountered during his days leading caravans around the Arabian Peninsula were largely Jewish Christians who survived among the Arabs.[22] So it is not coincidence that the Muslim understanding of Jesus is remarkably similar to Jewish Christian understanding. As mentioned previously, the understanding that Jesus was substituted on the cross is found in a verse in the Koran – Surah An-Nisa' number 157 – that says (interpreted), "And (because of) their saying: 'Surely we have killed the Massih – son of Maryam,' the messenger of Allah, and they could not kill him nor could they crucify him, even though a likeness of that was made for them."[23]

Chapter 14

The Unsung

Jesus was a Jew.

Most biblical scholars today acknowledge that he was raised in a Jewish household in Jewish Palestine, brought up in a Jewish culture, accepted the Jewish ways, learned the Jewish tradition and kept the Jewish law.

As an adult, he started preaching and gathering disciples who were all Jews, most of whom considered him to be the Jewish Messiah, come to deliver the Jewish people from the oppressive power of Rome. The power players in Jerusalem arrested and handed him over to the Roman governor who put him on trial for sedition for claiming to be the King of Jews.[1]

So, Jesus was a Jew.

Through sources dating back from the second to the fourth centuries, we know of Christians called the Ebionites, who were and understood themselves to be Jewish followers of Jesus.[2] The Ebionite/Nazarene movement was made up of mostly Jewish/Israelite followers of John the Baptist and later Jesus, who were concentrated in Palestine and surrounding regions and flourished between the years 30-80CE. In an attempt to capture the whole of this earliest movement, those original first-century largely Palestinian followers of Jesus gathered around James in Jerusalem; they were zealous for the Torah, but saw themselves as part of the New Covenant Way inaugurated by their "True Teacher" Jesus.[3]

What this regression pulls together and highlights is that James, the brother of Jesus, was an unsung hero of Christianity. As the blood brother of Jesus, authority and rights of guidance were passed on to him. He was a highly respected leader of the

Jewish church that Jesus headed. James was the undisputed leader of the Jerusalem church, from the time of Jesus' supposed crucifixion until the time of James' death. His was the unquestioned wisdom and vision at the Jerusalem Council and his exalted status in memory of the later Jewish Christian communities attest to the paramount role that he played in the struggles of his early Church to define its theology with both parent Judaism and Gentile Christianity. More than that, it shows that James and the Apostles were thoroughly Jewish in their beliefs and practices, and adhered to a stricter form of messianic Judaism.[4]

Why did history virtually wipe out the existence and the important role that the brother of the Messiah himself played?

We continue the regression to find out. James finds himself in the realms of light, reviewing his death and what happened afterwards, to his teachings and followers in the old country, Jerusalem, and Britannia.

Mia: Well, in the old country [sigh] no one was able to keep our movement in unity like I could. They were finding it difficult not because I was wonderful at it, but because the factions got more and more momentum. So Paul and the followers of Paul broke away, which made it convenient for them, because then they did not have to follow the old laws and they could just practice their version of what happened according to their belief system. That's what happened there. The Zealots, they just decided to do more uprising. They had had enough of the Roman occupation. They'd had enough of what's happening. And so the Romans came and invaded where we used to practice and our little church, and imprisoned those who did not manage to escape. Tortured them, killed them, executed them. The Romans politically got a stronger hold in Jerusalem. And then the third group, those who held on to the old laws a bit more, blended into the Pharisees and Sadducees. So, in Jerusalem, the Way melted away. Those who did manage to get away practiced the Way in their own way. But in little individual pockets as opposed to a bigger movement. This is Jerusalem.

This account is in line with historical references. Firstly, the siege of Jerusalem that occurred after the death of James (and Paul) in 70CE resulted in the dissolution of the Jerusalem church and scattered the Jewish Christian believers. With the loss of the Temple and central authority in Jerusalem, Gentile Christianity, which was building momentum, severed any lingering ties with Judaism and based its theology completely on Paul's teaching of faith in Christ as the replacement for the law.[5] Secondly, as the fledgling church of Gentile Christianity grew and evolved, it stressed the doctrine of the virgin birth and the perpetual virginity of Mary.[6] This was done to emphasize and highlight the divine nature of Jesus. A sibling, a brother, would have watered down this doctrine, and would have called Jesus' divine status into question.

At the end of the day, James and the Jewish Christians saw their mission as being almost exclusively to the Jews.[7] This particularism, while it does not dismiss the validity of the teachings, made it rather exclusive, and ended up fizzling out. Paul's Gentile Christianity had a more universal appeal and its fires raged on to become what it is today – one of the world's largest religious movements.

The regression continues.

Reena: What happened in Britannia?

Mia: In Britannia, things were progressing quite nicely because we had the support from the leaders of the tribe. The unity was there from the get-go. But there was no formal structure to those teachings because it was a way of Being. And so the tribe and the locals – they were Being. The men from the old country who worked for me in Britannia, they started to integrate more into the culture and it became very… it was not the strong movement that Paul was developing. We mixed it up with the pagan traditions, the local traditions and rituals. It was very localized. It did not spread very much. It's almost like it went into the essence of those who started it in Britannia because it was a way of life. Everything that they did had the essence of the teachings. It is an internal thing – which is what I was teaching everyone anyway – to come from within. To work within as opposed to focusing on what happens on the outside. It was also about integrating it with local traditions and local beliefs so there was a lot of unity. It's almost like it's within people's spiritual DNA.

These fascinating insights about how James' teachings were integrated in Britannia is substantiated by Laurence Gardner in his book *The Grail Enigma*. Not only was Christianity intermixed with the Druids in Britain at that time,[8] Gardner claims that the James and Jesus bloodline played an important role in upholding Jesus' teachings and the Davidic lineage in Britain.

Gardener's claims are further substantiated by the regression as James gets more information in the Spirit Realms.

Reena: OK. And what was the soul's plan behind the choice of being his [Jesus] brother? What did you want to achieve?

Mia: I feel quite separate from that life. It was not about my soul's evolution but being of service. But I went into that one with very little issues. I needed to be pure to get the job done… There were so many jobs. And maintaining the purity of the bloodline.

Reena: Did you do that by marrying Jesus junior with your daughter as well?

Mia: Mm. Maintaining the bloodline keeps the knowledge. It's so the knowledge was kept alive in a physical way. The knowledge had to be kept alive not just as being written because that could be destroyed. There was the need for the physical manifestation. We were able to maintain the purity of the message and not be corrupted or for the message not to be corrupted or destroyed.

In *The Grail Enigma*, Gardner claims that James' offspring married the descendant of a kingdom in Britain, whose children became rulers in Cumbria and Siluria (the greater area of southeast Wales).[9] One of their grandchildren, referred to as Lucius, King of the Britons in the *Anglo-Saxon Chronicle* in the year 167CE, became the instigator of Celtic Christianity in Britain by proclaiming his Christianity at the court of Winchester in 156CE. The *Anglo-Saxon Chronicle* also states that he sent a deputation to meet with the then Bishop of Rome, a claim confirmed in an entry in the Vatican's *Liber Pontificalis*.[10] He conducted the first restoration of the Wattle Chapel in Glastonbury and built the first St. Michael's Tower on Glastonbury Tor in 167CE.[11] There are records showing that he entered into correspondence with a leader of the persecuted Christians in Rome at that time.[12]

James also mentioned that Yesoo, or Jesus Jr., was with him in Britannia. According to Gardner, Jesus Jr. married in 73CE and bore a son, Jesus III, in 77CE, who became the head of the mission that James had started in Siluria. Jesus III seems to have died without children, so the mantle was passed to his cousin Josue, the son of Jesus and Mary's third child, Joseph.[13] Josue, who was also known as the Fisher King Aminadab, married the daughter of the King of the Britons.[14] Gardner then goes on to postulate how the lines of King Lucius and Fisher King Aminadab combined to produce the Pendragon line, of King Arthur, whose supposed tomb is marked at the Glastonbury Abbey to this day. So Judeo-Christianity was imbued into both the spiritual movement of the Druids as well as the monarchy in Britannia after James' time there.

The regression continues with James reuniting with Jesus in the Spirit Realms.

Reena: What do you say to him?

Mia: Sorry, I feel I failed to create a lasting message.

Reena: What does Jesus say?

Mia: He just smiles. And tells me it's OK. It's how it was meant to be.

Reena: And maybe he can shed some light about how it was meant to be?

Mia: There is only a small percentage of people that are really able to give themselves over to an enlightened way of living and so the message was there for those people to achieve this through this time. But the majority of people were not able for that. The value that James brought is that he upheld, to the best of his ability, the practice of Christ Consciousness [Divine Consciousness] within him. He moved with it. It is not his teachings that were important but the example that he led. James saw it as it was – that embodying the Christ Consciousness [Divine Consciousness] is a way of Being. It is not just receiving teachings. It is in everything he practiced. How he spoke to someone. How he behaved. His values. Everything he did, he did out of love and in service. He was in service to Jesus. He was in service to his sister. He was in service to Jesus' church. He was in service to the family when he became the merchant because there was no one else to do it. He lived his life in service, and he embodied the Way. He was the true example.

This is probably why James is best known as James the Just in church traditions because of his exceeding righteousness. James the Just, as Bishop Clement calls him in his writings, is a title organically bestowed upon James by the early Jewish-Christian Nazarene/Ebionite group that he led, who revered James for his outstanding righteousness under the law[15] and the Way.

Based on Mia's regressions, there is no doubt that Jesus had siblings, and that James was indeed his brother. It left very little doubt that James and Joseph of Arimathea were indeed the same person – Jesus' brother. I was struck by how selflessly James devoted himself to his brother, his brother's family and the cause. James was a key player in this story, both spiritually and practically.

Firstly, if James had not possessed the means, connections and wealth, the story of Jesus would have been very different indeed. Perhaps Jesus would have gone the way John the Baptist had – beheaded – and had his title of Messiah revoked. Who knows what would have happened to Mary Magdalene and her children.

Secondly, while James is not considered close to being Jesus' spiritual, esoteric equal, he symbolized living the Way authentically and righteously, embodying it in all areas of his life. He strived to be the best example he could be for his leadership and flock of the Jewish Church. Ultimately spirituality is a way of Being as opposed to a way of thinking and speaking. In being and practicing the Way faithfully, he was truly inspirational.

Conclusion

One of the key debates between the Gentile Church and the Judeo-Christian Church is whether the Divine Consciousness resides externally only in God and Jesus, the only Son of God, or internally, embodied by all the children of God, as Jesus the human did. This is one of the basic fundamental differences between the Gentile Church, led by Paul the Evangelist, and the Judeo-Christian Church, led by James, the brother of Jesus.

What is Divine Consciousness?

> *So God created man in his own image, in the image of God created he him; male and female he created them.*
> *Genesis 1:27*

God or the Divine (existence) is comprised of both consciousness and matter. Pure Consciousness or spirit needs a body or a vessel to express itself through. That is where we come in – we are the microcosm of the Divine because we are both consciousness (spirit) and matter (flesh). Divine Consciousness brings together a complex relationship between spirit and matter. So, we all hold the consciousness of the Divine within. We are all embodied Divine Consciousness and can therefore choose to express our divinity while in a body.[1]

The regression of Paul was very eye-opening in that it revealed that Paul, while an ardent, enthusiastic student of Jesus, took on the tough task of taking his teachings into the heart of Rome. Therefore, he had to adapt the teachings and Jesus' life story for people in Rome to accept and adopt those teachings. Paul's intentions were not selfish or mean or vile. His intentions were motivated by his enthusiasm to get the most number of people to adopt the teachings of someone Paul clearly idealized, was inspired by and believed in completely.

In Paul's fervor to get the Romans to accept Jesus and make

his teachings relevant, he elevated Jesus to a divine status. Jesus became the Son of God – thereby achieving the status of a God, like all the other pagan gods that the Romans believed in. Due to their cultural conditioning, if the Romans believed that Jesus was just a man – and a Jew at that – they would not have paid his teachings any notice as they would not have been relevant for them. So Paul made him a divine being to proselytize his teachings.

Paul also martyred Jesus, as the benevolent, loving divine being who sacrificed his mortal body for the salvation of people. This of course is in direct competition with the wrathful, vengeful polytheistic Roman gods who demanded sacrifices from people to prove their devotion. Paul portrayed a revolutionary loving God in Jesus to make him and the essence of love in his teachings widely embraced and accepted.

The regression of James, the brother of Jesus, also showed that he was another who had a very difficult role to play.

Jesus and James were thoroughly Jewish in their beliefs and practices. However, they wanted to break away from what they perceived to be the power struggles, corruption and control wrought by the other Jewish sects, the Sadducees and Pharisees. So Jesus, who was believed to be the true Messiah of Israel, along with John the Baptist, popularized a different set of spiritual teachings, while still incorporating the laws and beliefs of the Jewish custom. This grew to become the Judeo-Christian Church.

Many scholars regard James as the unsung hero of Christianity – the successor that Jesus chose, the true leader of Jesus' original Church after his death.

When Jesus died, after a brief sojourn in Britannia, James led and held together this original Church, in Jerusalem. At this time, there were various factions within the Judeo-Christian movement, splintering the Church. There were those holding on to the Pharisaic beliefs, arguing about how much of the Law and the Jewish customs they had to observe. There were also the Zealots, who wanted to be rid of the Romans and the Gentiles, and establish the true Messiah of Israel. James had the unenviable task of holding all the believers of these disparate factions together, in order to stop them from tearing the Church apart. He also had to manage confrontations of this Church with the established priesthood of the Pharisees, mediate with the Sanhedrin Council, and contend with the burgeoning non-Jewish Gentile Church in Rome.

James chose a novel way to maintain peace and balance within this Church. He became the embodiment of a righteous devotee and follower of Jesus. He diligently followed Jesus' teachings and methods to the letter, which included trying to imbue the message that the Divine Consciousness is within all men and women. If Jesus, a person like anybody else, could tap into his divinity and be a shining inspiration to all, then so can any person. It was a matter of choice, and being empowered to do so, just as James led through his example, choices and actions. This is how James earned his title – James the Righteous – bestowed on him by the followers of the Judeo-Christian Church.

So while Paul fanned the flames of looking for salvation and the Divine Consciousness externally in Jesus and God, James was true to the Essenes' teachings that the Divine Consciousness and salvation they seek are within themselves. From these disparate teachings, two separate Churches grew – the Gentile Church and the Judeo-Christian Church.

In order to build a structure around their beliefs and root their respective Churches to Jesus' teachings, they had many things in common:

1. They both developed and conducted rituals and ceremonies with their followers to help establish a practice. However, each Church attributed different interpretations to what the elements of the practices meant, in line with their respective ideologies.

2. They focused on storytelling to get the message and teachings across.
3. They established organized rules and laws for followers of their Church to adhere to.
4. They established a hierarchy of leadership as the respective movements grew.
5. Neither involved women very much in the leadership and teachings of their churches due to the patriarchal nature of both the Romans and the Jews.

In their fervor of growing and spreading their respective teachings, they broke away from one another. When comparing Judeo-Christianity and Gentile Christianity, the latter can be considered to be more liberal. Paul opened Jesus' teachings to non-Jews, whereas Judeo-Christianity wanted to maintain and observe their orthodox Jewish laws and rituals. In doing so, the Judeo Christians limited access to Jesus' teachings to only those who practiced Jewish law. Gradually, the Gentile and Judeo Christians moved further and further apart due to irreconcilable differences of the interpretation of Jesus' divine status, the meanings of the rituals and, of course, the teachings themselves.

The fall of the Judeo-Christian Church that occurred after the siege of Jerusalem by the Romans in 70CE resulted in the dissolution of the Jerusalem Church and the scattering of those who upheld Jewish Christianity. After which, Gentile Christianity severed any ties with Mother Judaism and based its theology on Paul's teachings as the replacement of the Jewish Law.[2] Marcion, a second-century evangelist, and his followers, the Marcionites, went even further, and removed everything Jewish from the Christian teachings and religion.[3]

According to Gardner, in the fourth century, under the influence of new leadership from Rome under Bishop Sylvester, Greek bishops had been appointed in Jerusalem, Antioch, Ephesus and Alexandria to continue to dislodge the Desposyni or bloodline heir from office. A revised history of Christianity was constructed, which claimed that it was St. Peter who was asked to lead the Church, to claim a figurative Apostolic Succession for its Popes instead of a Desposynic Succession. In 318CE, a delegation of eight men, representing the Jewish Church in Jerusalem, journeyed to Rome to object to this. They claimed that the Church should be centered in Jerusalem, and not Rome, and that the Bishop of Jerusalem needed to be the true hereditary Desposynos, just as Bishop Clement had recognized years earlier. They also demanded the reintroduction of Jewish customs. However, the then Bishop Sylvester dismissed their claims by claiming that this version of the teaching of Jesus had been superseded, and that the Mother Church was to be in Rome, which was more amenable to the imperial requirement of that time.[4] Thus, Gentile Christianity severed any ties with Jesus' humanness and his familial lineage.

It cannot be stressed enough that it is because of his untiring efforts that Paul laid the foundation for the growth of the largest religion in the world to date. Virtually all forms of modern-day Christianity go back to Paul's Church. Victorious in the theological conflicts in the second and third centuries, the modified and advanced form of Gentile-Christianity then decided what the "correct" Christian perspective was, who could exercise authority over Christian belief and practice, and which forms of Christianity to marginalize, set aside and destroy.[5] Furthermore, they rewrote the history of controversy, making it appear that there had not been much of a conflict at all. They claimed that their views were truly those of Jesus, his Apostles and the majority of Christians, and that other scriptural texts represented small splinter groups deliberately deceiving people.[6]

The victory of this so-called "true" Christian perspective, which scholars refer to as proto-orthodox Christianity, led to the formation of the New Testament. The Church has not always had the New Testament. According to Bart Ehrman, the books that came to be collected into the sacred canon were written by a variety of authors over a period of sixty or seventy years. Scholars do not have the "originals" of any of the books that came to be included in the New Testament. "Most of the surviving copies are hundreds of years removed from the originals themselves," he claims.[7] Furthermore, many theological scholars have abandoned the apostolic authorities of Matthew, Mark, Luke and John, and recognize that the books were written by well-educated but unknown Greek-speaking Christians during the latter half of the first century.[8] Over centuries, these 27 books went through a rigorous process, meeting selected criteria and agreement by the Roman Catholic, Eastern Orthodox and Protestant traditions, to be included into the New Testament. While most churches agreed on its contours in the fifth century, the canon of the New Testament was ratified by widespread consensus at the Council of Trent in the mid-sixteenth century. Even though the Council of Trent was a Roman Catholic council, binding only to Roman Catholics, these 27 books were already considered Scripture.[9]

There is also the broader politically historical implication of proto-orthodoxy, which led to its growth to be the largest religion on the planet. Since the inception of the religion in Rome by Paul, Christians have been subject to local persecution, as we saw in Greg's regression. However, this grew worse in the mid-third century. Paul's Christians refused to worship and sacrifice to the pagan gods. As a result they were blamed for any disaster that happened – drought, famine, economic and military setbacks, as well as disease. So, in 303CE, emperors Diocletian and Maximian released an official, empire-wide attempt to eliminate the religion. The persecution failed to force the majority of Christians to recant, and by 313CE official toleration for Christians was pronounced, as people were granted freedom of religious choice.[10]

The Emperor at the time was Constantine, and in 312CE he

began to attribute his military and political victories to the god of the Christians, and began to identify himself as a Christian. In 325CE, he called the Council of Nicaea, the first ecumenical council, where bishops from around the world were brought together to establish a consensus on major points of faith and practice. Constantine supported all decisions made by this council, and it is speculated by historians that he saw in the Christian Church a way to bring unity to his empire. As a result of the favors Constantine poured on the Church, conversion to the faith became prevalent. By the start of the fourth century, five to seven percent of the population of the Roman Empire were Christians. By the end of that century, Christianity had become the religion of choice for half the empire. It was Emperor Theodosius I who made Roman Christianity, based on the Gentile Church, the official religion of the state, and the Bishop of Rome the ultimate religious authority.[11]

One of the greatest tragedies of this story is that the common deeper essence of both James' and Paul's teachings got lost as people, politics and power got in the way, in pursuit of establishing their individual selves as part of the "true" and "rightful" Church. At the end of the day, both Churches shared the internal essence of Jesus' teachings – Love. However, the separation between the two Churches occurred due to external factors, including the hierarchy of leadership, differing views about ideologies, customs, rituals and ceremonies, and teachings. A series of political maneuverings, persecutions, inquisitions and forced conversions successfully dimmed the light on the rich, diverse teachings of the original Church as it was at the beginning.

Collaboration became competition.
Wholeness separated into Duality.
Pride overruled Hearts.
Egos prevailed.
Love forgotten.

In the words of Eckhart Tolle, "All religions are equally false and equally true, depending on how you use them. You can use them in the service of the ego, or you can use them in the service of the Truth. If you believe only your religion is the Truth, you are using it in the service of the ego. Used in such a way, religion becomes ideology and creates an illusory sense of superiority as well as division and conflict between people. In the service of the Truth, religious teachings represent signposts or maps left behind by awakened humans to assist you in spiritual awakening... that is to say, in becoming free of identification with form."[12]

Source, God or Consciousness has no name, apart from the ones we have given, yet so many of us believe through our faith, our intuition, our gut feel. The best ways to determine the authenticity of the claims in this book, or any other, is to ask – does it feel right for you? Do you resonate with the accounts? Do you resonate with the messages presented? How did the energy of the book make you feel?

The feeling, when something is in true resonance, creates a vibration and in remembering that vibration, there is just Joy and Peace.

It is up to you to decide.

The Methodology

While it is interesting debating the theological and spiritual elements of the stories that have emerged in the book, it is imperative to examine the methodology used to get this information.

Are these memories genuine?

While the majority of past-life regressions take clients back to ordinary lives, occasionally some souls go back to their genuine past life of people who are considered famous, like James, the Brother of Jesus, or Paul the Evangelist.

One question that is asked is why didn't the soul of Paul, for example, be incarnated as another great soul in this life – e.g. the current Pope. Why is it Greg? I then ask back, why can't Joe Blow have been James, or Sheila Smith have been Paul the Evangelist? After all, this book has shown that the biblical characters were all ordinary people, doing extraordinary things under extraordinary circumstances. Also, the hierarchy of the evolved soul is judged by our ego selves – in the realms of the spirit and divine, there seems to be more equality and mutual respect between the souls.

There are souls who have genuinely not experienced these biblical lives, yet visited them in regressions. There could be several explanations for this, as suggested below:

Collective Unconscious

In 1916, Carl Jung introduced the concept of the "collective unconscious" in his article "The Structure of the Unconscious." This is an idea that we all share instincts and Consciousness from collective memories of the past which we can all tap into. He went further and talked about it containing "archetypes." They are aspects of basic human behavior and situations that are explained simply to give meaning to the generalized instincts and behavior of people. Jung says that the collective unconscious does not develop individually but is inherited. The collective unconscious is distinguished from Freudian's "personal unconscious," where the latter represents an individual's personal repressed memories.[13]

In an altered state, regressees are able to tap into both their own personal unconscious and also into the collective unconscious. Sometimes the regressees tap into the past-life experiences stored in the collective and re-experience a life as if it was their own. Why? It depends on the individual – for some, it is for their own soul's growth and development to learn different aspects of emotions; for others it could be to just experience and gain insights on the archetype they are exploring.

How do we tell the difference between lives from the collective unconscious and genuine past lives, almost from the personal unconscious? It is very difficult to create an emotional reaction from the collective. It's almost like having an emotional reaction from watching an emotional scene in the movies versus actually experiencing the emotional scene. The more intense the emotion and body sensations, the more likely it is to be a personal memory.

Projection of Therapists' Thoughts

The experience of direct communication between two minds has been reported frequently. Sometimes we do it on a daily basis – knowing who's on the other end of the phone before picking it up (before the days of caller ID), thinking of someone and suddenly getting a text from them, for example.

These days, quantum physics has taught us that nothing is solid, and that everything is continuously vibrating energy. Quantum physicists refer to this as string theory – when physicists have broken down matter to the tiniest particle thus far, they theorize that it is just energy that vibrates so quickly, it behaves like string.

Based on these quantum theories, our thoughts are also energy vibrating. Whatever thoughts we choose, they vibrate at a certain frequency that is drawn to and attracts elements (including other thoughts) that vibrate at the same frequency. This can manifest in different ways in people's behaviors including thought transference.

One of the first "thought-transference" tests between distant hypnotized subjects was conducted in 1883 by British physicist Sir William Barrett, where he examined the correlation between what thoughts hypnotized subjects at a distance were sending and receiving. His experiment was reported to be successful and encouraged others to investigate on either side of the Atlantic.[14]

People are particularly susceptible to thought transference when their minds are in the alpha state, which is the state they are in under hypnosis. If the therapist has preconceived ideas and notions about the subject or story that the regressee is even beginning to tell them, then the therapist can inadvertently project these thoughts and the regressee can pick it up and reflect those thoughts back to the therapist as if it's their own experience.

Could I have transferred my thoughts to these regressees? Firstly, I have been trained to suspend judgement and not have any preconceived thoughts as a regression therapist.

Secondly, this project needed the regression of two souls, who have no knowledge of one another, with different levels of individual biblical knowledge. The only link between them was myself, who was born and brought up a Hindu, then became an atheist before moving on to the spiritual path. I had no prior knowledge of the biblical characters, story and context until I began to regress the subjects for this series of books. I had no prior knowledge to transfer to my subjects in the first place. All my research was done at the end of collecting all the accounts from clients to minimize bias during the sessions on my part.

Reflection of Souls' Deepest Desires

Sometimes the soul can manifest their deepest desires to experience or assume the role of one they have idolized for many years, or in this case, centuries. This can then be played out in the client's psyche and take the form of having experienced the life. Of course, under this topic, conscious mind confabulations are possible. The souls are merely remembering something they have read, seen or heard. The desire to assume the identity is so great that the mind creates scenarios and experiences that feed into the regressee's own desires. Even though I have only regressed one person to the life of Paul the Evangelist, for example, I have colleagues who have regressed multiple people who have experienced the lives of Mary Magdalene and Jesus Christ.

How can we tell the difference between a confabulated story and a genuine memory recollection? Again, it is the intensity of emotions and body sensations felt. Deep emotions and spontaneous body sensations and physical movements cannot be imagined – only recollected.

Cryptomnesia

Cryptomnesia is the condition where a forgotten memory returns to someone, who believes it is something new and original. It is a memory bias whereby a person may falsely recall experiencing a memory as if it were a new inspiration. So some critics could say that these regressees may have seen, heard or read accounts of the story somewhere else and, under hypnosis, regurgitated what they had received as second-hand information, as opposed to experiencing genuine memories.

While it is feasible that that's happened, this argument does not take into consideration two vital aspects of this methodology:

a. There were two people who experienced these lives. These clients had minimal, if any, connection to one another – and they do not discuss matters of private regression sessions with one another. They also had very limited prior information about the lives that they recounted.

b. The accounts included many tiny details that the clients would normally not have access to in second-hand accounts.

Name Anomalies

In collecting information from the regressions for this book, one of the most glaring challenges was the anomaly of names, given for the same character by the different regressees, and frankly the historical references. How do these affect the validity of the information gained?

When we, in our current lives, recall details that we have watched in films, read in books, or even our own memories from ten years ago, our strongest memories are the emotional situations that we are in. Names and things of that nature are far less important. For example, when you think back to your childhood, you are likely to remember the most highly-charged emotional memory of your seventh birthday party, but you may not be able to clearly remember the names of all the people who attended. Confusion is created when one tries to get several people to name the people who were at that seventh birthday party, therefore creating errors. Access to the names is hard in regression, typically because a different part of the brain is being accessed, and the regressees then consciously second-guess the name.

The same applies to past-life recall. Soul memories are comprised of the major events that occurred, the emotionally inspiring events, positive emotions and negative emotions. Those are the ones that are remembered in more detail.

Final Thoughts

Two thousand years ago marked the end of the Age of Aries, and the start of the Age of Pisces. It was a time of upheaval as the New Consciousness brought about change and challenged status quo. It was a time where cultural conditioning and belief systems were being challenged. It was during this time that Jesus, his teachings and his followers emerged with their controversial new teachings, which challenged the established powers of both the Roman and Jewish establishments. They challenged both the Jewish Laws and Ways of Being, as well as the rituals of polytheistic worship by the Romans. Those who wanted change were persecuted.

Today – two thousand years later – we are moving from the Age of Pisces to the Age of Aquarius. We are again confronted with the same changes and upheaval. However, now, as we now shift into the New Consciousness, we are in a position to move past the superficial grains, and look into the deeper layers of truth. We can now choose to look beyond what separated both branches of the Church – and go back to the core of Jesus' message. We can move from the Duality of which is right or wrong, true or false – to the wholeness of the essence of the teachings – Love and Oneness.

Duality is when two are set up in opposition and separate in some essential, irrevocable way. For example Good and Bad, Feminine and Masculine, Right and Wrong, True and Fake, Spirit and Body. "Non-duality" is actually a translation of the Sanskrit word "Advaita" from the Upanishads, which simply points to the essential Oneness of life, a wholeness and unity which exists here and now, prior to any apparent separation. There is only one universal essence, one reality. Oneness is all there is – and we are included.[15] It is only through love that we can access Oneness.

Two thousand years ago, there was a shift in the Web of Consciousness. Paul the Evangelist worked ceaselessly to lead a shift in the belief systems and cultural conditioning from the fear-based beliefs of the many vengeful Gods to the one loving God who resides externally. It cannot be denied how much comfort people got from the teachings perpetuated by the Gentile Church. Sure there was plenty of conflict and persecution as well, but there was also comfort.

Today, at the rise of the new vibrations, we have a choice. We can choose to stay in the belief of the one external loving God… or we could incorporate the knowing of the Divine Consciousness within – the original message of Jesus. Real divinity lies within love. Love lies within all of us. If, as James claimed and showed by example, Jesus was human who embraced the divine within, then so can we all.

As Mia concludes her regression:

> Mia: Now we are coming into a different period – a shift in Consciousness – where more people can open themselves to this spiritual love; where they can attain this God [Divine] Consciousness. Goddess Consciousness. Oneness. There have always been pockets that have carried this message in many faiths, but now there is an energy shift and an awareness where more people can feel the vibration and where more people can gain the knowledge, and the knowledge is to attain a feeling of love. One is able to vibrate one's energy level in peaceful accordance with the rest of the universe. This is what some religions call enlightenment. God [Divine] Consciousness. Oneness. We talk about God being within and without. It is around us and within us, because the illusion of separateness is an illusion. And this illusion falls away when we are able to energize at the same vibration. If we really want to gain balance, we must balance the God with the Goddess. We must combine the duality to create Oneness. Whole. It's not to be read, but to be practiced.

This sentiment is echoed by Jeffrey Butz, that people of all faiths can all surely agree that God was in Jesus as surely as God is within us all. This is something that was part of the foundation of James' ministry. Unfortunately, it was lost in Gentile Christianity when it lost the full humanity of Jesus and when it declared other ministries, including the Jewish Ministry, a heresy. However, since the middle of the last century, archaeological findings such as the Nag Hammadi Library and the Dead Sea Scrolls have brought to light the understanding of the common heritage of the Jews, Christians and Muslims, as well as a different perspective of Jesus' teachings that is not found in today's Church.[16] Maybe this is so that we can all be open to the Spiritual Love of all and Divine Consciousness within and around during this shift to the new consciousness.

If we all hold Spiritual Love and Divine Consciousness within, there is no separation between one another, and between us and God. There is only Oneness. Within the Oneness, there is even more love. In embracing our own divinity, we can rise and shine like the radiant beings that we are.

We have the choice.

Appendix

Past-Life Regression – The Process

Past-life regression is a technique that uses hypnosis to recover memories of past lives or incarnations. It is typically undertaken either in pursuit of a spiritual experience, or in a psychotherapeutic setting to resolve trauma or related difficulties in the current life.

The first step of guiding clients into past lives is to allow them to go into a deep state of relaxation – also known as hypnosis. There are so many misconceptions and definitions of hypnosis – but our focus here is therapeutic hypnosis. It is a process of deep relaxation that shifts a person's brain waves into the alpha/delta state. This is a similar state to when a person is meditating or is in deep sleep. In this state of focused attention, the client can access the subconscious mind a lot more easily than in the normal state.

Why do we need to access the subconscious mind? One of the main jobs of our subconscious mind is to store everything that has ever happened in a huge memory bank. Its capacity is virtually unlimited. Under hypnosis, older people can often remember, sometimes with perfect clarity, events from fifty years before, and even beyond their current life. It is by hypnosis that we tap into this inexhaustible memory bank to gather information needed for the session.

How do we get in touch with the subconscious? Using the analogy of the car – in our normal wakeful state, the conscious is driving the car, and the subconscious is in the passenger seat. Under hypnosis, the conscious mind is so relaxed, it drifts to the passenger side, and the subconscious mind takes over driving the car. Having more access to the subconscious, we can work with the deeper part of a person's psyche. The function of the subconscious mind is to store and retrieve data. The subconscious memory is virtually perfect. It is the conscious recall that comes into question. Just to add – the conscious mind that is in the passenger seat is not asleep. It is just relaxed. So, it is aware of everything that is happening around it, and what is being said. It is just so relaxed, it does not filter and interfere with the flow of information from the subconscious.

Have you ever been so deeply engrossed in an activity that you lost track of time? How about when you drive: do you sometimes get to the end destination without being aware of how you have got there? In these states, you are experiencing light hypnosis. Athletes, musicians and artists regularly enter this state while they are performing. A common term for this is being "in the zone."

Regression and PLR Therapy

The function of our subconscious mind is to store and retrieve data. Its job is to ensure that we respond in exactly the way we are programmed and it makes everything we say and do fit a pattern consistent with our programmed beliefs and patterns. It makes our behavior fit a pattern consistent with our emotionalized thoughts, hopes and desires.

The subconscious mind has what is called a homeostatic impulse for our basic survival. It keeps our body temperature at 37 degrees Celsius (98 degrees Fahrenheit), just as it keeps you breathing regularly and keeps your heart beating at a certain rate, without you even consciously thinking about it.

Our subconscious mind also practices homeostasis in our mental realm, by keeping us thinking and acting in a manner consistent with what we have done and said in the past. All our habits of thinking and acting are stored in our subconscious mind. It has memorized all our comfort zones and it works to keep us in them. Our subconscious mind causes us to feel emotionally and physically uncomfortable whenever we attempt to do anything new or different, or to change any of our established patterns of behavior.

In the hypnotic state, there is direct access to the subconscious, giving us the direct route to the source of our lives' programming. The source could be in our past life, current life or both. Therapeutically, transforming at this level thus gives us the fastest and most decisive point at which to change our programming, and as a result, change our lives.

To guide someone into a hypnotic state, I first ask them to make themselves comfortable – either in a reclining or lying position. With their eyes closed, I ask them to focus on their breathing and guide them to relax physically. Then, using my voice and certain words, I help them get into a state of both mental relaxation and alertness. As they move more and more inward, they leave external distractions outside, and slowly their brain wave shifts from the beta state to the alpha state – whereby they are able to access their subconscious, thereby accessing deeper and suppressed memories, either of the current life or their past life.

Past Life Regression Therapy works with the content of past experiences and extends the timeline to allow past-life stories to emerge. Clients are guided back and encouraged to relive and resolve the conflicts from the past that have been previously inaccessible to their Consciousness. Often these are experiences which are still influencing and distorting their mental and emotional stability.

In regression therapy, other psychotherapeutic models like psychodrama and gestalt therapy are incorporated within the sessions. Also, in most cases, the sessions extend into the current life, especially resolution through inner-child work, where the source issue normally first manifests in the current life. There is no doubt that many people have benefited from and been healed by Past Life Regression Therapy. This is not just based on my experience as a regression therapist, but that of the many pioneers and practitioners of this form of therapy.

Areas where regression therapy has had proven results

include unexplainable pains (including migraine, phantom pain syndrome), deep-seated emotional patterns (including feeling disempowered, depression), relationship problems, addiction, and also physical challenges that have an emotional issue behind them (including irritable bowel syndrome, inability to conceive).

In the therapeutic setting, it is not important for the therapist to prove that the past-life story is real. The most important thing that therapists focus on is using the experience that the client is undergoing to heal a deep-seated emotional challenge that has been plaguing them.

Spiritual Investigation via Past Life Regression

For this book, however, the sessions conducted were not so much therapeutic but information-gathering. The method used to collect details was therefore slightly different from the one used for conducting therapeutic sessions. It is still integral to work with the clients in the hypnotic state – that does not change. However, there is a refined way of questioning to ensure that the person still remains in the experience and the conscious mind of the person is not engaged.

Let's use gathering names as an example. In the therapeutic sense, the main thread that is followed is the emotional pattern, and experiences relevant to the pattern. The name of the past-life character is not required, for it does not affect the therapeutic experience of the client. Only when the name comes up spontaneously do we take note of it for future reference, if relevant.

However, in the case of this book, it was important to get information like names, dates, names of places, for the purposes of research, cross-referencing and to verify the validity of the stories that emerged. Asking the person under hypnosis, "What is your name?" will more often than not take the person out of the experience and into the conscious mind, which is not ideal as they may access the information from books or the Internet as opposed to the experience. What I do instead is, when they are at relevant points of the story, ask them, "How are you addressed?" This then keeps the person in the experience of the memory and gets a more authentic response. However, therein lies another problem: how they are addressed may not be the actual name (e.g. Jesus may have been addressed as teacher, son, brother, father, husband, or by a nickname by respective people) and so it was difficult to maintain the consistency of names especially. The way we tried to overcome that was to ask the person at multiple significant points in their regression, "How are you addressed?" and use the "majority rules" principle to then determine the name.

Age was another difficult detail to obtain. Even in our current life, we normally remember the experience, and we get slightly fuzzy about the age we were when it happened. The same principle applies for past-life recollection. For this we then ask questions like, "At what point of your life does this occur? Are you a child, a teenager, an adult or an elderly person?" Then we try as much as possible to home in on a reasonably small age range.

In both instances (for information-gathering or therapeutic purposes), the most authentic experiences elicit deep emotional responses. So for example, when using the torture of Jesus, most people we regressed felt deep emotions, and expressed them quite visually and audibly… by either crying, by softening their voice, or through silence, as they tried to manage the emotions in order to speak. Experiencing deep emotions as a reaction to events is one of the ways that we determine the authenticity of the experience.

Using the example of a child riding a bicycle for the first time as a trigger, let us just think about this. If we do not have a child, and we witness a child riding for the first time, our imagination is triggered at how we think the child feels and we may have a small smile on our face. However, if we have our own children, and we see another child riding for the first time, this will trigger a memory of our own child riding a bike, and the delight we feel will be far deeper and more intense because there is a personal experience we can relate to.

The same applies to past-life experiences. If the experience is made up by the conscious mind, there will be very little to no emotions displayed by the person. However, if they are experiencing a memory via the subconscious mind, then the emotions they exhibit are, more likely than not, deep, intense and totally authentic.

Intense emotion can also explain spontaneous recall of past lives, or any repressed memories in the current life. When there is a trigger of a highly-charged emotion, the associated memory will immediately be drawn up to the conscious awareness. For example, I had a friend who was terrified of the dark. She could not stay alone in the dark without becoming breathless and getting a panic attack. One day, she came back home late from work, fumbled around to turn the lights on and felt something furry (her cat) brush against her ankle. She immediately had a vision of herself being a man struggling with a giant bear, feeling intense fear and anxiety. When she came to me for a session, she saw herself as a burly hunter, who was so intently following his prey, he did not realize it had gone dark. So, he went to seek shelter in a dark cave, and stumbled on something quite furry and fell. The next thing he knew, there was an almighty roar, and a flash of white teeth, and he was mauled by a bear. In a disassociated state, he realized the cave was home to a mother bear and two cubs. She saw him as a threat and attacked. My friend brought that fear of darkness into her current life, not understanding it until the feeling of fur on her ankle in the darkness spontaneously triggered the intense emotion and brought the memory to her conscious awareness.

Memories can be triggered by positive emotions as well. Say you had a fabulous relationship with your grandmother, who always smelled of lavender, and every time you saw her you were filled with joy. She passes away when you are three. One day, in your thirties, you happen to chance upon a lavender garden and, as you take a deep breath, you are filled with joy and you see your grandmother's face. The scent of lavender is the trigger of the emotion and the memory.

The same principle applies to a past-life memory. If the experience was so deep and triggered such intense emotions (e.g. rape, torture) a subtle stimulus could trigger the same intense emotion, bypassing all rational filters, and bringing up the memory from the past life.

Skeptics

There is no end to what skeptics say against past-life regression. One of the arguments is that the use of hypnosis and suggestive questions make the subject particularly likely to hold distorted or false memories. They claim that the source of the memories is more likely cryptomnesia and confabulations that combine experiences, knowledge, imagination and suggestion or guidance from the hypnotist, rather than recall of a previous existence. Once created, the memories are indistinguishable from memories based on events that occurred during the subject's life.

There is also the assumption made that subjects undergoing past-life regression indicate that a belief in reincarnation and suggestions by the hypnotist are the two most important factors regarding the contents of memories reported.

However, let's look at it this way. The work of Dr. Ian Stevenson, Carol Bowman (in her book *Children's Past Lives*), and many others since, who have documented past lives of children is a strong indication of the existence and authenticity of past lives that has nothing to do with prior knowledge via mass media, suggestions by the researcher or even a belief in reincarnation.

While there are some memories reported during past-life regression that have been investigated and revealed historical inaccuracies, there have also been some where the information is fully in line with actual historical findings. I would ask the skeptics that if someone gets a memory detail of their childhood wrong, does this mean that all their childhood memories are unreal? If a detail in the past life is wrong, does that mean all the past-life memories are wrong? And also, who is to say that the research is more accurate than the past-life story? Historical research is normally based on intelligent deductions of physical evidence found and also stories told – but deductions nevertheless do not make an absolute truth.

Also, psychologically speaking, what we experience is a matter of perception. We will most likely retain the perception that has had the biggest impact on us. For example, let's say my husband and I went to the Formula 1 Grand Prix. The biggest impression that I had was the loud sounds every time the cars drove past, and the searing heat. If you asked me details later, I would not be able to remember the color of the cars or the names of drivers. My husband, whose background is engineering, was more interested in the speed, the corner turns and horsepower. If you asked him, he would not remember the heat, pollution and loud noises, but would give an enthusiastic monologue about the details and mechanics of the cars, as well as the driving strategies.

As for our book, some of the people we regressed had prior knowledge of the commonly told story of Jesus, preached by the Church, and some people went in with very little, if any, information. During the process, I made every attempt to keep the primary questions as open as possible, in the hope that at this level at least I would not be leading the subjects. During the session, the most asked questions were, "What happens next?" and "Tell me more about that" – to allow the clients to remember the experience. Even the entry into the experience was very open and did not presuppose the entry into the characters of the story. It was left open for them to experience the life authentically.

Moreover, as mentioned, all the regressees had spontaneously regressed to these biblical past lives through private therapy or as students on the course prior to regressing them for the book.

Another phenomenon that occurs in past-life regression that is very difficult for skeptics to challenge is xenoglossia – or the ability to speak in languages that have not been acquired by natural means in this lifetime. The phenomenon encompasses cases where the subjects speak languages to which they hadn't had any form of exposure. For example, someone has the ability to speak Telegu when they lived in a part of the world that has no relation to Telegu, nor has the person ever studied it, or read books referring to it, or conversed with someone who spoke it, or had any other form of exposure to it.

Dr. Ian Stevenson was one of the most respected academicians in the United States. He carried out specialized research into xenoglossy, and his book *Xenoglossy* (Stevenson, 1974) is one of the leading scientific studies in this area. In it, he documents a study he made of a 37-year-old American woman. Under hypnosis she experienced a complete change of voice and personality into that of a male. She spoke fluently in the Swedish language – a language she did not speak or understand when in the normal state of consciousness.

Dr. Stevenson's direct involvement with this case lasted more than eight years. The study involved linguists and other experts and scientists who meticulously investigated every alternative explanation. Fraud was ruled out for a number of substantive reasons which Stevenson outlines in his study. The subject and her physician husband were thoroughly investigated. They were under extreme and continuous close scrutiny, did not want publicity and agreed to the publication of the study only if their names were changed to protect their privacy. Both the husband and wife were considered by their local community to be honest and decent and their behavior exemplary. Certainly there was no motive for personal profit.

What makes xenoglossy so important for Past Life Regression Therapy is the fact that it offers direct validation to reincarnation and past-life regression. Often, when we regress our subject, the subject tends to stay skeptical. Even if they see things, their conscious mind so dominates their subconscious mind that they assume it must have been their imagination as opposed to a past-life memory. However, if the subject starts speaking in a language they did not know, it instils a lot more faith in the experience. It also provides a more intimate and intense experiential reliving of the past life, which is tough to dispute.

In April 2013, the Society for Medical Advance and Research with Regression Therapy (SMAR-RT) was founded. SMAR-RT is an international group specializing in past-life and regression-therapy research, and led by medical doctors from all over the world who share the vision to bring about the integration of complementary and holistic approaches into medicine. SMAR-RT is focused on conducting numerous medical research projects to gauge the effectiveness of Past Life Regression Therapy as a healing modality. These research projects are led and conducted by medical doctors and will be scientifically and medically measuring the effects of the therapy.

With regards to skeptics – at the end of the day, there is not one piece of evidence or research done that proves that past lives categorically do not exist or that regression therapy absolutely does not work. Until there are some, this leaves the many doors of possibilities open – including the existence of past lives.

Websites

For more information about past-life regression, please refer to the following websites:

Society for Medical Advance and Research with Regression Therapy (SMAR-RT)

This is a special-interest group in the Earth Association of

Regression Therapy of researchers led by medical doctors who share the vision to bring about the integration of complementary and holistic approaches into medicine. It conducts medical research using past-life and regression therapy and promotes regression therapy to the medical profession and the wider public. Through research, it also contributes to enhancing the effectiveness of regression therapy.

Website: http://www.smar-rt.com

Spiritual Regression Therapy Association (SRTA)

This is an international association of past-life, regression and life-between-lives therapists who respect the spiritual nature of their clients. They are professionally trained by the Past Life Regression Academy to international standards and work to a code of ethics that respects the clients' welfare.

Website: http://www.regressionassociation.com

The Past Life Regression Academy (PLRA)

The academy specializes in past-life and regression therapy, past-life regression, life-between-lives regression and hypnosis training in Europe, Asia, India, South Africa, Mexico, the United States and Australia. It awards internationally accredited qualifications enabling its graduates to belong to independent professional associations, including the Earth Association of Regression Therapy. The academy training director is Andy Tomlinson, a graduate in psychology, registered psychotherapist, certified past-life regression therapist, international trainer and author in this field.

Website: http://www.regressionacademy.com

Books

Healing the Eternal Soul, Andy Tomlinson, From the Heart Press

Turning the Hourglass: Children's Passage Through Traumas and

Past Lives, Christine Alisa, AuthorHouse

Between Lives Spiritual Regression

In 1994, Dr. Michael Newton caused a stir through the publication of his book *Journey of Souls*. This ground-breaking book documented ten years of research that he had undertaken to navigate souls through the between-life stages, where they can find out the plan that they had agreed to for their current life. This process can be incredibly insightful and poignant, as it gives the regressee a spiritual look at different events, relationships and circumstances of their lives, the pleasant and the not so pleasant, which they then gain a deeper understanding of and appreciation for. It has been known to be a life-changing experience. Since then, more than 15,000 successful between-lives sessions have been conducted worldwide by therapists who have been trained in this process.

Part of that process is called the Eternal Now – where clients communicate with their guides and other evolved Spirits of Light, to gain clarification and insights into specific areas of their life that they are having trouble with in their current existence.

The first step employed to get the best possible results is to make the intent to access the right vibrational frequency or spiritual being before putting the client into hypnosis. I also make sure that the communication will be for the highest good of the people involved. This is done bearing in mind that we are working with really subtle energies and making the right energetic connection is important. It is like dialing the right number on the telephone.

I also conscientiously clear any unwanted intrusive energies that could interfere with the channeling. This is to ensure that the energetic pathway to meeting our intent is clear. Once communication is established via hypnosis, normally the deeper the hypnosis the better, the question-and-answer session can commence; but all throughout, I am very vigilant of any intrusive energy, and will keep topping up the protection around the session. This is important to maintain throughout the entire session.

Once the session ends, we politely give thanks to all who helped us and I bring the client out of hypnosis slowly and gently, as they would have been quite deep in when this occurs.

A question I get asked frequently is, "Can anyone access these high vibrational spaces?" I refer back to the fact that there have been more than 15,000 people that have accessed higher frequencies during life-between-lives sessions, and many more who access them spontaneously or by intent in addition to that. If all these people can do it, I believe so can anyone, if they are open and trust the subtle energies, and the steps outlined above are followed.

Extra References on Between Lives Spiritual Regression

Exploring the Eternal Soul, Andy Tomlinson, From the Heart Press
Journey of Souls, Michael Newton, Llewellyn Publications, US
Destiny of Souls, Michael Newton, Llewellyn Publications, US

Bibliography

Books

Aslan, Reza (2013) *Zealot: The Life and Times of Jesus of Nazareth*. New York, NY: Random House

Butz, Jeffrey J. (2005) *The Brother of Jesus, and the Lost Teachings of Christianity*. Rochester, VT: Inner Traditions

Ehrman, Bart D. (2003) *Lost Christianities: The Battles for Scripture and the Faiths We Never Knew*. New York, NY: Oxford University Press

Ehrman, Bart D. (2003) *Lost Scriptures: Books That Did Not Make It into the New Testament*. New York, NY: Oxford University Press

Ehrman, Bart D. (2014) *How Jesus Became God: The Exaltation of a Jewish Preacher from Galilee*. New York, NY: HarperOne, Harper Collins Publisher

Ehrman, Bart D. (2016) *Jesus Before the Gospels: How the Earliest Christians Remembered, Changed and Invented Their Stories of the Savior*. New York, NY: HarperOne, Harper Collins Publisher

Elder, Isabel Hill (1999) *Joseph of Arimathea*, 10th Edition. UK: Glastonbury Abbey Shop

Gardner, Laurence (2005) *The Magdalene Legacy: The Jesus and Mary Bloodline Conspiracy*. San Francisco: Weiser Books

Gardner, Laurence (2008) *The Grail Enigma: The Hidden Heirs of Jesus and Mary Magdalene*. London: Harper Element

Jowett, George F. (2011) *The Drama of the Lost Disciples*. UK: The Covenant Publishing Company Ltd

Jung, Carl (1991) *The Archetypes and the Collective Unconscious*. Translated by RFC Hull. Princeton: Bollingen Series

Kumarasingham, Reena (2018) *Shrouded Truth: Biblical Revelations Through Past Life Journeys*. Wiltshire, UK: From the Heart Press

Lash, John Lamb (2006) *Not In His Image: Gnostic Vision, Sacred Ecology and the Future of Belief*. White River Junction, VT: Chelsea Green Publishing

Malachi, Tau (2006) *St. Mary Magdalene: The Gnostic Tradition of the Holy Bride*. Woodbury, Minnesota: Llewellyn Worldwide

Radin, D. (2009) *The Conscious Universe: The Scientific Truth of Psychic Phenomena*. New York: HarperOne

Tomlinson, Andy (2005) *Healing the Eternal Soul*. UK: From the Heart Press

Documentary

"Jesus, The Rebel?" *Jesus Conspiracies*. The Discovery Channel, Karga Seven Pictures Production Company, US (April 2012)

Websites

Carl Jung, 1939 lecture at the Eranos meeting. Previously retrieved from: <https://carljungdepthpsychology.wordpress.com>

Goldberg, Louis. "The Pharisees: Bad Guys Or…?" <https://jewsforjesus.org/publications/issues/issues-v06-n03/the-pharisees-bad-guys-or/>

Hopkins, Keith. "Murderous Games: Gladiatorial Contests in Ancient Rome." *History Today*, Volume 33, Issue 6, 6 June 1983: <http://www.historytoday.com/keith-hopkins/murderous-games-gladiatorial-contests-ancient-rome>

Jewish Virtual Library. "A Project of AICE; Ancient Jewish History: Pharisees, Sadducees and Essenes": <http://www.jewishvirtuallibrary.org/pharisees-sadducees-and-essenes>

OoCities.org. (Formerly GeoCities.com). Abu Samad, Nayeem Akhtar, MD: <http://www.oocities.org/abusamad/substi.html>

Penner, Todd. "Paul and Acts." *Bible Odyssey*, 2 May 2018: <https://www.bibleodyssey.org/en/people/related-articles/paul-and-acts.aspx>

Quartermaster of the Barque, Dispensing Orthodox Catholic Joy. *The Origins of Mandatory Private Confession in the Catholic Church*, October 30, 2013

Reincarnation After Death? <http://reincarnationafterdeath.

com/why DO people believe/>

Swami Sahajananda (2006) Barnabas Tiburtius: <http://www.livingspark.net>

Tabor, James. "Ebionites & Nazarenes: Tracking the Original Followers of Jesus." *Taborblog, Religion Matters from the Bible to the Modern World*, 29 December 2015: <https://jamestabor.com/ebionites-nazarenes-tracking-the-original-followers-of-jesus/>

Theopedia. "Pauline theology": <https://www.theopedia.com/pauline-theology>

Tilghman, J. "Christ Consciousness for the Christian," 2 March 2013: <www.spiritofthescripture.com>

Wikipedia contributors. "Ancient Israelite cuisine." Wikipedia, The Free Encyclopedia: <https://en.wikipedia.org/wiki/Ancient_Israelite_cuisine#Fish>

Wikipedia contributors. "Claudius." Wikipedia, The Free Encyclopedia, 5 June 2017

Wikipedia contributors. "James, brother of Jesus." Wikipedia, The Free Encyclopedia, 29 August 2017, 31 August 2017

Wikipedia contributors. "Jewish Christian." Wikipedia, The Free Encyclopedia, 4 September 2017

Wikipedia contributors. "Josephus." Wikipedia, The Free Encyclopedia, 28 August 2017

Wikipedia contributors. "Halakha." Wikipedia, The Free Encyclopedia, 16 December 2017, 8 January 2018

Wikipedia contributors. "Languages of the Roman Empire." Wikipedia, The Free Encyclopedia, 29 May 2017

Wikipedia contributors. "Paul the Apostle." Wikipedia, The Free Encyclopedia, 6 June 2017

Wikipedia contributors. "Zacchaeus." Wikipedia, The Free Encyclopedia: <https://en.wikipedia.org/wiki/Zacchaeus>

Wikipedia contributors. "Zealots (Judea)." Wikipedia, The Free Encyclopedia, 8 December 2017, 6 January 2018

Notes and References

Introduction

1. Ehrman, Bart D., 2003, *Lost Christianities*, New York: Oxford University Press, p. 27
2. Ehrman, Bart D., 2003, *Lost Christianities*, New York: Oxford University Press, p. 1
3. Ehrman, Bart D., 2003, *Lost Christianities*, New York: Oxford University Press, p. 4
4. Butz, Jeffrey J., 2005, *The Brother of Jesus*, Vermont: Inner Traditions, p. 10
5. Butz, Jeffrey J., 2005, *The Brother of Jesus*, Vermont: Inner Traditions, p. 15
6. Gardner, Laurence, 2005, *The Magdalene Legacy*, San Francisco: Weiser Books, p. 28
7. Ehrman, Bart D., 2014, *How Jesus Became God*, New York: HarperOne, p. 214
8. Ehrman, Bart D., 2016, *Jesus Before the Gospels*, New York: HarperOne, p. 3
9. http://reincarnationafterdeath.com/why DO people believe in reincarnation
10. *Ibid*
11. *Ibid*
12. http://reincarnationafterdeath.com/how-many-people-believe-in-reincarnation
13. Carl Jung, 1939 lecture at the Eranos meeting
14. https://www.theopedia.com/pauline-theology
15. Wikipedia contributors, "Jewish Christian," Wikipedia, The Free Encyclopedia, 4 September 2017

Chapter 1: The Meeting

1. Penner, Todd, *Bible Odyssey*, 2 May 2018, "Paul and Acts," https://www.bibleodyssey.org/en/people/related-articles/paul-and-acts

2. Acts 1:21-23
3. https://en.wikipedia.org/wiki/Zacchaeus
4. Acts 23:23, 25:1-13
5. https://en.wikipedia.org/wiki/Paul_the_Apostle

Chapter 2: The Parting
1. https://en.wikipedia.org/wiki/Ancient_Israelite_cuisine#Fish
2. Gardner, Laurence, 2005, *The Magdalene Legacy*, San Francisco: Weiser Books, pp. 38-9

Chapter 3: The Start
1. Ehrman, Bart D., 2014, *How Jesus Became God*, New York: HarperOne, pp. 135-7
2. Ehrman, Bart D., 2014, *How Jesus Became God*, New York: HarperOne, pp. 181-2

Chapter 4: Rome
1. Ehrman, Bart D., 2014, *How Jesus Became God*, New York: HarperOne, pp. 218-9
2. Gardner, Laurence, 2008, *The Grail Enigma*, New York: Harper Element, p. 206
3. Gardner, Laurence, 2005, *The Magdalene Legacy*, San Francisco: Weiser Books, p. 145
4. Ehrman, Bart D., 2016, *Jesus Before the Gospels*, New York: HarperOne, p. 122
5. Ehrman, Bart D., 2016, *Jesus Before the Gospels*, New York: HarperOne, p. 82
6. Ehrman, Bart D., 2003, *Lost Christianities*, New York: Oxford University Press, pp. 249-50
7. *Ibid*

Chapter 5: Son of God
1. Hopkins, Keith, *History Today*, Volume 33, Issue 6, 6 June

1983, "Murderous Games: Gladiatorial Contests in Ancient Rome," http://www.historytoday.com/keith-hopkins/murderous-games-gladiatorial-contests-ancient-rome

2. Ehrman, Bart D., 2003, *Lost Christianities*, New York: Oxford University Press, p. 137
3. Ehrman, Bart D., 2003, *Lost Christianities*, New York: Oxford University Press, p. 137
4. Ehrman, Bart D., 2016, *Jesus Before the Gospels*, New York: HarperOne, pp. 82-5
5. Gardner, Laurence, 2005, *The Magdalene Legacy*, San Francisco: Weiser Books, pp. 135-6
6. Gardner, Laurence, 2008, *The Grail Enigma*, London: Harper Element, p. 142
7. Gardner, Laurence, 2005, *The Magdalene Legacy*, San Francisco: Weiser Books, p. 144
8. Ehrman, Bart D., 2003, *Lost Christianities*, New York: Oxford University Press, p. 151
9. Ehrman, Bart D., 2003, *Lost Christianities*, New York: Oxford University Press, pp. 151-7
10. Ehrman, Bart D., 2014, *How Jesus Became God*, New York: HarperOne, p. 140
11. Ehrman, Bart D., 2003, *Lost Christianities*, New York: Oxford University Press, p. 140

Chapter 6: Rituals and Ceremonies

1. Wikipedia contributors, "Languages of the Roman Empire," Wikipedia, The Free Encyclopedia, 29 May 2017
2. Ehrman, Bart D., 2014, *How Jesus Became God*, New York: HarperOne, pp. 251-69
3. Ehrman, Bart D., 2003, *Lost Christianities*, New York: Oxford University Press, p. 141
4. Ehrman, Bart D., 2003, *Lost Christianities*, New York: Oxford University Press, pp. 141-3
5. Wikipedia contributors, "Claudius," Wikipedia, The Free

Encyclopedia, 5 June 2017

6. Wikipedia contributors, "Claudius," Wikipedia, The Free Encyclopedia, 5 June 2017
7. Wikipedia contributors, "Paul the Apostle," Wikipedia, The Free Encyclopedia, 6 June 2017
8. Ehrman, Bart D., 2016, *Jesus Before the Gospels*, New York: HarperOne, p. 86
9. Ehrman, Bart D., 2014, *How Jesus Became God*, New York: HarperOne, p. 92
10. Ehrman, Bart D., 2003, *Lost Christianities*, New York: Oxford University Press, p. 141
11. Ehrman, Bart D., 2014, *How Jesus Became God*, New York: HarperOne, p. 215
12. Gardner, Laurence, 2005, *The Magdalene Legacy*, San Francisco: Weiser Books
13. Quartermaster of the Barque, Dispensing Orthodox Catholic Joy, *The Origins of Mandatory Private Confession in the Catholic Church*, October 30, 2013

Chapter 7: The Evangelizer

1. Ehrman, Bart D., 2003, *Lost Christianities*, New York: Oxford University Press, pp. 144-5
2. Ehrman, Bart D., 2014, *How Jesus Became God*, New York: HarperOne, p. 227
3. Ehrman, Bart D., 2003, *Lost Christianities*, New York: Oxford University Press, p. 183
4. Butz, Jeffrey J., 2005, *The Brother of Jesus*, Vermont: Inner Traditions, p. 154
5. Butz, Jeffrey J., 2005, *The Brother of Jesus*, Vermont: Inner Traditions, p. 131
6. Gardner, Laurence, 2008, *The Grail Enigma*, London: Harper Element, pp. 82-3
7. Ehrman, Bart D., 2003, *Lost Christianities*, New York: Oxford University Press, p. 145

8. Butz, Jeffrey J., 2005, *The Brother of Jesus*, Vermont: Inner Traditions, pp. 74-5
9. Butz, Jeffrey J., 2005, *The Brother of Jesus*, Vermont: Inner Traditions, pp. 74-85
10. Butz, Jeffrey J., 2005, *The Brother of Jesus*, Vermont: Inner Traditions, pp. 88-9
11. Butz, Jeffrey J., 2005, *The Brother of Jesus*, Vermont: Inner Traditions, p. 113
12. Wikipedia contributors, "Paul the Apostle," Wikipedia, The Free Encyclopedia, 6 June 2017

Chapter 8: The Passing

1. Gardner, Laurence, 2008, *The Grail Enigma*, London: Harper Element, pp. 205, 206
2. Gardner, Laurence, 2005, *The Magdalene Legacy*, San Francisco: Weiser Books, p. 147
3. Gardner, Laurence, 2008, *The Grail Enigma*, London: Harper Element, p. 18
4. Gardner, Laurence, 2005, *The Magdalene Legacy*, San Francisco: Weiser Books, p. 145
5. Gardner, Laurence, 2008, *The Grail Enigma*, London: Harper Element, p. 19
6. Ehrman, Bart D., 2003, *Lost Christianities*, New York: Oxford University Press, p. 183
7. Ehrman, Bart D., 2003, *Lost Christianities*, New York: Oxford University Press, p. 173
8. Ehrman, Bart D., 2003, *Lost Christianities*, New York: Oxford University Press, p. 179
9. Ehrman, Bart D., 2003, *Lost Christianities*, New York: Oxford University Press, p. 227

Chapter 9: The Brother

1. Gardner, Laurence, 2005, *The Magdalene Legacy*, San Francisco: Weiser Books, p. 21

2. Gardner, Laurence, 2005, *The Magdalene Legacy,* San Francisco: Weiser Books, p. 58
3. Gardner, Laurence, 2008, *The Grail Enigma,* London: Harper Element, p. 90
4. Ehrman, Bart D., 2003, *Lost Christianities,* New York: Oxford University Press, p. 99
5. Gardner, Laurence, 2008, *The Grail Enigma,* London: Harper Element, p. 91
6. Butz, Jeffrey J., 2005, *The Brother of Jesus,* Vermont: Inner Traditions, p. 81
7. Butz, Jeffrey J., 2005, *The Brother of Jesus,* Vermont: Inner Traditions, p. 88
8. Gardner, Laurence, 2008, *The Grail Enigma,* London: Harper Element, p. 7
9. Gardner, Laurence, 2005, *The Magdalene Legacy,* San Francisco: Weiser Books, p. 179
10. Gardner, Laurence, 2005, *The Magdalene Legacy,* San Francisco: Weiser Books, pp. 122-3
11. *Jesus Conspiracies* – "Jesus, the Rebel?"
12. Wikipedia contributors, "Josephus," Wikipedia, The Free Encyclopedia, 28 August 2017
13. Tabor, James, "Ebionites & Nazarenes: Tracking the Original Followers of Jesus," *Taborblog, Religion Matters from the Bible to the Modern World,* 29 December 2015
14. Jowett, George F., 2013, *The Drama of the Lost Disciples,* UK: The Covenant Publishing Co. Ltd, p. 55
15. Tabor, James, "Ebionites & Nazarenes: Tracking the Original Followers of Jesus," *Taborblog, Religion Matters from the Bible to the Modern World,* 29 December 2015
16. *Jesus Conspiracies* – "Jesus, the Rebel?"
17. Gardner, Laurence, 2005, *The Magdalene Legacy,* San Francisco: Weiser Books, p. 21
18. https://en.wikipedia.org/wiki/Ancient_Israelite_cuisine#Meat

19. http://www.oocities.org/abusamad/substi.html – Abu Samad, Nayeem Akhtar, MD
20. Kelhoffer, James A., 2014, *Conceptions of "Gospel" and Legitimacy in Early Christianity*, Tubingen, Germany: Mohr Siebeck, p. 80
21. Ehrman, Bart D., 2005, *Lost Christianities*, New York: Oxford University Press, pp. 185-7
22. Ehrman, Bart D., 2005, *Lost Christianities*, New York: Oxford University Press, pp. 187-8
23. Gardner, Laurence, 2005, *The Magdalene Legacy*, San Francisco: Weiser Books, p. 245
24. Jowett, George F., 2013, *The Drama of the Lost Disciples*, UK: The Covenant Publishing Co. Ltd, p. 17
25. Gardner, Laurence, 2005, *The Magdalene Legacy*, San Francisco: Weiser Books, p. 31
26. Gardner, Laurence, 2005, *The Magdalene Legacy*, San Francisco: Weiser Books, p. 193

Chapter 10: Britannia

1. Elder, Isabel Hill, 1999, *Joseph of Arimathea*, Glastonbury Abbey Shop, p. 19
2. Gardner, Laurence, 2005, *The Magdalene Legacy*, San Francisco: Weiser Books, p. 23
3. Elder, Isabel Hill, 1999, *Joseph of Arimathea*, Glastonbury Abbey Shop, p. 20; Jowett, George F., 2013, *The Drama of the Lost Disciples*, UK: The Covenant Publishing Co. Ltd, pp. 31, 185
4. Elder, Isabel Hill, 1999, *Joseph of Arimathea*, Glastonbury Abbey Shop, pp. 6-10
5. Jowett, George F., 2013, *The Drama of the Lost Disciples*, UK: The Covenant Publishing Co. Ltd, p. 40
6. Elder, Isabel Hill, 1999, *Joseph of Arimathea*, Glastonbury Abbey Shop, p. 12
7. Jowett, George F., 2013, *The Drama of the Lost Disciples*, UK:

The Covenant Publishing Co. Ltd, p. 70

8. Gardner, Laurence, 2008, *The Grail Enigma*, London: Harper Element, p. 245
9. Gardner, Laurence, 2008, *The Grail Enigma*, London: Harper Element, p. 90
10. Tabor, James, "Ebionites & Nazarenes: Tracking the Original Followers of Jesus," *Taborblog, Religion Matters from the Bible to the Modern World*, 29 December 2015
11. Butz, Jeffrey J., 2005, *The Brother of Jesus*, Vermont: Inner Traditions, p. 10
12. Wikipedia contributors, "Halakha," Wikipedia, The Free Encyclopedia, 16 December 2017, 8 January 2018
13. Gardner, Laurence, 2008, *The Grail Enigma*, London: Harper Element, p. 167
14. Jowett, George F., 2013, *The Drama of the Lost Disciples*, UK: The Covenant Publishing Co. Ltd, pp. 70-77
15. Gardner, Laurence, 2008, *The Grail Enigma*, London: Harper Element, p. 168
16. Gardner, Laurence, 2005, *The Magdalene Legacy*, San Francisco: Weiser Books, p. 108
17. Lash, John L., 2006, *Not In His Image*, Vermont: Chelsea Green Publishing, p. 74

Chapter 11: Leading the Flock

1. Elder, Isabel Hill, 1999, *Joseph of Arimathea*, Glastonbury Abbey Shop, pp. 13-14
2. Gardner, Laurence, 2005, *The Magdalene Legacy*, San Francisco: Weiser Books, pp. 201-2
3. Gardner, Laurence, 2005, *The Magdalene Legacy*, San Francisco: Weiser Books, p. 200
4. Elder, Isabel Hill, 1999, *Joseph of Arimathea*, Glastonbury Abbey Shop, pp. 13-14
5. Butz, Jeffrey J., 2005, *The Brother of Jesus*, Vermont: Inner Traditions, p. 74

6. Gardner, Laurence, 2008, *The Grail Enigma*, London: Harper Element, p. 90
7. Gardner, Laurence, 2008, *The Grail Enigma*, London: Harper Element, p. 91
8. Gardner, Laurence, 2005, *The Magdalene Legacy*, San Francisco: Weiser Books, p. 146
9. Goldberg, Louis, "The Pharisees: Bad Guys Or...?" https://jewsforjesus.org/publications/issues/issues-v06-n03/the-pharisees-bad-guys-or/
10. Goldberg, Louis, "The Pharisees: Bad Guys Or...?" https://jewsforjesus.org/publications/issues/issues-v06-n03/the-pharisees-bad-guys-or/
11. Malachi, Tau, 2003, *St. Mary Magdalene*, Minnesota: Llewelyn Publications, p. 77
12. Tabor, James, "Ebionites & Nazarenes: Tracking the Original Followers of Jesus," *Taborblog, Religion Matters from the Bible to the Modern World*, 29 December 2015
13. Gardner, Laurence, 2005, *The Magdalene Legacy*, San Francisco: Weiser Books, p. 66
14. Gardner, Laurence, 2008, *The Grail Enigma*, London: Harper Element, p. 15
15. Jewish Virtual Library, "A Project of AICE; Ancient Jewish History: Pharisees, Sadducees and Essenes," http://www.jewishvirtuallibrary.org/pharisees-sadducees-and-essenes
16. Jewish Virtual Library, "A Project of AICE; Ancient Jewish History: Pharisees, Sadducees and Essenes," http://www.jewishvirtuallibrary.org/pharisees-sadducees-and-essenes
17. Jewish Virtual Library, "A Project of AICE; Ancient Jewish History: Pharisees, Sadducees and Essenes," http://www.jewishvirtuallibrary.org/pharisees-sadducees-and-essenes
18. Wikipedia contributors, "Zealots (Judea)," Wikipedia, The Free Encyclopedia, 8 December 2017, 6 January 2018
19. Gardner, Laurence, 2008, *The Grail Enigma*, London: Harper Element, p. 79

20. Gardner, Laurence, 2008, *The Grail Enigma*, London: Harper Element, pp. 82-3

Chapter 12: Jerusalem

1. Gardner, Laurence, 2008, *The Grail Enigma*, London: Harper Element, pp. 244-5
2. Butz, Jeffrey J., 2005, *The Brother of Jesus*, Vermont: Inner Traditions, p. 97
3. Gardner, Laurence, 2008, *The Grail Enigma*, London: Harper Element, p. 243
4. Tabor, James, "Ebionites & Nazarenes: Tracking the Original Followers of Jesus," *Taborblog, Religion Matters from the Bible to the Modern World*, 29 December 2015

Chapter 13: The End

1. Butz, Jeffrey J., 2005, *The Brother of Jesus*, Vermont: Inner Traditions, p. 138
2. Ehrman, Bart D., 2003, *Lost Christianities*, New York: Oxford University Press, pp. 100-1
3. Butz, Jeffrey J., 2005, *The Brother of Jesus*, Vermont: Inner Traditions, p. 69
4. Ehrman, Bart D., 2003, *Lost Christianities*, New York: Oxford University Press, pp. 144-5
5. Ehrman, Bart D., 2003, *Lost Christianities*, New York: Oxford University Press, p. 101
6. Ehrman, Bart D., 2003, *Lost Christianities*, New York: Oxford University Press, p. 145
7. Butz, Jeffrey J., 2005, *The Brother of Jesus*, Vermont: Inner Traditions, p. 132
8. Butz, Jeffrey J., 2005, *The Brother of Jesus*, Vermont: Inner Traditions, pp. 75-6
9. Gardner, Laurence, 2008, *The Grail Enigma*, London: Harper Element, p. 142
10. Butz, Jeffrey J., 2005, *The Brother of Jesus*, Vermont: Inner

Traditions, pp. 69-71

11. Butz, Jeffrey J., 2005, *The Brother of Jesus*, Vermont: Inner Traditions, p. 86
12. Butz, Jeffrey J., 2005, *The Brother of Jesus*, Vermont: Inner Traditions, pp. 90-5
13. Butz, Jeffrey J., 2005, *The Brother of Jesus*, Vermont: Inner Traditions, pp. 88-9
14. Jowett, George F., 2013, *The Drama of the Lost Disciples*, UK: The Covenant Publishing Co. Ltd, pp. 173, 232
15. Jowett, George F., 2013, *The Drama of the Lost Disciples*, UK: The Covenant Publishing Co. Ltd, pp. 173, 232-240
16. Butz, Jeffrey J., 2005, *The Brother of Jesus*, Vermont: Inner Traditions, p. 96
17. Butz, Jeffrey J., 2005, *The Brother of Jesus*, Vermont: Inner Traditions, p. 95
18. "Fragments from the Acts of the Church; Concerning the Martyrdom of James, the Brother of the Lord, from Book 5," Wikipedia contributors, "James, Brother of Jesus," Wikipedia, The Free Encyclopedia, 29 August 2017, 31 August 2017
19. Wikipedia contributors, "James, Brother of Jesus," Wikipedia, The Free Encyclopedia, 29 August 2017, 31 August 2017
20. Butz, Jeffrey J., 2005, *The Brother of Jesus*, Vermont: Inner Traditions, pp. 171-2
21. Butz, Jeffrey J., 2005, *The Brother of Jesus*, Vermont: Inner Traditions, p. 175
22. Butz, Jeffrey J., 2005, *The Brother of Jesus*, Vermont: Inner Traditions, p. 176
23. http://www.oocities.org/abusamad/substi.html – Abu Samad, Nayeem Akhtar, MD

Chapter 14: The Unsung

1. Ehrman, Bart D., 2003, *Lost Christianities*, New York: Oxford University

Press, p. 96

2. Ehrman, Bart D., 2003, *Lost Christianities*, New York: Oxford University Press, pp. 99-100
3. Tabor, James, "Ebionites & Nazarenes: Tracking the Original Followers of Jesus," *Taborblog, Religion Matters from the Bible to the Modern World*, 29 December 2015
4. Butz, Jeffrey J., 2005, *The Brother of Jesus*, Vermont: Inner Traditions, pp. 168-9
5. Butz, Jeffrey J., 2005, *The Brother of Jesus*, Vermont: Inner Traditions, p. 171
6. Butz, Jeffrey J., 2005, *The Brother of Jesus*, Vermont: Inner Traditions, p. 169
7. Butz, Jeffrey J., 2005, *The Brother of Jesus*, Vermont: Inner Traditions, p. 172
8. Gardner, Laurence, 2008, *The Grail Enigma*, London: Harper Element, p. 247
9. Gardner, Laurence, 2008, *The Grail Enigma*, London: Harper Element, p. 246
10. Gardner, Laurence, 2008, *The Grail Enigma*, London: Harper Element, p. 247
11. Gardner, Laurence, 2008, *The Grail Enigma*, London: Harper Element, p. 248
12. Gardner, Laurence, 2008, *The Grail Enigma*, London: Harper Element, p. 246
13. Gardner, Laurence, 2008, *The Grail Enigma*, London: Harper Element, pp. 253-60
14. Gardner, Laurence, 2008, *The Grail Enigma*, London: Harper Element, pp. 253-9
15. Butz, Jeffrey J., 2005, *The Brother of Jesus*, Vermont: Inner Traditions, p. 154

Conclusion

1. Tilghman, J., "Christ Consciousness for the Christian," 2 March 2013, www.spiritofthescripture.com

2. Butz, Jeffrey J., 2005, *The Brother of Jesus*, Vermont: Inner Traditions, p. 171
3. Ehrman, Bart D., 2003, *Lost Christianities*, New York: Oxford University Press, p. 103
4. Gardner, Laurence, 2008, *The Grail Enigma*, London: Harper Element, p. 83
5. Ehrman, Bart D., 2003, *Lost Christianities*, New York: Oxford University Press, p. 4
6. Ehrman, Bart D., 2003, *Lost Christianities*, New York: Oxford University Press, p. 4
7. Ehrman, Bart D., 2003, *Lost Christianities*, New York: Oxford University Press, p. 217
8. Ehrman, Bart D., 2003, *Lost Christianities*, New York: Oxford University Press, p. 235
9. Ehrman, Bart D., 2003, *Lost Christianities*, New York: Oxford University Press, p. 231
10. Ehrman, Bart D., 2003, *Lost Christianities*, New York: Oxford University Press, p. 249
11. Ehrman, Bart D., 2003, *Lost Christianities*, New York: Oxford University Press, pp. 250-1
12. Tolle, Eckhart, 2009, *A New Earth*, UK: Penguin Books
13. Jung, CG, 1991, *The Archetypes and the Collective Unconscious*, translated by RFC Hull, Princeton: Bollingen Series
14. Radin, D., 2009, *The Conscious Universe: The Scientific Truth of Psychic Phenomena*, New York: HarperOne
15. Swami Sahajananda, 2006, Barnabas Tiburtius, http://www.livingspark.net
16. Butz, Jeffrey J., 2005, *The Brother of Jesus*, Vermont: Inner Traditions, p. 190

An Author Biography

Reena Kumarasingham is a therapist whose practice, *Divine Aspect*, has clients spanning Asia, Australia and Europe. She is a certified trainer and supervisor for the Past Life Regression Academy in the training of therapists in the UK, Australia and the USA. She has given talks internationally including the World Congress of Regression Therapy in Turkey and the Past Life Regression Convention in India. Reena is the author of *Shrouded Truth* and *The Magdalene Lineage.* She also contributed two chapters on advanced regression therapy techniques to *Transforming the Eternal Soul*.

Website: www.reenakumarasingham.com
Facebook: @rkumarasingham
Instagram: @reenakumarasingham
Twitter: @DivineAspect

Thank you for purchasing *Divine Consciousness*. My sincere hope is that you derived as much from reading this book as I have in creating it. If you have a few moments, I would be grateful if you could add your review of the book on your favorite online site. Also, if you would like to connect with other books that I have coming in the near future, please visit my website.

Sincerely, Reena Kumarasingham

Previous Titles

Shrouded Truth:
Biblical Revelations Through Past Life Journeys
978-0-9567887-5-7

Two thousand years ago, the Biblical time, was a time of great change. Jesus and those closest to him were inspiring in their ability to tap into their inner radiant light to navigate a challenging period of chaos. Over time, their heroic and heartwarming stories have been cloaked in shadow... Until now. Through the past-life journeys of eight souls, *Shrouded Truth* unveils the dramatic adventures and emotional experiences of those closest to Jesus, in a quest to unravel false entanglements while pursuing a path of spiritual purity.

Backed by tradition and documentary evidence, discover little-known information that will challenge previously-held beliefs about the Biblical Era, answer some questions and raise a few new ones. Explore revelations that inspire the recognition and embodiment of our own radiant light. *Shrouded Truth* is the first book in the Radiant Light Series, which helps us to explore the true relationship between the spirit of man and the spirit of the God. It challenges us to look deeply into our inner core to illuminate the biggest shrouded truth of them all – our own radiant divinity.

"*Shrouded Truth* is a unique, highly recommended Biblical study that should be included in any serious historical and cultural examination of Jesus' life and times."

D. Donavan, *Midwest Book Review*

The Magdalene Lineage:
Past Life Journeys into the Sacred Feminine Mysteries
978-1-78904-300-6

NOW IS THE TIME FOR THE DIVINE FEMININE.
For two thousand years, Mary Magdalene has been a veiled silhouette, a shadow of her vibrant self. An enigmatic figure, she was shrouded in mystery, a feminine caricature of either the purest of saints or the most repentant of sinners.
Two thousand years have buried her, her lineage and her legacy. Through past-life regression, backed by academic research and oral tradition, journey with Mary Magdalene from the age of six to sixty. Discover intimate knowledge of her as a daughter, a sister, a wife, a mother and a spiritual teacher. Her daughter Tamar, the product, initiate and bearer of her legacy, continues her sacred teachings.
This is their story – the story of the feminine in spirituality.

Connect with Reena

Empowering Divine Feminine Online Course

The Divine Feminine is now experiencing a reemergence – a rebirth into the collective consciousness. It is time to understand and empower the Divine Feminine within us all, men and women – as we move towards Oneness and Wholeness, both within and without.

Drawing from the wisdom of past lives, *The Magdalene Lineage: Past Life Journeys into the Sacred Feminine Mysteries,* this online course will share simple tips and techniques of how we can empower the Divine Feminine within us, men and women. It is about bringing to balance the spiritual, energetic aspect of both the Divine Feminine and the Sacred Masculine, as we move into the New Consciousness.

www.reenakumarasingham.com

Advanced Vibrational Technique in a New Plane

We are going through an intense shift in vibration, from the third dimension to a higher dimension. This shift has enabled us to access stronger, more potent energies. Having access to these new energies gives us a different tool, in accordance with the new vibrational plane that we find ourselves in. We find ourselves having access to many new ways of Being.

Reena facilitates a seven-day training course that not only helps participants access and apply these high vibration energies, but also gives participants a taster of what it is to BE in the new Consciousness. The course is highly practical, and includes lectures, interactive discussions, demonstrations and practice sessions.

www.reenakumarasingham.com/advanced-vibrational-healing-training

www.vibrationnewplane.com

Past Life Regression Academy

The Past Life Regression Academy specializes in past-life regression therapy, regression therapy, between-lives spiritual regression and hypnosis training in Europe, Asia and the United States, as well as Soul Evolution workshops. Reena is a trainer for the Academy, specializing in teaching therapists between-lives spiritual regression in Australia, Singapore, the UK and the US.

www.reenakumarasingham.com/between-lives-regression-training

www.regressionacademy.com/life-between-lives-training.htm

SPIRITUALITY

O is a symbol of the world, of oneness and unity; this eye represents knowledge and insight. We publish titles on general spirituality and living a spiritual life. We aim to inform and help you on your own journey in this life.

If you have enjoyed this book, why not tell other readers by posting a review on your preferred book site?

Recent bestsellers from O-Books are:

Heart of Tantric Sex

Diana Richardson

Revealing Eastern secrets of deep love and intimacy to Western couples.

Paperback: 978-1-90381-637-0 ebook: 978-1-84694-637-0

Crystal Prescriptions

The A-Z guide to over 1,200 symptoms and their healing crystals

Judy Hall

The first in the popular series of eight books, this handy little guide is packed as tight as a pill-bottle with crystal remedies for ailments.

Paperback: 978-1-90504-740-6 ebook: 978-1-84694-629-5

Take Me To Truth
Undoing the Ego
Nouk Sanchez, Tomas Vieira
The best-selling step-by-step book on shedding the Ego, using the teachings of *A Course In Miracles*.
Paperback: 978-1-84694-050-7 ebook: 978-1-84694-654-7

The 7 Myths about Love...Actually!
The Journey from your HEAD to the HEART of your SOUL
Mike George
Smashes all the myths about LOVE.
Paperback: 978-1-84694-288-4 ebook: 978-1-84694-682-0

The Holy Spirit's Interpretation of the New Testament
A Course in Understanding and Acceptance
Regina Dawn Akers
Following on from the strength of *A Course In Miracles*, NTI teaches us how to experience the love and oneness of God.
Paperback: 978-1-84694-085-9 ebook: 978-1-78099-083-5

The Message of A Course In Miracles
A translation of the Text in plain language
Elizabeth A. Cronkhite
A translation of *A Course in Miracles* into plain, everyday language for anyone seeking inner peace. The companion volume, *Practicing A Course In Miracles*, offers practical lessons and mentoring.
Paperback: 978-1-84694-319-5 ebook: 978-1-84694-642-4

Your Simple Path

Find Happiness in every step

Ian Tucker

A guide to helping us reconnect with what is really important in our lives.

Paperback: 978-1-78279-349-6 ebook: 978-1-78279-348-9

365 Days of Wisdom

Daily Messages To Inspire You Through The Year

Dadi Janki

Daily messages which cool the mind, warm the heart and guide you along your journey.

Paperback: 978-1-84694-863-3 ebook: 978-1-84694-864-0

Body of Wisdom

Women's Spiritual Power and How it Serves

Hilary Hart

Bringing together the dreams and experiences of women across the world with today's most visionary spiritual teachers.

Paperback: 978-1-78099-696-7 ebook: 978-1-78099-695-0

Dying to Be Free

From Enforced Secrecy to Near Death to True Transformation

Hannah Robinson

After an unexpected accident and near-death experience, Hanna Robinson found herself radically transforming her life, while remarkable new insight altered her relationship with her fathe practising Catholic priest.

Paperback: 978-1-78535-254-6 ebook: 978-1-78535-255-3

The Ecology of the Soul

A Manual of Peace, Power and Personal Growth for Real People in the Real World

Aidan Walker

Balance your own inner Ecology of the Soul to regain your natural state of peace, power and wellbeing.

Paperback: 978-1-78279-850-7 ebook: 978-1-78279-849-1

Not I, Not other than I

The Life and Teachings of Russel Williams

Steve Taylor, Russel Williams

The miraculous life and inspiring teachings of one of the World's greatest living Sages.

Paperback: 978-1-78279-729-6 ebook: 978-1-78279-728-9

On the Other Side of Love

A woman's unconventional journey towards wisdom

Muriel Maufroy

When life has lost all meaning, what do you do?

Paperback: 978-1-78535-281-2 ebook: 978-1-78535-282-9

Practicing A Course In Miracles

A translation of the Workbook in plain language, with mentor's notes

Elizabeth A. Cronkhite

he practical second and third volumes of The Plain-Language *A Course In Miracles*.

Paperback: 978-1-84694-403-1 ebook: 978-1-78099-072-9

Quantum Bliss

The Quantum Mechanics of Happiness, Abundance, and Health

George S. Mentz

Quantum Bliss is the breakthrough summary of success and spirituality secrets that customers have been waiting for.

Paperback: 978-1-78535-203-4 ebook: 978-1-78535-204-1

The Upside Down Mountain

Mags MacKean

A must-read for anyone weary of chasing success and happiness – one woman's inspirational journey swapping the uphill slog for the downhill slope.

Paperback: 978-1-78535-171-6 ebook: 978-1-78535-172-3

Your Personal Tuning Fork

The Endocrine System

Deborah Bates

Discover your body's health secret, the endocrine system, and 'twang' your way to sustainable health!

Paperback: 978-1-84694-503-8 ebook: 978-1-78099-697-4

Readers of ebooks can buy or view any of these bestsellers by clicking on the live link in the title. Most titles are published in paperback and as an ebook. Paperbacks are available in traditional bookshops. Both print and ebook formats are available online.

Find more titles and sign up to our readers' newsletter at http://www.johnhuntpublishing.com/mind-body-spirit

Follow us on Facebook at https://www.facebook.com/OBooks/ and Twitter at https://twitter.com/obooks